RAILS to the SEA

A CELEBRATION OF
RAILWAY JOURNEYS
PAST AND PRESENT

JOHN HADRILL

To Julia, Lisa, and Mark, for your many contributions to this ambitious venture, and in memory of three former educators whose vision and dedication to the pursuit of excellence encouraged countless creative endeavours. Their enduring influence is far greater than they could ever have known:

J.H.Leakey,   Dulwich College Preparatory School;
G.H.Stainforth,   Oundle School; and
N.A.M. MacKenzie,   University of British Columbia.

And in remembrance of Rosina Muriel Oliver (1896-1994), who loved those journeys to the sea.

RAILS
to the SEA

TRANSPORT

Atlantic

PUBLISHERS

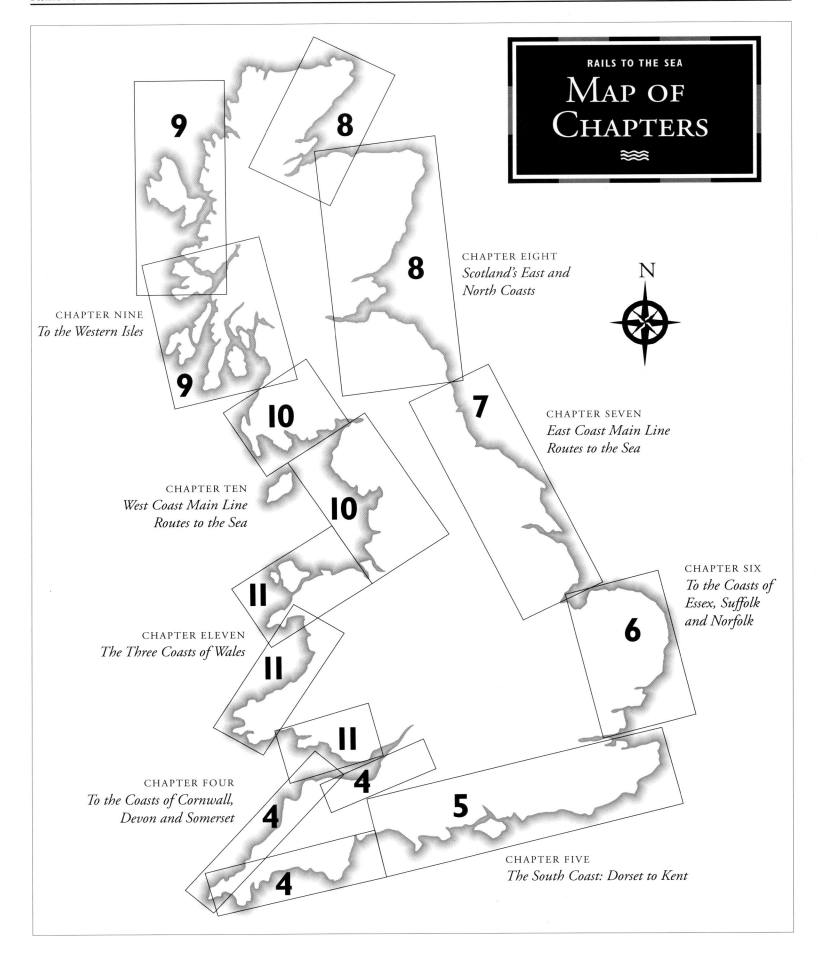

RAILS TO THE SEA

MAP OF CHAPTERS
≈≈≈

9

8

CHAPTER EIGHT
*Scotland's East and
North Coasts*

N

8

CHAPTER NINE
To the Western Isles

9

7

10

CHAPTER SEVEN
*East Coast Main Line
Routes to the Sea*

CHAPTER TEN
*West Coast Main Line
Routes to the Sea*

10

CHAPTER SIX
*To the Coasts of
Essex, Suffolk
and Norfolk*

11

6

CHAPTER ELEVEN
The Three Coasts of Wales

11

11

4

CHAPTER FOUR
*To the Coasts of Cornwall,
Devon and Somerset*

4

5

4

CHAPTER FIVE
The South Coast: Dorset to Kent

Contents

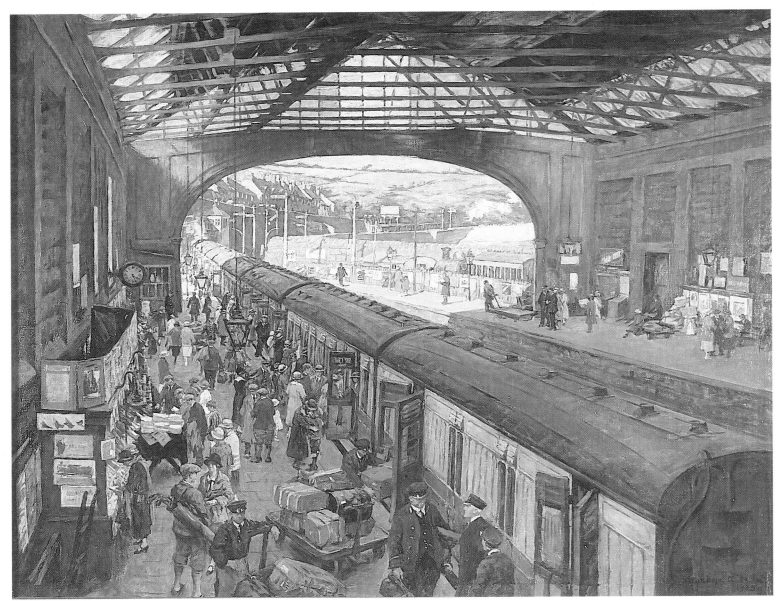

Penzance station - from an oil painting by Stanhope Alexander Forbes (NRM/Science & Society)
Pages 2 and 3: Barmouth viaduct (Colour-Rail/BRW 64)

Atlantic Publishers,
Trevithick House, West End, Penryn, Cornwall TR10 8HE

First published 1999

© John Hadrill and Atlantic Publishers, 1999
The moral right of the author has been asserted

ISBN: 0 906899 86 9

Graphics: Lisa Birrell
Layout and design: Richard Joy & Elizabeth Rodriguez, Paris

Reproduction and printing by The Amadeus Press Ltd, Huddersfield, West Yorkshire

British Cataloguing in Publication Data: A catalogue record for this book is available from the British Library.

Introduction

As we approach the end of the twentieth century, this book celebrates more than 160 years of railway journeys to the sea, based to a large extent on the author's travels by train throughout mainland Britain during the past fifty years. It has been said that second only to religion, railways have been the most civilizing influence the world has ever known. Many people still enjoy the pleasures of travel by train to the coast, where the more remote regions offer two of today's most precious commodities, namely tranquillity and permanence. While some branch lines to the sea may have disappeared, there are places where former trackbeds now provide access to scenic coastal areas, such as those along the route of the former 'Atlantic Coast Express' near Padstow and Ilfracombe.

There are over 6,000 miles of coastline in Britain, and a rail network of nearly 2,500 passenger stations, of which more than 200 are beside or near the sea. Starting at London, the journeys in this book take the reader first to Cornwall, Devon, and Somerset, thence counterclockwise round the coast from Dorset to South Wales, concluding at the Severn estuary, Britain's great tidal and geographical divide.

From the remarkable cavalcade of trains since 1825, past and present journeys are described as we travel around Britain, using services provided by the various train operating companies, or by preserved and narrow-gauge railway companies. Several journeys in this book may appear unusual, or perhaps eccentric in routes chosen to reach the sea. The choice is a personal one, which may rekindle happy memories or encourage journeys of exploration by readers.

Charles Dickens, in wonder and delight at the sight of a speeding express train, marvelled at "the greatest power in nature and art combined." Railways have been the source of more literature, architecture, sound recordings, documentary films, archival material and archaeology than any other industry in Britain. Famous writers and artists who found inspiration in their visits by train to the sea include Virginia Woolf and Barbara Hepworth at St Ives; Tennyson at Freshwater Bay on the Isle of Wight; Galsworthy, R.L.Stevenson, and Disraeli at Bournemouth; Charles Dickens on the Kent coast; Augustus John at Tenby; John Betjeman at Padstow; and George Orwell on Jura in the Inner Hebrides.

Most of Britain's railways were built by small private companies in the 19th century. In 1923, four major railway companies were formed and known as the London, Midland and Scottish (LMS); the London and North Eastern Railway (LNER); the Great Western Railway (GWR); and the Southern Railway (SR) .

This grouping marked an era of growth and prosperity, when the 'Big Four' railway companies took great pride in their services to the coast, notably with famous trains titled 'Cornish Riviera', 'Atlantic Coast Express', 'Bournemouth Belle', 'Golden Arrow', 'Brighton Belle', 'Torbay Express', 'Pines Express', and 'Eastern Belle', among many others. In 1948, the four major companies were nationalized to form British Railways, and subsequently privatized into 25 passenger train operating companies during the 1990s.

Today, after decades of hard work by staff and supporters of preservation groups, railway excursions may be taken on trains hauled by steam locomotives designed, built, and operated in Britain during the great years of train travel between the two World Wars, when performance, service, and route miles were at their peak. Some brief accounts of memorable high speed runs to and from the sea are included, in tribute to those who devoted most of their working lives to the railways, and to those who drove their locomotives with such skill and panache.

In Britain, the statute mile is set permanently on trackside markers, in railway timetables and reference books. Distances are therefore quoted in miles; heights above sea level are given in feet; and times are referenced to the 24 hour clock. In planning any travel by train the reader is advised to obtain current information from the respective train operating companies for journeys based on those described in this book. Timetables may change, but the impression of Britain's coastline upon the those who take a train to the seaside fortunately endures.

Several walks and occasional bus rides from railheads near interesting parts of Britain's coastline are included in the text. Knowledge of incoming tides is essential for safety when walking beside the sea. For those who wish to explore pathways built upon former railway trackbeds, the existence of a right of way should be verified before entering any such pathway or railway property.

Each of us has been influenced in one way or another by train journeys we have taken, and whatever happens to the railways in the 21st century, their impact and usefulness will surely endure. It is hoped that this book will inspire those now managing the privatized railways of Britain to show the vision, leadership and pride of service to the travelling public that were evident prior to nationalization half a century ago.

Above all, this book is a celebration of the achievements of Britain's railways, of the pleasures, memories, sights and surprises of past journeys, and of the many enjoyable trips we can take by train to the seaside today.

Vancouver, British Columbia January 1999.

Britain's Railways to the Sea

"One day we shall endow chariots with incredible speed without the aid of any animal."

Roger Bacon (1214-1294)

In 1814, the year that George Stephenson built his first steam locomotive, Paddington was described as "a village situated on the Edgeware Road, about a mile from London." Horse-drawn barges glided along the Grand Junction canal to Paddington basin, bringing merchandise and passengers to the city from towns and villages on the extensive canal network in Britain.

Far away, in Cornwall, south Wales and the north of England, wagons on rails were hauled by primitive steam locomotives, whose invention and subsequent development owed much to the insight and ingenuity of men such as Richard Trevithick, James Watt, and William Murdock, all working in Cornwall at the time.

When the Stockton & Darlington Railway inaugurated the world's first steam-hauled passenger train on 27 September 1825, with Robert Stephenson's seven-ton 'Locomotion' providing the motive power, the railway age had arrived, and with it the first rail speed record of 15 mph. The locomotive was the most developed industrial product of the time, a technological wonder soon to be seen operating on railways all over the world.

The first inter-city line to the sea, between Manchester and Liverpool, was opened in 1830, as was the Canterbury & Whitstable line to the Kent coast. On 14 December 1836, a train crossed the 851 arches of a viaduct into London's first railway terminus at London Bridge, on the line to Greenwich. By the autumn of 1838, London was linked to Preston, 209 miles from Euston, and to the coast at Fleetwood by July 1840, giving a shorter sea link to Scotland. In the south, Brunel's main line west to Bristol opened in 1841, and by 1844 the main lines to

Dover, Brighton and Southampton had been completed.

Through the spread of these ribbons of steel, the railways made their great contribution to the industrial revolution in Britain. Powerful men of vision and courage had planned and negotiated the routes, and armies of tough navvies had created them, using implements from a previous agricultural age. The labourers building the London to Birmingham railway shifted more rock, earth, and stones in five years than all the Egyptian slaves toiling for twenty years to build the Great Pyramid. After the printed word, no other creation of man had such a wide impact upon the world as the widespread introduction of railways in Britain and elsewhere.

In 1830 there were 120 miles of railways in Britain; by 1840 the network had grown to nearly 1,500 miles, and two years later the railways were carrying almost sixty million passengers a year. The Railway Mania of 1845 had produced 650 Acts of Parliament authorizing the construction of nearly 9,000 miles of track, not far short of Britain's total route mileage today.

The west coast main line to Scotland was completed in 1848, and the final link on the east coast main line was made when the high level bridge over the river Tyne from Gateshead to Newcastle was opened in 1849.The temporary railway bridge at Berwick, built in 1848, was replaced in 1850 by the famous Royal Border bridge, whose massive stone structure enabled heavier and faster trains to cross the estuary of the Tweed.

In 1829 the fastest mail coach from London to Edinburgh took three uncomfortable days and required many changes of horses during the 400 mile journey. By 1848, the same journey by train took twelve hours in a clean and spacious

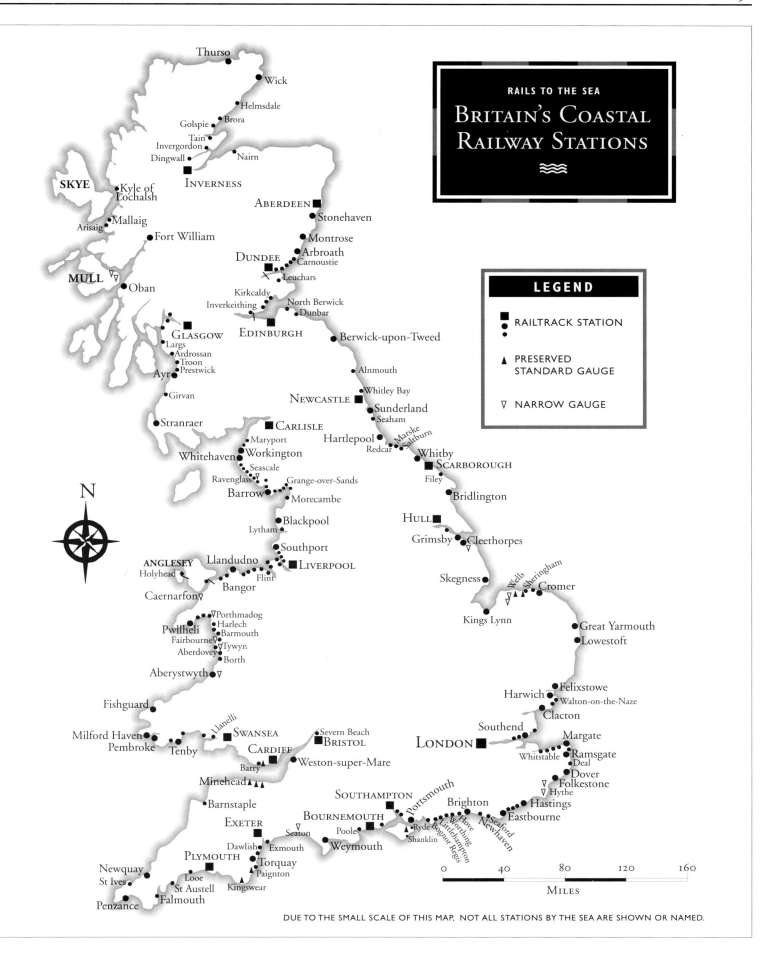

RAILS TO THE SEA
BRITAIN'S COASTAL RAILWAY STATIONS
≈

LEGEND

■ RAILTRACK STATION

● RAILTRACK STATION

• RAILTRACK STATION

▲ PRESERVED STANDARD GAUGE

▽ NARROW GAUGE

Thurso
Wick
Helmsdale
Brora
Golspie
Tain
Invergordon
Dingwall
Nairn
INVERNESS
SKYE
Kyle of Lochalsh
Mallaig
Arisaig
Fort William
MULL
Oban
ABERDEEN
Stonehaven
Montrose
Arbroath
DUNDEE
Carnoustie
Leuchars
Kirkcaldy
Inverkeithing
North Berwick
Dunbar
GLASGOW
EDINBURGH
Largs
Ardrossan
Troon
Prestwick
Ayr
Girvan
Berwick-upon-Tweed
Alnmouth
Whitley Bay
Stranraer
NEWCASTLE
Sunderland
Seaham
CARLISLE
Hartlepool
Maryport
Workington
Redcar
Marske
Saltburn
Whitehaven
Seascale
Whitby
Ravenglass
Grange-over-Sands
SCARBOROUGH
Barrow
Filey
Morecambe
Bridlington
Blackpool
Lytham
HULL
Southport
Grimsby
Cleethorpes
ANGLESEY
Llandudno
LIVERPOOL
Holyhead
Flint
Bangor
Skegness
Wells
Sheringham
Cromer
Caernarfon
Porthmadog
Harlech
Pwllheli
Barmouth
Kings Lynn
Fairbourne
Tywyn
Aberdovey
Great Yarmouth
Borth
Lowestoft
Aberystwyth
Fishguard
Felixstowe
Harwich
Walton-on-the-Naze
Clacton
Milford Haven
Llanelli
SWANSEA
Severn Beach
Southend
Pembroke
Tenby
CARDIFF
BRISTOL
Margate
Barry
Weston-super-Mare
LONDON
Ramsgate
Whitstable
Deal
Minehead
Dover
SOUTHAMPTON
Portsmouth
Folkestone
Barnstaple
BOURNEMOUTH
Brighton
Hythe
Hastings
EXETER
Seaton
Poole
Ryde
Hove
Seaford
Eastbourne
Dawlish
Exmouth
Weymouth
Shanklin
Worthing
Littlehampton
Bognor Regis
Newhaven
PLYMOUTH
Torquay
Paignton
Newquay
St Ives
Looe
St Austell
Kingswear
Penzance
Falmouth

0   40   80   120   160
MILES

DUE TO THE SMALL SCALE OF THIS MAP, NOT ALL STATIONS BY THE SEA ARE SHOWN OR NAMED.

Dawlish in 1957 - a view epitomising the heyday of railway journeys to the sea. Miniature golf is in full swing and no doubt there is lots of good clean fun on the sands. 5004 Llanstephan Castle *is bringing yet another train-load of holiday-makers to the West Country. (P.W. Gray/Colour-Rail BRW942)*

Two swans complete the picture as an ex Great Western pannier tank brings a boat train down to Folkestone Harbour in June 1960. The point where the steep grade eases is clearly discernible. (C. Hogg/Colour-Rail BRS960)

The idyllic harbour setting of Whitby Town with the abbey prominent on the skyline. Steam has been a rare visitor to the resort in recent years, but an exception was October 1987 when 9F 92220 Evening Star shunted stock beneath a gloriously sunny sky. (R. Jones/Colour-Rail P229)

Today's steam to the sea. 'King' class locomotives never ventured over the Royal Albert Bridge in normal service, so the sight of one in Cornwall on 19 September 1998 was a novel experience. 6024 King Edward I was making light work of Lostwithiel bank as it headed west with an enthusiasts' special 'The Penzance Pirate'. (Jon Bennett)

compartment, with meals provided at stations along the way. In that same year a new speed record of 78 mph was set by a train of the Great Western Railway, a world record for steam trains which stood for 56 years.

By 1860 there were more than 200,000 labourers at work building railways throughout Britain, and 112,000 persons operating them. Route mileage had increased to 15,560 miles by 1880, and one of the largest construction projects of that decade was the building of Britain's longest railway tunnel, with over four miles of double track beneath the Severn estuary and adjacent land on each side. The tunnel was completed by the GWR in 1886, and greatly improved rail services into south Wales.

Meanwhile, in its efforts to attract more passengers, the Midland Railway was the first in Britain to introduce third-class accommodation on all its trains in 1872, quickly followed by the other rail companies, for their second-class was about the same standard as the Midland's third-class. It was a brilliant move, and second class soon disappeared, leaving the peculiar first- and third- class fare structure for travel on Britain's railways until the mid-20th century.

In the summer of 1888, fierce rivalry between railway companies operating between London and Edinburgh led to the most exciting demonstration of locomotive power and speed seen in Britain since the Rainhill trials of 1829. Sixty years of railway construction had produced a network of routes that included three main lines from London to Scotland. The first to be completed was the west coast line via Carlisle to Glasgow; the second was east coast line via York and Newcastle to Edinburgh. These routes are the busiest long distance main lines in Britain today.

The third route to Scotland was constructed by the Midland Railway across the Pennines via Leeds, Settle and Carlisle to Glasgow, a route that could not compete with the others in terms of speed, but the Midland's trains offered the most luxurious accommodation, and the first dining cars in Britain. The real contest for fastest trains and greatest revenue was therefore between east and west coast companies. Prior to 1887, trains from Euston took ten hours to reach Edinburgh via the west coast main line, while those from King's Cross took nine hours on the shorter and more level east coast route.

In the 'Race to the North' of August 1888, the travel time from King's Cross to Edinburgh was cut from 8h 30min to 7h 27min (including a luncheon stop of 20 minutes at York), and from 8h 30min to 7h 38min on the west coast line from Euston, with a luncheon stop at Preston. This was a prelude to even faster timings, when new routes beyond Edinburgh set the stage for another round of even more exciting railway races seven years later.

By 1890 there were over 17,000 route miles in mainland Britain, and the massive Forth Bridge had opened up a shorter east coast route to Aberdeen and northeast Scotland, where builders of the Caledonian Railway had constructed over 200 bridges and 23 viaducts in laying track through the hills and across the rivers of Fife and Angus. It was inevitable that the opening of the Forth Bridge would provoke renewed railway rivalry, this time for fastest services between London and Aberdeen, in competition for the lucrative passenger traffic to the north of Scotland.

The famous overnight contests between east and west coast railway companies in July and August 1895, around the time of 'the Glorious Twelfth' shooting season in Scotland, resulted in final honours going to the west coast express, which on the night of 21/22 August covered the 540 miles from Euston to Aberdeen in 512 minutes, including stops at Crewe, Carlisle and Perth to change locomotives and crews.

This record run, notably the long high speed climbs up to the line summits at Shap (915ft) and Beattock (1,015ft) from near sea level at Morecambe Bay and Carlisle respectively, was a truly heroic achievement in terms of human effort and endurance by men heaving tons of coal into the locomotive fireboxes to produce the necessary high power for over eight hours of passenger train racing. Since then, no other train has beaten this start-to-stop speed record from London to Aberdeen via the west coast route.

In May 1892, the last of Brunel's famous broad-gauge lines in Devon and Cornwall were removed by 5,000 men deployed along 200 miles of track. The mammoth task of converting all GWR broad gauge lines to a standard gauge was exceptionally well organized in a remarkable two-day operation. Huge stacks of uprooted tracks occupied more than fifteen miles of sidings in and around Exeter, the railway crossroads of south Devon. Britain now had one standard gauge throughout its railway network, so that passengers would no longer have to endure the tedious and time-consuming 'change of gauge' interruptions of their cross-country journeys at places such as Bristol.

As a result of improvements in track construction and locomotive power in the 1890s, the quest for speed among railway companies intensified. In the south, fast new trains were introduced between London and Bournemouth, covering the 107 miles in a respectable 125 minutes. But it was difficult for steam trains between London and the south coast to maintain high speeds on busy commuter lines with many station stops, compared to long distance routes leading north from London to Scotland.

In the exuberance of speed and service during the 1890s, the railways that linked London to Aberdeen on the west coast main line, having set the speed record between these cities, decided to celebrate the Diamond Jubilee of Queen Victoria's reign in 1897 with a patriotic display of locomotive power, using the colours of the Union Jack as livery.

From Euston to Crewe, the LNWR assigned the locomotive

DISTRIBUTION OF RAILWAY STATIONS
AROUND BRITAIN'S COASTLINE

CHAPTER	SECTION OF COAST	STATIONS
4	WESTON-SUPER-MARE – NEWQUAY – ST IVES – PENZANCE – FALMOUTH – LOOE – PLYMOUTH – PAIGNTON – TORQUAY – TEIGNMOUTH – DAWLISH – EXMOUTH	17
5	WEYMOUTH – POOLE – BOURNEMOUTH – PORTSMOUTH – ISLE OF WIGHT – WORTHING BRIGHTON – EASTBOURNE – HASTINGS – DOVER – RAMSGATE – MARGATE – WHITSTABLE	49
6	LEIGH-ON-SEA – SOUTHEND – CLACTON – WALTON-ON-THE-NAZE – HARWICH – FELIXSTOWE – LOWESTOFT – GREAT YARMOUTH – CROMER – SHERINGHAM – KING'S LYNN	18
7	SKEGNESS – CLEETHORPES - BRIDLINGTON – SCARBOROUGH – WHITBY – SALTBURN – HARTLEPOOL – WHITLEY BAY – ALNMOUTH – BERWICK-UPON-TWEED	19
8	DUNBAR – NORTH BERWICK – EDINBURGH – DUNDEE – ARBROATH – MONTROSE – ABERDEEN – INVERNESS – TAIN – GOLSPIE – BRORA – HELMSDALE – WICK – THURSO	23
9	KYLE OF LOCHALSH – MALLAIG – ARISAIG – FORT WILLIAM – OBAN – CRAIGENDORAN – GOUROCK – WEMYSS BAY – LARGS – ARDROSSAN	14
10	TROON – AYR – STRANRAER – WHITEHAVEN – SEASCALE – RAVENGLASS – GRANGE-OVER-SANDS – MORECAMBE – BLACKPOOL – LYTHAM – SOUTHPORT – LIVERPOOL – WEST KIRBY	35
11	FLINT – PRESTATYN – RHYL – LLANDUDNO – HOLYHEAD – PWLLHELI – PORTHMADOG – BARMOUTH – ABERYSTWYTH – FISHGUARD – PEMBROKE – TENBY – SWANSEA – PENARTH	43
	TOTAL	218

THESE FIGURES ARE BASED ON THE AUTHOR'S COUNT. OTHER TOTALS MAY VARY SLIGHTLY. THERE ARE ALSO TWENTY STATIONS NEAR THE SEA ON THE PRESERVED AND NARROW GAUGE RAILWAYS SHOWN IN APPENDIX 3. *The photo of Penzance station was taken by the author in 1993.*

TITLED TRAINS TO THE SEA

Although it is 1957, the scene looks very Great Western as 'Castle' 5069 Isambard Kingdom Brunel prepares to leave Penzance with the up 'Cornish Riviera'. The pedigree of this famous train dates back to 1897 when its forerunner completed the world's longest non-stop journey from London to Exeter at an average speed of 52mph. (J Spencer Gilks collection/Colour-Rail BRW1160)

The 'Pines Express' from Manchester and Liverpool to Bournemouth was the fastest train on the late lamented Somerset & Dorset line. Even so, its average speed over this scenic route with much single line was only a shade over 30mph. The down service is seen coming off Midford viaduct in August 1962 behind the characteristic combination of 4MT 75023 and 'West Country' 34043 Combe Martin.
(W. Potter/Colour-Rail SD141)

The legendary 'Golden Arrow', running from London to Dover where passengers boarded the ferry to Calais for the onward journey to Paris. Introduced in 1929, it ran for the last time in June 1961. 'West Country' 34079, complete with headboard and all the trimmings, is ready to leave London Victoria in April 1949.
(J.M. Jarvis/Colour-Rail BRS196)

Sir Laurence Olivier was among the many loyal patrons who protested when the 'Brighton Belle', the world's first and only all-electric Pullman train, was withdrawn in 1972. Four years earlier the up service prepares to depart from Brighton. (T.J. Edgington)

"Greater Britain" painted in red; for the Crewe to Carlisle section, "Queen Empress" was painted in a creamy white; and northwards from Carlisle, the Caledonian Railway had no need to change the colour of their bright blue locomotives for the royal progress to Aberdeen, and westwards to Ballater station, for Balmoral Castle.

It is not recorded if the Queen was amused, but she was very supportive of railway rituals which enhanced her prestige. From the time of her first train journey from Slough (for Windsor) to Paddington in June 1842, Queen Victoria gave orders that the maximum speed of royal trains was not to exceed 40 mph by day and 30 mph at night.

She did, however, travel much faster in death than in life, for when she died at Osborne on the Isle of Wight in 1901, her funeral train from Portsmouth was delayed, and in order not to keep the new king waiting in London, a maximum speed of 80 mph was recorded after the train left Fareham en route to London (Victoria). Her son, King Edward VII, was an enthusiastic railway traveller, and during his reign he set some speed records of his own, notably during a non-stop run from Paddington to Kingswear on the Devon coast.

The railways were the greatest industrial creation of Queen Victoria's reign, and we have to acknowledge her contribution in prototyping such on-board conveniences as flushing toilets, improved heating and lighting, inter-carriage walkways, sleeping cars, bathrooms, and communications between coaches and locomotive while in motion. She had no interest in dining facilities, for she never took a meal on a train, preferring to have her meals at stations such as Perth en route to Aberdeen and Balmoral.

When the superintendent of the LNWR retired in1895, he recalled that during his 112 journeys on board the royal train, he had avoided as far as possible unpleasant encounters with Her Majesty's personal attendant John Brown, whom he aptly described as "the Queen's coarse phonograph", a reference to Brown's habitual opening words: "The Queen says".

Such was the progress in railway building and travel as the nineteenth century came to a close, with many rural workers moving to a new metrocentric way of life created by the railways out of the agrarian past. Over 18,000 miles of railway had been built across Britain, and in the first year of the new century, the fastest speed yet reached by a scheduled passenger train was recorded by the Midland Railway, with a speed of 90 mph near milepost 34 from London's St Pancras station.

Between 1901 and 1910 the Great Western Railway constructed 140 miles of new track to provide shorter routes to the sea, notably from London to Devon, Cornwall and South Wales. From London's main line termini railway lines spread like a spider's web to all points of the compass, most ending ultimately at the coast. The magazine 'Punch' poked fun at the many railway companies and their titles by suggesting that

there should be a "John o'Groats and Land's End Junction Railway, with branches to Ben Lomond and Battersea," since at the time there were over 40 large and 60 smaller railway companies in Britain, several competing for passengers on different lines between the same cities and towns.

By 1911, the railway network was virtually complete, and all routes to the sea had been built. Appendix 1 lists the opening dates for railways to some of the coastal destinations covered in Chapters 4 to 11. Railway business was booming, and trains were getting longer as well as faster, with more powerful locomotives entering service. In the Highlands of Scotland on the night of 11 August 1912 more than 800 coaches passed through Perth station en route to Aberdeen and Inverness for the 'Glorious Twelfth' in those golden years prior to the First World War.

At the outbreak of WW1 in August 1914 the government established a Railway Executive Committee, with overall control of most railway companies operating in Britain. This ensured that the entire railway system and infrastructure were operated in the best interests of a nation at war. From experiences gained during this temporary form of nationalization, the seeds were sown for later amalgamation.

After the war, the Railway Act of 1921 legislated a merger of companies that had been controlled by the government since August 1914. On 1 January 1923 a total of 123 separate railway companies were grouped into the 'Big Four', namely the London, Midland & Scottish (LMS); the London & North Eastern Railway (LNER); the Great Western Railway (GWR); and the Southern Railway (SR). A new railway era in Britain had begun.

Bradshaw's Railway Guide of 1923 listed the trains run by these new companies. In first place on the timetable was the Great Western Railway, the only company to retain its original name from 1835 to 1948. Even in 1923, many long distance journeys were tiring and tedious, usually with several changes of train en route. For example, Bradshaw's Guide showed the southbound 'Scottish Express' leaving Inverness at 0740 and reaching London at 0500 the next day, some fourteen hours slower than today's 'Highland Chieftain'.

By 1926, the rail network had reached its peak of about 21,000 miles, and the railways had created or developed seaside resorts at Blackpool, Brighton, Bournemouth, Ramsgate, Southend, Margate, Rhyl, Tenby, Weston-super-Mare, Scarborough, Newquay, St Ives, Paignton, Dawlish, Southport, Lowestoft, and Skegness, as well as many other places around Britain's coastline. The railways also brought prosperity to isolated coastal communities in Scotland, notably those at the Kyle of Lochalsh, Mallaig, Wick, Thurso, and Oban, all of which are served by train today.

To provide fast, comfortable, and environmentally clean services to the south coast, the line from London to Brighton was electrified in 1933, followed by the line to Portsmouth in

1937, the former much appreciated by those fortunate to live by the sea and work in London, and the latter for its frequent fast services from Waterloo to Portsmouth Harbour, for ferries to the Isle of Wight.

When the Southern Railway completed electrification of the south coast line from Portsmouth to Brighton, travel to the many resorts along this route increased considerably, and it is on this line that the greatest concentration of coastal railway stations in Britain is to be found: five stations in 3.5 miles, centered at Worthing in Sussex.

The only other seaside lines with closely grouped stations are from Ryde Pierhead to St John's Road on the Isle of Wight, with three stations in 1.5 miles; the Cumbrian coast line with three stations in two miles near Whitehaven; Blackpool with four stations (North, South, Pleasure Beach, and Squires Gate) in three miles; and the very popular St Erth to St Ives line in Cornwall, with five stations in four miles, including a summer 'park and ride' station at Lelant Saltings.

Britain's railways achieved their greatest feats of speed and endurance by steam trains in the years from 1936 to 1939, when rival express trains on the east and west coast main lines made many exceptional high speed runs. Powerful new locomotives were driven by men who had spent decades working up the railway ladder to reach the rank of 'top link driver', whose skill and panache usually ensured 'on time' arrival at their destination.

In pursuit of the absolute speed record for a steam-hauled train, the LMS and LNER recorded some outstanding runs. On 9 June 1937, the LMS streamlined locomotive 'Coronation' and its seven coaches reached a maximum speed of 112.5 mph between Madeley Bank and Crewe on the west coast main line, coming close to disaster as it hurtled towards the station. This was a result of continuing its acceleration far too close to Crewe for safety, then braking violently as it approached the platforms where horrified spectators were standing.

The LMS officials claimed 114 mph, which would have just beaten the existing LNER record of 113 mph, but independent recorders agreed that 112.5 mph was the maximum. The footplate crew had been asked to attempt to reach 120 mph, and the locomotive certainly had the power, but acceleration was both slow and late, considering how close they were to the maze of tracks leading into Crewe station.

On 3 July 1938, the A4 Class locomotive 'Mallard', hauling a seven-coach train including a dynamometer car to give absolute proof of maximum speed, attained 126 mph southbound on the east coast main line near milepost 90 between Little Bytham and Essendine. The location is marked by a large sign placed beside the tracks on the 60th anniversary of this record run. While most speed records are made to be broken, both 'Mallard' and its world speed record survive to this day, and hopefully will endure for all time.

At the outbreak of WW2, and during the war years, speeds were reduced and journey times lengthened. One daily scheduled service whose timing was affected by the war more than any other was the 'Thames-Clyde Express' from St Pancras to Glasgow (St Enoch). At the best of times it was a slow train, but with heavy wartime loads the journey was scheduled to take twelve hours, and it often took much longer.

The route to Scotland was via Kettering, Leicester, Nottingham, Derby, Leeds, Settle, Carlisle, Dumfries, and Kilmarnock to Glasgow, a distance of 444 miles, the longest distance travelled by a daily scheduled train between London and Glasgow. No other train in Britain passed daily through so many tunnels: there were 40 in all, totalling fifteen asphyxiating miles, and six of these tunnels were over a mile in length.

Journeys on Britain's railways reached a peak in 1944, when passenger traffic, including military trains, was 50 percent greater than in 1930. The evacuation from Dunkirk in 1940 required 525 extra trains to and from south coast stations, and many of these trains converged on Redhill station, where a record turnaround time of two minutes per train was set, as the wounded were transferred to hospitals around Britain.

By 1945 the railways had done much to save Britain, providing 110,000 railway personnel to the armed forces, and suffering over ten thousand aerial attacks. It was a period of austerity for every railway enterprise, although approval was obtained during the war to build the innovative and controversial 'Merchant Navy' class of locomotives, containing many prototype features. It was only when rebuilt by British Railways after WW2 that the essential combination of power, reliability, and minimal maintenance was finally achieved for these remarkable locomotives.

After WW2, the railways struggled to recover some of their past glory, with a huge backlog of maintenance work required for locomotives, coaches, and permanent way. Just four of Britain's seventy titled trains had run throughout the war, and all went to the coast: the 'Cornish Riviera', the 'Aberdonian', the 'Flying Scotsman', and the 'Night Scotsman'. From 1945 onwards, many famous named trains were restored, and those to the seaside are described in Chapters 4 to 11.

At midnight on 31 December 1947, locomotive whistles were sounded by drivers of night trains throughout Britain to mark the start of national ownership of the railway system. After years of bitter political wrangling, the LMS, LNER, GWR, and SR were amalgamated to form British Railways. It had taken two world wars to forge the railways of Britain: from over 100 companies in 1914, to the 'Big Four' in 1923; then 45 years later the four were nationalized into one. Only the former GWR managed to retain some semblance of the great days of steam, for it had by far the finest pedigree of all main line railways, and from 1835 to 1948 had established an enduring tradition of reliability and pride in serving its passengers.

The development of diesel-powered high speed trains (HSTs) transformed railway journeys to the sea. Apart from London to Penzance services operated by Great Western, they are also used for important cross-country expresses such as the 'Cornishman', 'Devonian' and 'Dorset Scot'. (John Hadrill)

With some 8,000 stations, 15,000 locomotives, and 40,000 coaches on inventory in 1948, it took several years for BR to implement livery changes, so the well-known colours of the 'Big Four' were seen on passenger trains for decades after nationalization. Even in the 1990s, the popular GWR 'chocolate and cream' colours could still be seen on branch lines in Cornwall, giving railway travellers a nostalgic ride to the seaside on what was affectionately known as 'God's Wonderful Railway'.

When the main line from London's Liverpool St station to the Essex coast was electrified in 1963, high speed electric trains serving seaside resorts at Clacton and Walton-on-the-Naze had the fastest timings of any short distance rail service in Europe. From start-to-stop beween Shenfield and Chelmsford, a distance of 9.5 miles, the timetable allowed 8.5 minutes, giving an average speed of over 67 mph. No steam or diesel service could match the awesome acceleration of 3,384 horsepower in each lightweight ten-coach electric train on this short section of a busy Great Eastern commuter line.

Between 0530 and 0930 on Mondays to Fridays during the 1990s, over 140 passenger trains passed through or stopped at Shenfield station en route to London from Southend, Braintree, Southminster, Colchester, Clacton, Walton-on-the-Naze, Harwich, Ipswich, Felixstowe, Lowestoft, Norwich, Great Yarmouth, Cromer, and Sheringham. While signs on the platforms at Clapham Junction proclaim it to be Britain's busiest station, Shenfield station on the Great Eastern line rates highly among Britain's busy stations during the rush hours into and out of London.

In contrast to the 1950s, when Britain's nationalized railways showed a profit, huge deficits in the 1960s inevitably resulted in closures of many unprofitable lines identified in the Beeching Report of 1963, which recommended withdrawal of passenger services on 5,000 route miles, and closure of 2,350 stations.

From a maximum route mileage of over 21,000 in the 1920s, by 1952 there were 19,000 route miles and 8,212 stations on Britain's rail network. By 1972, route mileage had been reduced to 11,500, with only 2,735 stations open to serve passengers, resulting in the railways carrying only a small fraction of the travelling public. There was clearly a need for radical improvements in rail services to attract more passengers, especially on long distance routes to and from London, the world's greatest railway metropolis.

On 6 May 1974, British Rail inaugurated its first long distance electric service on the west coast main line from London to Glasgow, reducing travel times to Scotland and places en route, as well as providing a more environmentally friendly form of traction than steam or diesel. The long climbs up to Shap and Beattock summits were relatively quiet and seemingly effortless; one could only marvel, for relative silence did indeed give fast ascent compared to the slow and polluting climbs of heavy freight and passenger trains hauled by steam or diesel locomotives for over a century on this steeply graded line.

Of even greater impact to rail travellers in Britain during the 1970s was the development and introduction of diesel-powered high speed trains (HSTs) on main line services. On a test run in June 1973, a prototype HST achieved a maximum speed of 143.2 mph between Northallerton and Thirsk, maintaining 140 mph for over twelve miles. The HSTs successfully combined high sustained speeds with the very best in comfort and space for standard-class passengers, and when placed in revenue service their smooth riding capabilities were outstanding compared to trains hauled by older types of diesel locomotives.

After a number of improvements based on prototype evaluation, the HST was introduced into main line revenue passenger service on 5 May 1975 between London, Bristol and Weston-super-Mare. Services to Cardiff and Swansea followed in October 1976, and to the west of England, Plymouth and Penzance in 1979. Cross-country HST services between Penzance and Edinburgh, the longest sea-to-sea route in Britain by one through train, were introduced in 1981.

The HSTs have carried more passengers on more long-distance routes to the sea than any other type of train. They average 250,000 miles each year, and some are expected to travel over ten million miles before they are replaced. Their great advantage over electric traction is that they can go almost anywhere in Britain, or operate on any standard-gauge railway abroad, and in this regard they are the most versatile, productive, and successful passenger trains ever built.

Journeys to the sea by HSTs on cross-country services enable thousands of passengers to travel daily from Scotland and the north of England to the southwest and south coasts (or vice versa) on through trains such as the 'Cornish Scot', 'Devonian', 'Sussex Scot', 'Armada', 'Dorset Scot', 'Cornishman', and 'Wessex Scot'. For example, a journey by HST from Inverness in the north of Scotland to Brighton in Sussex, requires only one change of train, usually at the same platform at Edinburgh's Waverley station, with timings (1998):

The Highland Chieftain:	dep. Inverness 0755; arr. Edinburgh 1121
The Sussex Scot:	dep. Edinburgh 1136; arr. Brighton 2022

These titled trains are so popular that reservations are recommended at all times of the year to ensure a seat. On certain cross-country services from Edinburgh, trains to the south coast may depart from Waverley in either direction, one train taking the east coast route, the other taking the west coast route. The 'Sussex Scot' takes the longer west coast route from Edinburgh to Brighton, giving a total journey time from Inverness to Brighton (674 miles) of 12h 27min, with a respectable average speed of 54.1 mph, including the change of trains at Edinburgh.

The sustained speed capability of HSTs in revenue service has been impressive. On 7 May 1977, an InterCity HST covered the 118 miles between Bristol and Paddington at an average speed of 103.3 mph from start to stop, and returned to Bristol at an average speed of 104.4 mph. On 30 August 1984 a top speed of 129.2 mph was attained between these two stations, with an average speed of 121.7 mph recorded for 107 miles. Isambard Brunel, builder of this line, would certainly have been impressed by HST performance on the route he selected between London and Bristol over 150 years ago.

By 1977, over 2,260 miles of track in Britain had been electrified, and plans were in hand for electrification of the east coast main line between King's Cross and Edinburgh, a great route for sustained high speed runs. On 27 September 1985, six years before electrification of this line was completed, a diesel-powered 'Tyne-Tees Pullman' HST sprinted from Newcastle to King's Cross in 2hr 19min 37sec at an average speed of 115.4 mph for the 268.5 miles.

During this journey, a maximum speed of 144 mph was recorded, the fastest speed ever achieved by a trainload of passengers on a scheduled service in Britain. At Finsbury Park, just over two miles from the buffer stops at King's Cross, the train was travelling at 103 mph. All 320 tons of train and passengers arrived safely at the platform after this exuberant display of HST power, speed, and smooth braking capability.

On the former SR main line out of Waterloo, with its extensive network of third rail electrified track dating back to the 1930s, and commuter trains serving the London suburbs and south coast, it was not possible to achieve such high sustained speeds. Nevertheless, on 14 April 1988 a 'Wessex Express' from Waterloo to Southampton recorded a maximum speed of 110 mph.

After electrification of the east coast route to Scotland was completed in 1991, and the new InterCity 225 (km/h) electric trains introduced, a new record run was inevitable on the main line that had produced many speed records by steam trains for over a century, and by diesels since the 1960s. On 26 September 1991, all previous British railway start-to-stop speed records between London and Edinburgh were shattered by an InterCity 225 train which covered the 393.5 miles in 3hr 29 min, averaging 112.9 mph on a special high-speed run.

This record was all the more remarkable considering the severe speed restrictions at York, Durham and Newcastle. Past milepost 90 (from King's Cross), where the southbound steam locomotive 'Mallard' with seven coaches reached the world record speed of 126 mph on 3 July 1938, the northbound InterCity 225 reached a top speed of 162 mph while climbing up to Stoke summit.

After the 1991 record run from London to Edinburgh, the 'Scottish Pullman' was timed to leave King's Cross at 0800 and reach Edinburgh at 1159, with stops at York and Newcastle. However, the year-round popularity of this service on a very busy main line with station stops, resulted in a more realistic arrival in Edinburgh at 1216. Subsequent competition with the airlines, and the rivalry for revenue between privatized railway companies serving Scotland, restored the 3h 59min timings in 1997 for the 0600 train from Edinburgh and the 1500 train from King's Cross, giving a start-to-stop average speed of 98.8 mph for 393.5 miles, with station stops at York and Newcastle en route.

In June 1995, a GNER train recorded a top speed of 154 mph on the east coast main line, setting a new British record for a scheduled passenger train in revenue service. Yet, although the east coast main line could claim Britain's fastest speeds and longest non-stop runs for many years, the three trains with longest non-stop timetabled service on 23 May 1998 were:

1. The Cornish Riviera:
   (diesel) from Paddington to Plymouth
   225.5 miles

2. The Royal Scot:
   (electric) from Euston to Preston
   207 miles

3. The Scottish Pullman:
   (electric) from King's Cross to York
   188 miles

Britain's railway companies operating from London a century ago built huge stations, cathedrals of the industrial age, to impress passengers and to intimidate rival companies. London has twelve main line termini, and from ten of these stations trains travel, or travelled, to the coast. They are:

WATERLOO: This is the only London terminus where trains start and end their journeys by travelling beside the Thames. High-rise buildings have unfortunately obscured many of the fine views of the Houses of Parliament, the Victoria Tower, and other historic buildings across the river, but there are still brief glimpses of some of this architectural splendour on the right side after departure, before the train veers away from the Thames towards Clapham Junction.

It was from Waterloo that famous trains such as 'Atlantic Coast Express', 'Devon Belle' and 'Bournemouth Belle' departed for the seaside. With its main station, East station, and Eurostar terminus, Waterloo has a total of 28 platforms, making it London's largest and busiest. In the heydays of transatlantic travel by luxury liners, 'Boat Train' specials left Waterloo several times each week for Southampton's Ocean Terminal. Platform 12 at Waterloo is where the 'White Star' boat train departed with passengers for the 'Titanic' on its maiden, and final, voyage in April 1912.

Trains from Waterloo still travel the route of the 'Atlantic Coast Express' to Exeter and, with change of train, to the Devon coast at Exmouth and Barnstaple. In July 1998, Waterloo station celebrated 150 years of rail service to the public. When opened by the London & South Western Railway it was larger than any other station in Britain, covering over 24 acres, with 21 platforms spread across its grand concourse.

VICTORIA: In addition to its many trains to the south coast, the ghosts of two famous titled trains still linger here. At Platform 8 stood the 'Golden Arrow', whose passengers passed under its bright and enticing archway. Even more beguiling was the 'Night Ferry', whose sleeping cars travelled all the way from Victoria to Paris, with through service to Brussels and Geneva.

On 25 May 1982, passengers at Platform 8 boarded the restored Venice Simplon Orient Express for the 926-mile journey to Venice. In the spirit of competition between rail and road travel dating back to the 1920s, a Ferrari driven by an enthusiastic British sportsman raced the VSOE from Victoria to Venice in 1997, and won. The VSOE has proved so popular that 'British Pullmans' now offer excursions from Victoria to famous places around Britain. Some of these trains are steam-hauled.

The 'Brighton Belle' Pullman, Britain's most luxurious commuter train, travelled to the sea and back several times each day from Victoria until its demise in 1972. The train now runs in a late-1990s version, without Pullman coaches. The journeys of these and other famous titled trains in Britain are covered in the respective coastal sections of this book.

PADDINGTON: On 24 May 1862, the world's first underground railway was inaugurated between Paddington and Farringdon Road in the City. This marked the dawn of the commuter age in Britain.

The station is one of Brunel's masterpieces, a huge trainshed completed in 1854, and inspired in part by Paxton's Crystal Palace of 1851, combining decorative cast iron and glass in what was then a daring design, reflecting Victorian artistic styles and engineering confidence. The Great Western Royal Hotel adjacent to the concourse was built in 1854 and was the largest and most luxurious in London. It is now an oasis of comfort and quiet, rare commodities these days for rail travellers in most of London's main line stations.

Paddington is the departure point for most seaside resorts in Cornwall, Devon, Somerset and south Wales. Trains from Paddington travel on Brunel's famous 'billiard table' tracks, for they are the most level of all long-distance main lines from London.

Two of Paddington's platforms (15 and 16) are used by Underground trains on the Hammersmith Line, accessed by the shortest above-ground walk between a main line train and a 'tube' train. No other terminus in London can offer such fast accessibility to the 'tube', or to Heathrow airport. In June 1998, 'Heathrow Express' services commenced between Paddington and the world's busiest international airport, with a journey time of 15 minutes, compared to about an hour by Underground.

EUSTON: The oldest of London's main line termini (1827), Euston was enlarged in 1838 to include Britain's first railway hotel for the comfort and convenience of passengers. The first bookstall in a railway station was opened here in 1848 by William Henry Smith, who also chartered special overnight trains to carry newspapers from Euston to cities around Britain. By 1850, W.H.Smith was operating more than thirty

EUSTON

Glasgow ▸ Fort William ▸ Mallaig ▸ Oban ▸ Gourock Wemyss Bay ▸ Largs ▸ Troon ▸ Ayr ▸ Stranraer Grange-over-Sands ▸ Morecambe ▸ Blackpool Lytham ▸ Southport ▸ New Brighton ▸ Prestatyn Rhyl ▸ Abergele ▸ Llandudno ▸ Bangor ▸ Holyhead Pwllheli ▸ Barmouth ▸ Aberdovey ▸ Aberystwyth

KING'S CROSS

Edinburgh ▸ Inverness ▸ Kyle of Lochalsh Wick ▸ Thurso ▸ Aberdeen ▸ Dundee Berwick-upon-Tweed ▸ Whitley Bay Saltburn ▸ Whitby ▸ Scarborough ▸ Filey Bridlington ▸ Cleethorpes ▸ Skegness

LIVERPOOL STREET

Southend ▸ Clacton ▸ Frinton Walton-on-the-Naze ▸ Harwich Felixstowe ▸ Lowestoft ▸ Gt Yarmouth Cromer ▸ Sheringham ▸ King's Lynn

To the Sea **FROM LONDON**

PADDINGTON

Penzance ▸ St Ives ▸ Newquay Falmouth ▸ St Austell ▸ Looe Saltash ▸ Plymouth ▸ Paignton Torquay ▸ Teignmouth ▸ Dawlish Exmouth ▸ Weston-super-Mare Milford Haven ▸ Pembroke ▸ Tenby Swansea ▸ Cardiff ▸ Penarth

FENCHURCH ST

▸ Leigh-on-Sea
▸ Southend
▸ Shoeburyness

CHARING CROSS
VICTORIA
CANNON ST
LONDON BRIDGE

DESTINATIONS SHOWN BELOW MAY BE SERVED BY TRAINS FROM ONE OR MORE OF THE ABOVE LONDON TERMINI.

Bognor Regis ▸ Littlehampton Worthing ▸ Brighton ▸ Hove Newhaven ▸ Eastbourne Hastings ▸ Folkestone ▸ Dover Deal ▸ Ramsgate ▸ Margate Herne Bay ▸ Whitstable

WATERLOO

Weymouth ▸ Bournemouth Poole ▸ Lymington Pier Southampton ▸ Portsmouth Isle of Wight

NOTE

THE STATIONS LISTED ARE A SELECTION BY THE AUTHOR.

A CHANGE OF TRAIN MAY BE NECESSARY TO REACH SOME STATIONS ON THE COAST.

THROUGH TRAINS TO INVERNESS DEPART FROM KING'S CROSS BY DAY AND FROM EUSTON BY NIGHT.

Photo: King's Cross (John Hadrill)

station bookstalls, and had exclusive sales rights at stations along 2,000 miles of track.

When the London & North Western Railway completed its main line to Scotland in 1848, the company created at Euston the most impressive and dignified entrance of any station in London. A massive Doric arch was built to emphasize the importance of Euston as London's gateway to the north, and inside the station was Hardwick's Great Hall, both demolished by British Rail when the station was rebuilt in 1962.

Thirty years later, four seats of stone quarried from Portland in Dorset, Elterwater and St Bees in Cumbria, and Merrivale in Devon, were placed by British Rail near to the spot where the famous arch stood, as if in penance for its destruction. A statue of Robert Stephenson stands nearby to mark his great achievements as locomotive builder and engineer for the London & North Western Railway.

Euston is one of London's busiest stations, with frequent fast services on the electrified west coast main line to Scotland, the northwest, midlands, North Wales and Holyhead (for Ireland).

ST PANCRAS: With its vast neo-gothic facade designed by Sir George Gilbert Scott, and completed in 1893, the station stands high above its neighbour, King's Cross. Compared to the subterranean platforms at Euston, the platforms at St Pancras are the highest above street level of any main line terminus in London.

This was necessary for trains to cross the Regent's Canal, resulting in a huge storage space below the platforms, put to good use by creating the largest beer cellar in London, 4.5

acres under one roof. The Midland Railway linked London with Burton-on-Trent, and the directors confidently expected good profits to be made in transporting ale by rail. It was said at the time that the height of the platforms above the street was determined by the size of stacked barrels in the station's cavernous cellar.

The station hotel was named 'The Midland Grand Hotel', and with 600 rooms it was the largest and finest in Britain. It was hoped that guests travelling on the 'Thames-Clyde Express' would stay here, lured by the patriotic words: "St George for England, St Pancras for Scotland." But it was difficult to compete with the much faster LMS and LNER expresses, so the hotel was closed down and converted into offices in 1935.

In contrast to Euston and King's Cross stations, St Pancras is an oasis of relative tranquillity and emptiness. This will change when the new Channel Tunnel Rail Link, Britain's first new main line for over a century, reaches St Pancras in the year 2007.

KING'S CROSS: William Cubitt, builder of this terminus, declared that he could build the whole structure for less than twice the cost of Euston's huge entrance arch, and he did. Standing beside the gothic magnificence of St Pancras, King's Cross is a utilitarian building, looking remarkably modern for a mid-nineteenth century station, under whose Platform 8, according to archaeologists, lies the grave of chariot-borne Queen Boadicea, who died in AD 61.

History was made here on 27 September 1935, when Britain's first streamlined train left for a test run to the north, exactly 110 years after George Stephenson had driven Locomotion No.1 on the Stockton & Darlington Railway. The new train was named the 'Silver Jubilee' to mark the reign of King George V. In June 1977, the name was revived briefly to mark the Silver Jubilee of Queen Elizabeth II.

King's Cross is terminus for the Great North Eastern Railway, with frequent fast electric services to Scotland on titled trains such as the 'Flying Scotsman', 'Aberdonian', 'Highland Chieftain' and 'Scottish Pullman'. The station has a long history of departures and arrivals of many high-speed trains from 1885 to the present day, as well as for unique luxury train cruises offered by the LNER's 'Northern Belle' in the 1930s.

In the 1996/97 judging of Britain's 2,500 stations, King's Cross won the 'Station of the Year' award. The independent panel of judges commented on the high standard of services, effective station signs, and arrangement of the concourse and platforms.

LIVERPOOL STREET: After a century of accumulated smoke and grime, making it one of the dreariest and dirtiest main line stations in London, this railway terminus has been transformed into London's newest and brightest, serving the coasts of Essex, Suffolk and Norfolk.

Until WW2, it was the starting point for one of the longest railway journeys in the world to the sea and beyond, from England to Japan. This marathon journey, made by many commercial travellers and adventurers in the 1920s and 1930s, started each day with departure of the 'Flushing Continental' at 1000 from Liverpool St to Harwich. Seventeen days later, weary passengers who had set out from London reached Tokyo, a journey of 7,600 miles by train plus 91 miles by sea.

Liverpool Street is one of London's busiest stations, with more than 100,000 passengers arriving and departing each weekday. Before WW1, the two-penny early morning return ticket from Enfield to Liverpool Street, a distance of 21 miles, was said to be the best miles-per-penny bargain in Britain. For those who could not travel to the sea, the Great Eastern Railway would deliver a large can of sea water to any address in London for sixpence, calling the next day to collect the empty can at no extra charge.

CHARING CROSS, LONDON BRIDGE, CANNON STREET: Grouped close to the Thames in the centre of London, these three termini provide frequent electric train services to stations on the south coast.

The diagram on page 21 shows some of the stations around Britain's coastline that are served by trains from one or more of London's main line termini.

Origins and growth of the Railway excursion

I cannot rest from travel:
I will drink Life to the lees.
I am part of all that I have met;
Yet all experience is an arch wherethro'
Gleams that untravell'd world, whose margin fades
For ever and for ever when I move.

Tennyson: "Ulysses"

The first railway in Britain to carry fare-paying passengers on a seaside excursion was horse-drawn, and ran along the coast of south Wales near Swansea, between Oystermouth and the Mumbles in 1807. It operated until 1960, and was unique in that it used five forms of power during its 153 years: horse, steam, electric, diesel, and even an early experiment with wind propulsion under sail.

At the opening of the London to Birmingham railway in 1838, Dr. Arnold, Headmaster of Rugby School, wrote: "I rejoice to see the railway, and to think that feudality is gone forever; it is so great a blessing to think that any one evil is really extinct." Three years later, the London & South Western Railway advertised its first combined rail and sea excursions, offering 200 miles of travel by land and water, including the Isle of Wight, for one pound.

Organized group travel by train on a grand scale began with Thomas Cook (1808-1892), who started life as a carpenter's apprentice, then became a printer in Market Harborough and leader of a temperance movement. In the late 1830s he covered some 2,000 miles a year, mostly on foot, holding meetings in towns and villages around Britain. After many tiring and tedious journeys, it was only a small step from proselytizing to creating a commercial enterprise specializing in railway excursions.

Cook left the podium in 1840, convinced that there was more money to be made from a career as travel agent than from sermons against the devil gin. He opened a railway travel business, and organized his first rail excursion on 5 July 1841 for 570 temperance members and their families, offering a day trip from Leicester to Loughborough, with tea, cricket and sandwiches for ticket holders, who paid one shilling (5p) per person.

This was so popular that other destinations served by railways around the country were added, and Cook wrote in his journal: "From the heights of Snowdon, my thoughts took flight to Ben Lomond, and I determined to get to Scotland." He was not alone in his plans, and in 1844 Sir Rowland Hill, founder of the penny post, and a director of the London & Brighton Railway introduced the first excursion train between these two stations. Four locomotives were needed to haul the 45 carriages that left Norwood junction, and by the time the train left Croydon, twelve more had been added, together with two more locomotives. The eight hundred passengers reached Brighton at 1330, four and a half hours after setting out.

During the railway mania of the 1850s, with hundreds of companies seeking approval for new routes, Sir Rowland Hill, a great innovator and philanthropist, proposed legislation in parliament for national ownership of Britain's railways, nearly a century before British Rail was established.

Meanwhile, encouraged by his success, Cook arranged his first tour to the Scottish lowlands in 1846, travelling from Leicester to Fleetwood by train, then by steamer to Ardrossan, where trains took his clients to Glasgow and Edinburgh, all for the cost of one guinea per person. In 1850 'The Times' observed: "There are thousands of our readers, we are sure, who in the last three years have travelled more and seen more than in all their previous life taken together." By 1866, Thomas Cook's company had taken 40,000 tourists to Scotland, of whom 4,000 had visited the Western Isles, Iona, and Fingal's Cave, while another 10,000 had sailed around Loch Lomond.

Those who had taken excursions with Thomas Cook's company were soon persuaded of the value and quality of his service, and he quickly expanded his business, offering 'Cook's Tours' to Paris, Italy, Geneva, and Mont Blanc. Over 100,000 Mohammedans made their pilgrimage to Mecca through the travel arrangements of Thomas Cook, who also organized the first 'round the world' trip in 1872, using newly opened railway routes, and inspiring Jules Verne to write his famous novel.

In the industrial north of England, whole trains were booked by companies to enable their workers to have a day beside the sea. In 1844 a factory manager in Lancashire arranged a day trip by train to Fleetwood for 650 of his employees, most of whom had never been on a train, nor visited the seaside until then. Initial fears of the iron monster were soon overcome, and the delight of so many happy people seeing places their ancestors had never seen in their lifetime was shared with friends and neighbours who came along on the next excursions. During Whitsun Week of 1850, a total of 202,543 passengers left Manchester and nearby towns for a holiday at Blackpool.

Until the coming of the railway, the record for distance travelled in one day by a human was held by the Roman emperor Tiberius who covered 200 miles, employing many horses and chariots of the imperial administration to achieve this distance, circa 30 AD. Nearly 1,800 years later it took over thirty hours travel time for a passenger to cover 200 miles from Gloucester to York by stagecoach, requiring several days, with overnight stops at inns en route for food, rest, recovery from the rough journey, and change of horses.

Certainly the railways were the greatest single cause and visible sign of progress, offering wider horizons to more people than any other invention had ever done. The completion of a railway line to the coast enabled seaside resorts to grow, welcoming tourists, daily newspapers at dawn, prompt arrival of the mail, fast delivery of perishable goods, and all the necessities of life which were not readily available by other means of transportation. A family holiday by train to the seaside was indeed one of the happiest inventions of the industrial revolution.

When the Great Exhibition of 1851 opened on May Day in London's Hyde Park, excursion trains from all over Britain brought tens of thousands to the capital, many for the first time in their lives, to gaze in wonder at artifacts of the age. This was the first exhibition of its size and scope in the world, and Thomas Cook arranged for more than 165,000 people from the north of England to travel there by train during the exhibition season. It was reported at the time that pawnbrokers held hundreds of silver watches pledged to pay for the special five-shilling return tickets issued for travel between Leeds/Bradford and London.

Employers sent large groups of their workers to the Great Exhibition by train on the one shilling entrance days, and thousands of poor folk took the only holiday in their lives in order to see the Exhibition. By the time it closed in mid-October, over six million people had attended, and most had come by train, with several railway companies declaring handsome dividends at the close of that profitable year of travel in Britain.

Railway companies pioneered the hotel industry across Britain, and spent 145 years as hoteliers, starting at London's Euston station in 1838 and selling off their last hotel in 1983. Railways were also the first large-scale users of the electric telegraph along their extensive routes, and a fare of one penny per mile was established by parliament on certain early morning and evening trains to provide workers with travel at reasonable cost. The 'workman's ticket' survived for more than a century, and was given the more socially acceptable title of 'early morning return' in the 1950s before being replaced by a new fare structure in 1961.

By 1852 a person could travel by train all the way from Plymouth to Aberdeen, with several changes en route. This is a long journey today even by HST, but this illustrates how rapidly the rail network had expanded in just over twenty years.

Boston, Lincolnshire, was a favourite destination in the 1850s for sea trips across the Wash to Hunstanton, or round the coast to Skegness. Railway excursions from the Midlands to Boston in 1859 brought 6,000 visitors on one day in July, including a train of forty carriages from Doncaster and Lincoln containing over 1,500 passengers. The first official Bank Holiday was legislated in 1871, enabling those who had never taken a railway journey to go to the seaside in the summer, "when England leaves her centre for her tide-line," as poet laureate John Betjeman later wrote in his poem 'Beside the Seaside.'

An excursion train carrying over 500 hundred people to the sea, like the steam locomotive itself, was a British invention. And while Brighton as a 'watering place' pre-dated the railways, many resorts were developed, if not created, by the arrival of trains at the coast. In 1871 there were 48 seaside resorts listed in the official census of Britain, and by 1900 there were over 200.

With few visitors each day in 1831, Blackpool welcomed 50,000 on a single summer's day in 1900, most of them arriving by train. Bournemouth had 905 residents in 1841, and by 1931 this had increased to 120,000, largely as a result of convenient train services from London, the midlands, and the north.

When the Paris Exposition of 1878 opened, Thomas Cook organized the first international excursions from London to Paris. He booked over 75,000 clients for tours to the continent from all over Britain, using hundreds of special trains for what

were to become 'Cook's Tours'. The public's appetite for such events was as insatiable then as it is now.

Perhaps the Duke of Wellington summed it up best. He was not a railway enthusiast, although he did attend the opening of the Liverpool & Manchester railway in 1830. Regarding railways he noted accurately, if somewhat snobbishly: "They allow the lower classes to move about." While Britain's class system remained rigidly in place, travel by train at reasonable cost was so popular that it soon became the great liberator of all levels of society.

For the Preston Guild Week of 1882, over 375,000 persons travelled by hundreds of trains which left for the seaside every two minutes at peak periods. Destinations included Blackpool, Lytham, St Annes-on-Sea, and Southport. To handle the huge crowds, all platforms and even cattle landing stages in the goods yards at some coastal stations were used to enable passengers to disembark as quickly as possible. This annual event in Lancashire was so popular that by 1922 over 500 trains were needed to carry a total of 555,434 passengers to and from the seaside during one week that summer.

Blackpool quickly became a favourite venue for railway excursions, no less than 50,000 visitors arriving on a single summer's day in 1900. Equally remarkable was this scene four years earlier, with trains lined up in Talbot Road station waiting to take participants in the annual Bass Brewery outing back to Burton-on-Trent. The famous Tower is just visible in the background. (NRM - 251/87)

A few discriminating travellers were able to choose their destination and travel in a unique railway coach. After the accession of King Edward VII in 1901, a new royal train was built for him, and one of the coaches used on Queen Victoria's old train was set aside for hire. Twelve first-class return fares to any station in Britain were sufficient to book it for a journey, so long as the departure was from a station on either the LNWR or Caledonian Railway. This coach offered the most luxurious form of transportation that could be booked for an excursion on the railway network in the Edwardian era.

During WW1, when excursion trains were replaced by

The LNER encouraged families to stay at holiday camps opened by Billy Butlin beside the sea in the 1930s and '40s. That at Filey was served by its own branch line and station, at which a crowd of war-weary holiday-makers is arriving in 1947, ready for the cheery wake-up calls and all sorts of jollification. (NRM - 292/82)

'military specials', through trains were run from Plymouth to Invergordon, the longest journey in Britain by one train at that time. The train left Plymouth at 0945 and reached Invergordon at 1030 the following day, with Thurso (for Scapa Flow) another four hours away.

At that time, the longest railway journey one could take in Britain from south to north using the most direct route was from Penzance to Lybster on the north-east coast of Scotland, 935 miles from Penzance, and 743 miles from London, via Wick. The journey took 31h 20min and required travel on six trains. Lybster is no longer on the railway network, and Wick is now the furthest station in mainland Britain from Penzance or London.

In 1921, a daily through coach for Penzance was attached to the southbound Aberdeen-King's Cross express, travelling with this train as far as York, where it joined an express linking York with Swindon, via Sheffield, Nottingham, Leicester, and Banbury. A GWR sleeping car train then took the coach for the remainder of the journey from Swindon to Penzance, a total distance of 785 miles from sea to sea.

This was the longest railway excursion that a person could take across Britain in one carriage, requiring a good measure of patience and stamina. The service was given the title 'Aberdeen to Penzance Express', though it was hardly an express, and it ran only until WW2. In summer, a coach from Glasgow and one from Edinburgh joined the Aberdeen coach for the long haul to Penzance.

Departure from Aberdeen was at 1020, with arrival in Penzance at 0740 the next day, a total journey time of 21h 20min. Those adventurous enough to travel the entire route, yet wishing to sleep in comfort, were allowed to book berths on the overnight sleeper from Paddington to Penzance, boarding at Swindon ten minutes before midnight, giving nearly eight hours in a comfortable berth on the journey to Britain's most westerly rail terminus.

In the reverse direction, the through coach for Aberdeen left Penzance with the 1110 express to Paddington as far as Westbury, where a train was waiting to take it to Swindon. At 1820 another train took the coach to York, arriving at 2335, in time for those with reservations to board the sleeping car train from King's Cross to Aberdeen, arriving at 0740 the next day.

During peak summer months in the 1930s, congestion at Penzance made it necessary to start the Penzance-Aberdeen service at St Erth, the only village station in Britain to be the starting point for an overnight rail service linking the south of England with the far north of Scotland. For those on holiday at St Ives and Carbis Bay, this start at St Erth was more convenient than going into Penzance, and it remains so today for fast direct cross-country services by HST from St Erth to Scotland.

At the high tide of rail excursions during the 1920s and 1930s, the four major railway companies published a wide range of pocket guides for ramblers and hikers, encouraging travel by train to many areas of outstanding natural beauty. At sixpence (2.5p) a copy, these excellent railway travel guides were a real bargain, and quickly sold out each year.

The most unusual excursions to the seaside in the 1920s were run by the LMS, LNER, and GWR on 29 June 1927, to witness an event that lasted only 24 seconds and created much excitement around the country. The objective was to see a total eclipse of the sun, the first to be observed in Britain since 1724, with an arc of totality extending from North Wales to Middlesbrough and Hartlepool on the northeast coast. The LMS claimed a large share of eclipse territory, and advertised that the best viewing place was at Southport in Lancashire, so this was their primary destination.

Special excursion trains were also run by the LMS to seaside resorts at Bangor, Blackpool, Carnarvon (as the station was then spelt), Colwyn Bay, Fleetwood, Liverpool, Llandudno, Rhyl, Lytham, and Morecambe. Over 70,000 people were carried on these excursions, and three special posters were issued by the LMS for this event, as well as leaflets and other publicity material. For those travelling from London, a procession of trains left Euston to reach the seaside in good time to watch this once-in-a-lifetime phenomenon.

In 1929, the LNER introduced a day excursion train from Liverpool St, which ran from the end of May to the end of September, using Pullman coaches, for which a supplement had to be paid, 10/6 for first class, and 6/6 for third class. The title of this train was the 'Eastern Belle', and it was unique in that it ran to a different seaside resort each day of the week except on Saturdays, when Clacton was the usual destination. Such was the wide choice of east coast destinations that each week a different set of resorts would be selected from a list

that included Felixstowe, Lowestoft, Great Yarmouth, Cromer, Sheringham, Frinton, Walton-on-the-Naze, Skegness, Clacton, Hunstanton, Heacham, Aldeburgh, Thorpeness, and Harwich.

Most of the trains ran non-stop to the coast, while the Cromer 'Belle' called at Wroxham and North Walsham for Norfolk Broads passengers . Of all the resorts served by this train, Clacton proved to be the most popular, being closest to London and allowing more time for visitors to enjoy its fine beaches and entertainments before returning home in comfort on the LNER's unique multi-route 'Eastern Belle' Pullman service.

Some 'day excursions' required stamina as well as sleepless nights. In 1932, the LMS and the 'Glasgow Herald' sponsored what was advertised as 'a day excursion over the sea to Skye', which involved two nights' travel to spend a day on Skye. The train left Glasgow at 2350 on Tuesday 19 July, and travelled through the night via Stirling, Perth, Forres, Nairn, Inverness, and Achnasheen, to reach the Kyle of Lochalsh at 0907.

Passengers landed on Skye at 0945 and stayed until 2145, enjoying the long northern daylight on the island before returning to the train, which departed at 2230, travelling through the night to reach Glasgow at 0805 on Thursday. The third class return fare was 22 shillings. For an extra 63 shillings, a first class compartment, sleeping car berth, and dining car services were provided for those who preferred these luxuries during two nights of travel on a crowded excursion train.

The Southern Railway, with the greatest number of seaside resorts within easy reach of London, arranged many varied day trips and weekend outings, while the Great Western Railway, whose trains had to travel much further to the sea from London, ran its 'Hiker's Mystery Expresses' from Paddington, where passengers were invited to 'join the great adventure'. Many did, resulting in lasting friendships, for it was all part of the fun, mystery, and adventure in which enthusiasm led the way, and nostalgia brought the hikers back year after year.

Half-day and evening train trips became popular in the 1930s. During the summer of 1934, the LMS ran 1,616 half-day excursion trains, many with restaurant car facilities. Evening excursions to Blackpool in 1935 attracted 637,000 visitors travelling in 1,878 trains. The last night of the famous illuminations brought visitors all the way from Birmingham on an evening excursion, a round trip of 242 miles for 4/6 return - a very late return, but certainly excellent travel value.

The variety of excursions offered by railway companies was almost limitless. In 1936 the LNER, proud of its railway station gardens in rural areas, ran rail tours to several of its prize-winning stations, using the newest coaches and buffet cars in a very successful public relations exercise. This was repeated in 1937, when eight 'garden specials' were arranged and 1,700 tickets sold to enthusiastic gardeners who toured the colourful horticultural displays at stations along LNER tracks.

For those who wished to stay a week or longer at their favourite holiday location served by train, camping coaches were provided by railway companies at seaside and country stations throughout Britain. Introduced by the LNER in 1933, and by the GWR in 1934, each camping coach was offered for hire to parties of six, at a cost of three pounds a week including linen, cooking facilities, crockery, utensils, and fuel. These coaches were very popular, and families had to book early each year to ensure they could return to the camping coach in their favourite location, just as they would to a cottage or guest house by the sea.

The LNER also encouraged families to stay at holiday camps opened by Billy Butlin beside the sea at Skegness in 1937, and at Clacton in 1938. Butlin borrowed his motto from Shakespeare: "our true intent is all for your delight", and most of his clients would probably have agreed. The growth of holiday camps in the 1930s and late 1940s provided good business for the railways, and Butlin made sure that all his seaside camps were close to railway lines at Ayr, Clacton, Filey, Minehead, Mosney (Ireland), Pwllheli, and Skegness. The LMS, not to be outdone, built its holiday camp at Prestatyn in partnership with Thomas Cook in 1939, and had just one summer of operation before the army requisitioned it for the duration of WW2.

Throughout the past 150 years, countless railway excursions to the seaside around Britain have brought pleasure, excitement, health and happy memories to millions of holidaymakers. From 1923 to 1947 the four large railway companies commissioned artists to design hundreds of posters, promoting travel to a coastal resort on the rail network. Most of the posters used the irresistible combination of sunshine, golden sands, colourful promenades, and happy swimmers in the surf. It was a formula that worked very well, and in one year during the 1930s the LNER commissioned the finest graphic artists in Britain to produce a series of 34 new posters based on themes that proclaimed the joie de vivre of holidays by the sea.

Few works of art evoke memories of happy holidays as vividly as railway posters, successfully combining fantasy with reality, and enthusiasm with nostalgia for those high summers of travel by train to the seaside in the 1920s,1930s and 1950s. The colourful and bold detail of the posters provide us with a vivid time capsule from those years, and they may now be seen in the collection at the National Railway Museum in York, whose archives hold over 6,000 railway posters dating from the 1890s to the present. As we look at them today, they do indeed appear to be pictures of paradise.

In the years before motorways and proliferation of private cars, the train was the preferred means of travel for most families going to the seaside. It was a comfortable, carefree way to travel, and special family rates offered by the railways made the prospect of a summer holiday by the sea even more attractive. The GWR was very ambitious in promoting the virtues of its resorts even in winter when it issued a travel poster headlined 'Bathing in February in the Cornish Riviera', with photographs of a bathing beauty frolicking in the sea off St Agnes during that month. With British weather so unpredictable, this was perhaps a little too optimistic for most people.

The summer of 1939 was to prove a high water mark for Britain's railways, whose passenger trains travelled on a greater variety of rail routes to the sea than in any subsequent year. As the war clouds gathered over Europe, and the future seemed uncertain, many people decided to seize the moment and take a holiday at their favourite resort during that last summer of the decade. Extra trains were run at weekends to seaside destinations all over Britain in the peak months of July and August, using all available coaches and locomotives to carry passengers on what would probably be their last excursion for several years.

The following table shows the total route mileage of each of the 'Big Four' companies and their inventory of locomotives in 1939, to give an indication of the relative size of their territories, and resources available to operate scheduled services and excursions that year. All numbers are rounded off to the nearest hundred:

Company	Route Miles	Locomotives
LMS	7,500	10,200
LNER	6,700	7,400
GWR	3,800	3,900
SR	2,200	2,300

On the first day of September 1939, two days before the declaration of war, the government placed Britain's railways under the control of the Railway Executive Committee, composed of the General Managers of the four main line railways. For a while it was mostly business as usual for rail travellers, and fortunately by the end of August most families had already taken their annual summer vacations.

In the shift from peace to war, most railway posters on billboards and hoardings all over Britain were removed, or covered up by wartime posters and propaganda. One text could be seen almost everywhere: "Is your journey really necessary?" But some nostalgic posters remained in stations around Britain, with scenes recalling memories of happy holidays by the sea. In the darkest years of the war, and in the gloom of old Euston station, high on the wall near Platform 12 was an evocative LMS poster by Norman Wilkinson inviting travellers to take the train to the Kyle of Lochalsh and over the sea to Skye. One wonders how many people, as they waited for their train in the blitz, wished they could have done so.

At the start of WW2, excursion trains became evacuation trains. Two examples of the ability of the railways to respond to urgent wartime needs for the mass transit of people will serve to illustrate the vital roles played by Britain's trains in 1939 and 1940. In the evacuation of children from London during September 1939, the railways took 607,635 passengers to destinations around Britain in just four days, using 1,577 special trains. Similar evacuations took place at Merseyside, Glasgow, and Manchester, using every locomotive and coach that could be put into service.

During the evacuation from Dunkirk at the end of May 1940, under codename 'Dynamo', a total of 186 trains carried 294,948 military personnel from ports along the south coast to places all over Britain in just nine days. The control centre for this operation was Redhill, the 'grand junction' for troop trains at that time, where incredible feats of train management were directed by telephone, for there was no time to write down messages ordering train movements. As O.S.Nock wrote of the railway's contribution to the success of 'Operation Dynamo': "Never in a thousand years of the stormy history of these Islands did the British genius for improvisation come more dramatically to our aid."

After the war, food, petrol, and essential materials were still rationed, and for those planning a trip to the seaside for their holidays, the train was the only practical mode of long distance travel. In retrospect, the total war effort of Britain's railways from 1939-1945 was the greatest achievement in railway transportation in the history of the world, but with peace came the enormous task of reconstruction.

Trains, tracks, stations, signalling, and communications, all needed repair. The railways were like an exhausted giant whose vision was blurred, in a country where post-war austerity and economy dominated every effort to restore the nation's pride in its railway system.

A welcome postwar sign was the return of several titled trains serving Britain's coasts. One of the first was the 'Royal Scot' from Euston to Glasgow (for Mallaig, Oban, and the Ayrshire coast) in October 1945, followed by the LNER's 'Hook Continental' from Liverpool Street to Harwich (Parkeston Quay) in November 1945. On 15 April 1946 the 'Golden Arrow' once again departed from Victoria Station's Platform 8, with its Pullman coaches bound for Dover, where passengers boarded the ferry to Calais, and the 'Fleche d'Or' to Paris.

The 'Cornish Riviera' had run throughout WW2, and on 31 December 1945 this famous train was re-equipped with new restaurant cars of more modern design. The 'Torbay Express' returned in the summer of 1946, taking holiday crowds to

Torquay, Paignton, and Kingswear. Other titled trains to the sea that were restored in October 1946 included the 'Pines Express', the 'Devonian', and the 'East Anglian'.

On 16 June 1947, the Southern Railway inaugurated an all-Pullman service between London and Devon resorts, naming its new train the 'Devon Belle', whose primary destination was Ilfracombe. It was so popular on summer weekends that 14 coaches were filled to capacity on most trips during its first season. On 7 October 1947, several pre-war titled trains returned to the timetables, including two other famous 'Southern Belles': the 'Bournemouth Belle' with its ten Pullmans, and the 'Brighton Belle' with its all-electric Pullman sets, which had been safely stored in remote sites around Britain during WW2, and renovated before re-appearing on the south coast.

The first postwar 'Night Ferry' left Victoria on 4 December 1947 for Dover, Dunkirk, and Paris. This was the only British train to travel across the sea to mainland Europe, linking the two capitals with daily scheduled service all year. The 'Atlantic Coast Express' had run incognito with slower timings throughout the war, and by the end of 1947 it had regained its pre-war title, with restaurant cars attached to most of the nine sections serving resorts in Devon and Cornwall.

After nationalization on 1 January 1948, British Rail introduced a new luxury train, the all-Pullman 'Thanet Belle' between London (Victoria) and Whitstable, Herne Bay, Margate, Broadstairs, and Ramsgate, the most popular resorts on the north Kent coast. This titled train included ten Pullman coaches in high season, and also ran in the winter with a mix of Pullman and standard coaches. Its name was later changed to the 'Kentish Belle'.

Another new train which entered service in September 1948, was the 'Tyne-Tees Pullman', leaving London (King's Cross) at the same time (1730) as the famous pre-war 'Silver Jubilee', but taking more than an hour longer to reach Newcastle, offering the popular 'Hadrian Bar' as a pleasant diversion en route. Further down the east coast, a new express train named the 'Norfolkman' was introduced in October 1948, running between London and Norwich in the winter, with through service to Cromer and Sheringham during the summer season.

In 1949, the longest (426 miles) and most scenic railway line between London and Scotland, from St Pancras to Glasgow (St Enoch) once again echoed to the sound of the comfortable and well-provisioned 'Thames-Clyde Express', with its renowned restaurant cars providing excellent food and service on its journey across the Pennines to Scotland. With the revival of many pre-war services, and some new titled trains on the horizon, an exciting decade of railway heydays was about to begin, heralding the second half of the twentieth century.

RAILWAY HEYDAYS:
From the 1950s to the 1990s

"And O what transport of delight…"

H.W. Baker (1868)

Nostalgia for the heydays of travel by train to the seaside is usually strongest when just within living memory. For some readers this will relate to the 1950s, the last full decade of steam train services on Britain's rail network; for others, their most vivid memories are from later years. This chapter recalls railway journeys from the 1950s to the 1990s, when privatized train operating companies took over British Rail's passenger train services.

In contrast to lingering austerity in the years immediately following WW2, the surge in passenger travel during the 1950s encouraged British Railways to restore more express trains to the coast, and to introduce some new ones. For rail travellers it was a decade of pleasure for the price of a cheap-day return ticket, or better still, the freedom of a 'Holiday Runabout' rail pass. It was also a time of optimism, enthusiasm, and a yearning to re-visit favourite resorts after the hiatus of the war years. All over Britain, railway posters proclaimed: "It's Quicker By Rail", and this was true for travel to most resorts, especially those on the coasts of Devon, Cornwall, and Somerset before motorways to the west country were built.

Travel by train reached a post-war peak in the 1950s, when the quintessential scenes at railway stations during summer holidays were of crowds surging towards departure platforms; children with buckets and spades, assorted baggage, food for the journey, beach balls, cricket bats, etc.; parents queueing for tickets, then rushing along the platform to find a carriage with enough seats for the whole family, hopefully near to a window facing the sea when their train finally reached the coast.

A ritual for many families with more baggage than they could manage on crowded trains of the 1950s was to use the railway's 'Passenger Luggage in Advance' services. For the modest sum of two shillings, a suitcase or other large article would be accepted at a local station and delivered to the specified destination for collection on arrival. For a small additional charge, the railway company also offered door-to-door service for PLA, which was popular not only for seaside holidays, but also for long-distance moves or return to boarding school after the holidays.

For those setting out on a cycling holiday, bicycles loaded with panniers and saddle bags were ridden to the station, ticketed, and put in the guard's van. On long journeys with several stops en route, owners could be seen rushing through corridor coaches to the guard's van, or along the platform on arrival at each station, to ensure that the bicycle had not been unloaded by mistake, for those were the days of spacious guard's vans on almost every train, with enough room for dozens of bikes of similar appearance. It was always a great relief to find that the bicycle had reached its destination safely, ready for its owner to jump on and pedal away with a feeling of freedom and independence before other people loaded with heavy baggage had struggled out of the station to a taxi, car, or bus.

In the 1950s, a popular holiday destination on the south coast was the Isle of Wight, served by frequent British Rail ferries that crossed the Solent from Portsmouth Harbour station to Ryde Pierhead. For the sum of one shilling, plus four pence for a bicycle, ferries with names of resorts on the IOW such as 'Shanklin', 'Brading', and 'Ryde' provided holiday-

EXPRESS TRAIN ARRIVALS AT TORQUAY

with through coaches to Paignton and Kingswear on most trains

SUMMER SATURDAYS IN THE 1950s

ARRIVAL	ORIGINATING STATION AND DEPARTURE TIME	
1115	Bristol	0940
1250	London	0850
1326	Birmingham	0810
1347	London	0900
1435	Cardiff	1055
1445	London	1045
1510	Birmingham	1010
1520	Swansea	0945
1528	London	1200*
1600	Manchester	0805
1620	Bristol	1345
1630	Manchester	0910
1645	Wolverhampton	1055
1713	Liverpool	0900
1718	Cardiff	1255
1725	Manchester	1020
1740	London	1315
1748	Bradford	1005‡
1815	Liverpool	1020
1825	Nottingham	1110
1910	London	1525

* THE TORBAY EXPRESS

‡ THE DEVONIAN

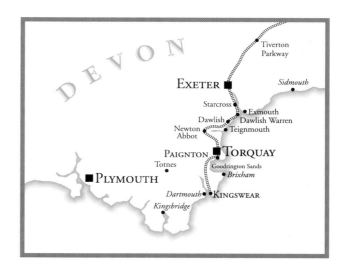

THE TORBAY EXPRESS

With its pedigree dating back to pre-WW1 days, the *Torbay Express* was a fast and popular train to the three Devon resorts of Torquay, Paignton and Kingswear (for Dartmouth).

On summer Saturdays in the 1950s, the *Torbay Express* ran non-stop from Paddington to Torquay, a distance of 199.6 miles, in 3 hours 28 minutes, speeding through Exeter and Newton Abbot en route to Torbay.

Photo: The sea front at Dawlish (John Hadrill)

BOAT TRAINS ON THE "SHORT SEA ROUTE" IN THE HEYDAYS OF THE 1950s

LONDON (Victoria) DEPART	ARRIVAL AT COAST		CONTINENTAL DESTINATION
0900	1042	Folkestone	Paris
1030	1255	Dover	Brussels
1100	1235	Dover	Paris *(Golden Arrow)*
1400	1535	Dover	Paris
1500	1655	Dover	Brussels
1630	1809	Folkestone	Paris
2200	2337	Dover	Paris *(Night Ferry)*
2300	0100	Dover	Brussels

The illustration is a 1950s snapshot of the Golden Arrow *charging down Polhill near Sevenoaks, Kent, en route to Dover. It was taken by the author with his first camera on a frequent trackside rendezvous with this famous train.*

makers with a pleasant journey across the Solent. Exhilarating sea breezes added to the enjoyment of a fine panorama of Hampshire's coastline from the upper deck, a seascape that was brilliantly captured in a 1950s poster issued by British Rail, titled 'Racing Off Ryde'. In those days, a ferry ticket also entitled the holder to a free train ride along the pier to Ryde Esplanade station.

The leisurely pace of life on the Isle of Wight in the 1950s was also evident on trains that served the island's resorts. Several old steam locomotives no longer suited to the hard driving at other places in Britain were put out to pasture on the island and given the distinctive prefix 'W' on their brass number plates. As with rail ferries across the Solent, they carried the names of towns and seaside resorts on the island, and it was always a pleasure to step off the ferry at Ryde Pierhead straight on to a train, with one of the well-preserved locomotives ready to steam away towards Shanklin and Ventnor, or Cowes, Yarmouth and Freshwater Bay.

After their new lease of life on the island, lasting some fifteen years, the 'W' class locomotives made their last runs for British Rail on 31 December 1966. Fortunately, W24 'Calbourne' has survived and is now in service with the IOW Steam Railway. Passengers may take a steam train between Smallbrook Junction and Wootton on an island where time seems to stand still - except for catching a ferry to the mainland from the far end of Ryde's long pier, when no train to the Pierhead Station is in sight.

British Rail's Southern Region, which had the greatest concentration of seaside resorts served by train in Britain, proudly punned in a 1950s poster that its 'Four Belles Ring The South Coast - and they did, from Ilfracombe and Plymouth in Devon to Margate and Ramsgate on the Kent coast. The four 'Belles' were the famous Pullman trains named 'Devon Belle', 'Bournemouth Belle', 'Brighton Belle', and 'Kentish Belle'.

Six more seaside destinations to the south and west were served by the Southern Region's 'Atlantic Coast Express' from London, and although the train had no Pullman coaches, it travelled further than any of the 'Belles' on its route to Padstow, 260 miles from Waterloo, hauling well-stocked restaurant cars for most of the way.

In the summer of 1951, the 'Festival of Britain' exhibition was held on the south bank of the Thames near Waterloo station, celebrating a century of progress since the Great Exhibition of 1851 in London's Hyde Park. The choice of a blitzed site for the 1951 festival resulted from attacks by the Luftwaffe on Waterloo station during WW2, when most of the bombs aimed at London's largest railway terminus landed on what was a densely populated south bank, creating a large open space beside the Thames, an ideal location for displaying Britain's industrial renaissance after six years of war.

Prominent among exhibits at the festival was the newest 'Britannia' Class locomotive 'William Shakespeare', which was to haul the 'Golden Arrow' on many occasions in the 1950s between Victoria and Dover. In contrast to this huge and handsome locomotive on static display, two miles upstream from Waterloo the locomotive 'Neptune' on the 'Far Tottering and Oystercreek Railway' took its passengers around the Festival Pleasure Gardens at Battersea, in a Rowland Emmet fantasy seaside excursion, an enchanting ride amidst all the delights of the greatest funfair ever held beside the Thames.

While trains from all over the country were carrying millions of passengers to London for the festival, British Rail offered some interesting rail tours to scenic areas around Britain. A popular one-day tour took a circular route in North Wales, starting at Llandudno and proceeding eastwards along the coast to Rhyl, then south along the delightful Vale of Clwyd through St Asaph to Denbigh, Ruthin, and Corwen. Here the train joined the line from Llangollen before turning west to Bala, where it ran along the shore of Bala Lake, then through the Cambrian Mountains to Dolgellau and along the Mawddach estuary to Barmouth for lunch and some sightseeing.

From Barmouth, the train headed north along the coast to Harlech, Minffordd (for Portmeirion), then westwards to Porthmadog and Criccieth, branching off northwards to Caernarfon, Bangor, Conwy, and Llandudno - two coasts of Wales in one day. The total distance was 152 miles, and the fare was 15 shillings. Seating was limited to 180 people, half of whom sat in saloon coaches with individual chairs. For the 1951 and 1952 seasons, this rail tour was advertised as the 'North Wales Land Cruise', and in 1953 it was given the title 'Coronation Land Cruise'. From 1954 it was called the 'Cambrian Radio Cruise', with a commentary during the journey.

Train services on several scenic rail lines in Wales were withdrawn in the 1960s and the only sections of the 'Cruise' route that remain on the railway network are Barmouth-Criccieth and Bangor-Rhyl. The narrow-gauge Bala Lake Railway now runs on part of the trackbed that linked Llangollen with Dolgellau, while the Welsh Highland Railway is in process of restoring rail service to Caernarfon on a narrow-gauge line from Porthmadog, which has trains in operation at each end, but a long mid-section has yet to be rebuilt to link the two coasts. There are more great little railways in Wales than in any other part of Britain, and those that go to the sea are described in Chapter 11.

When Coronation Year dawned in 1953, memories of the famous 'Coronation' trains of 1937 prompted BR's executives to introduce the 'Elizabethan' non-stop express between London and Edinburgh. With the fastest post-war timing between the two capitals, at almost a mile a minute for the 393-mile journey, this was one of the most exacting duties for an A4 class locomotive hauling much heavier trains than the

'Coronation'. It was a year of pride, ceremony, and revelry, with many patriotic ventures in what was seen as a new Elizabethan age, and British Railways marked the occasion with locomotive names and titled trains that recalled Britain's greatness during the reign of Elizabeth I.

In the weeks leading up to Coronation Day on 2 June 1953, thousands of trains brought a million people to London, and over 200,000 overseas visitors came to join in the celebrations. While the 'Festival of Britain' in 1951 marked the recovery from hardships and shortages of WW2, the coronation of Queen Elizabeth II was the most expensive celebration in Britain's history, and BR reported a profit of some £30 million in 1953, resulting in part from the surge in rail journeys all over Britain during that festive year.

In 1955, Britain led all of western Europe with the introduction of trains that combined sleeping accommodation and transportation of cars on the same 'Motorail' train. The idea had originated at BR's Eastern Region HQ, and was first used on a twice-weekly night express between King's Cross and Perth, bypassing Edinburgh. This service enabled passengers to get a good night's sleep, enjoy a hearty Scottish breakfast at Perth's fine Station Hotel, and then drive away to the Highlands, or to harbours such as Oban, Mallaig, and the Kyle of Lochalsh for ferry services to the Western Isles.

Overnight 'Motorail' trains to the West Country from the midlands and north were introduced in 1956, while motorists from the London area had to send their cars ahead by special freight trains until 'Motorail' trains linked Surbiton with Okehampton in Devon on a 'Saturdays only' service in the 1960s. By the early 1970s, before motorways had taken away most of BR's car and freight traffic, there were 57 'Motorail' terminals around Britain. Now there are six.

Those halcyon years of the 1950s produced a strong surge of nostalgia in the boardrooms of BR's Western Region, resulting in the introduction of several new trains painted in the venerable GWR chocolate and cream livery. Two of these trains deserve mention, the first appearing in January 1955 with title 'Royal Duchy', carrying a heraldic headboard of the Duchy of Cornwall, with consent of the Queen. The train left Paddington at 1330 for Penzance, taking a comfortable six hours for the journey, and the name survived until 1965, when revisions to BR's main line services deleted several titled trains from the timetable. Tradition was not enough to save this and other titled trains from oblivion during the first two decades of BR management.

The second named train to the sea was the 'Mayflower', departing Paddington at 1730 on its four-hour journey to Plymouth. It had a relatively short life, from July 1955 until the end of summer 1965, although it was revived briefly in 1970 as the 0730 Paddington-Plymouth service to mark the 350th anniversary of the Pilgrim Fathers' sailing for America.

Latter day pilgrims from the USA arriving early in the morning at Heathrow could, if lucky, board the 'Mayflower' at Reading by using the 'Railair' coach from the airport, and avoid London altogether.

One of Britain's most interesting and nostalgic sea-to-sea railway journeys, dating back to 1904 and still running in the early 1950s, was a cross-country service between Newcastle and Swansea. It was given the unofficial title of 'Ports-to-Ports Express', since it served ports around the Tyne as well as Cardiff and Swansea in Wales. Its route between Banbury and Cheltenham was through sleepy little Cotswold villages with stations at Chipping Norton, Stow-on-the-Wold and Bourton-on-the-Water.

For 45 miles the train meandered along a single track through valleys and villages which had never seen an express until the 'Ports-to-Ports' arrived on the scene. It took 82 minutes for the 'express' to travel through this tranquil heart of England; fortunately there was a restaurant car on the train, so passengers could enjoy tea, toast, and cakes between Banbury (dep. 1530) and Cheltenham (arr. 1652). The 397 mile journey from England's north coast to the south coast of Wales took almost twelve hours in those days, but who would wish to hurry on such a delightful journey across the heart of England?

It was at King's Sutton station on the Banbury-Cheltenham section of the 'Ports-to-Ports' express route that one of the most nostalgic moments in British railway lore occurred. It was reported that a child who had purchased the first ticket here in 1887 on the opening day of the line returned as an old man to purchase the last ticket issued on the final day of service in 1951.

Nearly a half century later, this single-track branch line across the Cotswolds may be found only as a thin spidery line in old atlases, perhaps encouraging railway archaeologists to explore this former branch line, although clues become harder to find as the years pass. In 1952 a new and faster train service between Cardiff and Newcastle was inaugurated via Gloucester, Birmingham, Derby, and York, with a journey time of 8h 25min, bypassing the old route whose character is best understood by reading David St. John Thomas' book 'The Country Railway'.

On most rail routes in the 1950s there was plenty of traffic other than passengers. For example, food and other perishable goods were carried on trains that in some instances were faster than many passenger trains. On the route of the 'Atlantic Coast Express', special milk trains transported huge quantities of milk each day from Devon, Dorset, and Somerset to dairies in and around London.

In 1957, stations around Chard Junction (now closed) in Somerset sent 18.6 million gallons to the capital, and received the empties back the next day. Those huge milk churns, part of a bygone age and yet still within living memory, may be seen

TITLED TRAINS RESTORED OR INTRODUCED
IN THE HEYDAYS OF THE 1950s

DATE RESTORED OR INTRODUCED	TITLE	DESTINATION *from London unless otherwise shown*
1950	*Broadsman* *Tynesider*	Cromer and Sheringham Newcastle
1951	*Kentish Belle* *Cambrian Coast Express*	Whitstable, Herne Bay, Margate, Ramsgate Aberystwyth, Barmouth, Pwllheli
1952	*Cornishman*	Wolverhampton–Penzance Leeds/Bradford–Penzance
1953	*Coronation** *Elizabethan*	Newcastle, Edinburgh Newcastle, Edinburgh
1954	*Emerald Isle Express*	Holyhead (for Ireland)
1955	*Royal Duchy* *Mayflower* *South Wales Pullman*	Plymouth, Penzance Plymouth Cardiff and Swansea
1956	*Talisman*	Edinburgh and Perth
1957	*Fair Maid* *Waverley*	Edinburgh and Perth Edinburgh
1958	*Essex Coast Express*	Clacton & Walton-on-Naze
1959	*Thames-Tees Express*	Middlesbrough & Saltburn

*Restored for Coronation year only   THIS IS A PARTIAL LISTING SELECTED BY AUTHOR.

today on platforms of several preserved railway stations around Britain, together with enamelled signs advertising Colman's Mustard, Lyons' Cakes, Wills Capstan and Gold Flake cigarettes, Stephens Inks, and other consumables from long ago.

A survey in the 1950s of preferred places for a holiday in Britain showed that four out of every five persons gave their first choice as 'somewhere by the sea'. This confirmed the popularity of journeys to the coast at a time when traffic congestion on Britain's roads, particularly those to resorts in Devon, Cornwall, and Somerset, convinced many travellers that the train was indeed the best way to get to their destination.

On Saturday 27 July 1957, a peak day of summer travel by passenger trains, over half a million journeys were made on the Western Region of British Rail. In one hour around mid-day at Exeter St David's station, 26 trains heading to resorts in Cornwall and Devon were counted, while at Newton Abbot, 80 trains passed through the station between 0824 and 2137 that day on their way to the sea.

In response to demand for faster services to the West Country, a new titled train, the 'Golden Hind' was introduced in 1964, running between London and Plymouth, whose maritime history had also provided the name 'Mayflower'. With its well-chosen title, the 'Golden Hind' was faster than any previous train between London and Plymouth, departing Paddington at 1730 and reaching Exeter (174miles) in 2h 34min. Seat reservations were compulsory, and the service proved so popular that it was extended to Penzance, with faster timings than the famous 'Cornish Riviera' express.

Mystery excursions that proved popular in pre-war years were revived by British Rail after WW2, one example being a 1965 'Mystery Train' which started from Weston-super-Mare, with the lure: 'Over 250 miles for one pound', and the clue: 'Journey time 3 hours 25 minutes each way'. Tenby was the destination, and five hours were allotted to enjoy the attractions of this fascinating medieval town and seaside resort on the Pembrokeshire coast.

The summer of 1968 marked the end of steam train services throughout Britain's standard-gauge rail network, and although all BR's steam locomotives were officially withdrawn during the week ending August 3, the determination of railway enthusiasts to prolong steam operations as long as possible resulted in several steam train excursions running on August 4. There was one 'final steam special' the following weekend, which in the past thirty years has become a railway legend.

On Sunday August 11, the last steam excursion train operated by British Rail on its main line network involved no less than five steam locomotives on a circular tour starting and ending at Liverpool, where the first steam trains had reached the sea from Manchester 138 years earlier.

Known as the 'Fifteen Guinea Special', BR's official farewell to standard-gauge steam took its passengers first to Manchester, then to Blackburn, Hellifield and Carlisle, before returning along the same route to Liverpool. It was a sad occasion for train enthusiasts, and especially for those who had devoted most of their lives to serving the railways. Although many steam locomotives were put to the torch, some were saved and restored to operate on preserved lines throughout the country, while their owners negotiated with British Rail management to allow them to run again with excursions on main line routes.

Three years later, a steam train returned for its first main line excursion in October 1971, when a survivor from the steam locomotive meltdown, GWR No. 6000 'King George V', hauled a train with 115 passengers aboard on a journey from Birmingham to London, returning to Hereford via Swindon. Once again, steam as white as linen floated over Britain's railway tracks, and the success of this restoration to main line operation resulted in approval for further steam excursions on routes that included Birmingham-Didcot, York-Scarborough, Newcastle-Carlisle, Shrewsbury- Newport, and Carnforth-Barrow. In due course, other routes were added for steam specials, including the famous Settle-Carlisle line across the Pennines.

Since then, thousands of rail excursions under steam have operated on main lines from which they had once been banned. Campaigns to re-open stations closed by British Rail, or to open new ones, resulted in over 100 station names added to the railway map of Britain since 1970, largely as a result of the efforts of the Railway Development Society. The ultimate irony was that twenty years after British Rail's elimination of steam on its network, and the refusal to allow steam locomotives on its standard-gauge tracks, British Rail ran its own scheduled steam trains during the summer months on the popular West Highland Line from Fort William to Mallaig.

During the past 25 years, more than seventy steam locomotives have been certified for main line excursions, representing forty different classes, and every design since the 1930s. Steam specials have been run on virtually every scenic line in Britain, and steam locomotives have returned to eight of London's main line termini to haul excursions all over the country, including the entire east and west coast main lines.

On midsummer day in 1975, the steam locomotives 'Flying Scotsman' and 'Mayflower' hauled a 16-coach excursion train on the Cumbrian coast line between Barrow and Carnforth. This was one of the longest trains to carry passengers in the steam preservation era, a memorable sight in an impressive setting, and a tribute to the dedication, devotion, and hard work of preservation groups, without whom these excursions would not be possible on the scale we see them today.

Meanwhile, with its large inventory of diesel locomotives,

British Rail advertised excursions and charter trains under several brand names, among which the euphemistic 'Merry-maker' was one of the most popular, with demand often exceeding resources available, and inevitable delays en route for some long distance railtours when diesels failed. Passengers arriving home three hours late in the middle of the night must surely have wondered whether, as British Rail proclaimed at the time "This is the age of the train."

Weather can play havoc with some railway excursions. In March 1970, British Rail, hoping to attract more passengers to Weston-super-Mare in the face of stiff competition from road traffic, ran a 'Holiday Preview Express' from Paddington to this popular Somerset resort. The 230 passengers paid one pound for the return trip of 270 miles, a rail travel bargain for a day beside the sea. However, unseasonal blizzard conditions and icy blasts up the Bristol Channel delayed the train en route and made this excursion to the seaside rather unpleasant, confirming the old weather lore of waiting until March is out before attempting such ventures.

Among the many special excursion trains run since early railway days, those to music and choral festivals, brass band contests and orchestral concerts generated considerable revenue for the railway companies. Organizers of the 1972 Brighton Festival chartered the 'Brighton Belle' for a musical trip from London to Brighton, the first time that a Pullman train had been used for such an event. Two hundred passengers were served dinner in the Royal Pavilion, followed by a performance of Berlioz's 'Railroad Song' by a military band and choir on the concourse of Brighton station before returning to London.

In that same year, the Cornwall Birdwatching and Preservation Society hired a special excursion train to travel slowly and quietly up and down the single track beside the River Fowey between Lostwithiel and Fowey. The train proved to be a great railway 'hide' for birdwatchers on this quiet branch line to the sea, now used only for freight, mostly china clay shipments. Perhaps, in a railway renaissance under privatization, this line will again carry passengers down to a part of the Cornwall coast that has a large gap in railway access to the sea, from Looe in the east to Falmouth in the west.

To provide rail charter and excursion services for the so-called VIP market, British Rail set up the InterCity Charter Unit in 1984 to operate 'scenic land cruises' (SLCs), for which it assembled five complete ten-coach sets, all first class and painted with white roofs to distinguish them from other trains. The SLCs offered luxury travel to various destinations around Britain, including select coastal resorts. On occasion, these charters used some unusual coaches, including a modified coach with lounge and dining saloon previously used by the Queen.

Of the many SLCs operated by BR in the 1990s, the 'West Highlander', with up to sixteen coaches including seven first class sleeping cars, was one of the most popular. Each rail cruise left London on a Friday and accommodated 156 passengers, all given a window seat, which made the train too long for the platforms at King's Cross, so the train departed from St Pancras, with routing via Derby and the east coast main line to Edinburgh, then on the West Highland line to Crianlarich and Oban (for Craignure on the Isle of Mull, and Iona), returning to Crianlarich for Rannoch Moor and Fort William. The train then continued westwards to Mallaig, followed by a cruise on Loch Nevis and a stop at Glenfinnan, then back to Fort William, Glasgow, Edinburgh, and St Pancras, returning in London on a Monday evening.

One of today's most ambitious railway excursions, starting and ending at the sea, is the railway marathon: over 1,000 miles by train in less than 24 hours without using any route more than once. Like most excursions, this is recommended during the summer months when daylight is longest, and best of all around the summer solstice. A rail pass is useful for this type of excursion, and there are several possible routes. Here are two based on the 1998 summer timetable, requiring good timekeeping by the selected trains in order to complete one thousand miles in a day:

The Golden Hind	Depart. Penzance: 0515 Arrive.London (Paddington): 0956 Miles: 305.2
The Royal Scot	Depart.London (Euston): 1040 Arrive.Glasgow (Central):1539 Miles: 401.3
InterCity Shuttle	Depart.Glasgow (Queen St):1600 Arrive.Edinburgh: 1650 Miles: 47.3
InterCity 225	Depart.Edinburgh:1730 Arrive.London (Kings X):2219 Miles: 393.2
(untitled)	Depart.London (Waterloo):2353 Arrive.Bournemouth: 0203 Miles:111.4
Total Time: 20hrs 48min	Total Miles: 1258.4

Here is another route, again starting and finishing beside the sea:

The Golden Hind	Depart.Penzance: 0515

	Arrive.London (Paddington): 0956 Miles:305.2
InterCity 225	Depart.London (Kings X): 1100 Arrive.Glasgow (Central): 1645 Miles:450.1
InterCity	Depart.Glasgow (Central): 1700 Arrive.London (Euston): 2215 Miles:401.1
(untitled)	Depart.London (Waterloo): 2250 Arrive.Portsmouth: 0036 Miles:77.0

Total Time: 19hrs 21min   Total Miles: 1233.4

The only person known to have travelled over every railway line in Britain on which scheduled passenger services were available throughout the year was Thomas Perkins (1872-1952). He began his prodigious task of exploring the entire railway network in 1893 and completed it in 1932 after travelling over 22,000 route miles, making detailed notes of all his journeys. No one can now match this distance record, for the total system mileage open for passenger traffic is much less than in the 1920s when most of Perkins' railway odyssey was accomplished.

Privatization of railway passenger services in 1997 introduced the 'Rail Charter Partnership' among the train operating companies to provide complete excursion packages, ranging from high-capacity trains for sporting events, to high quality wine-and-dine charters, and long distance land cruises. Three types of charter train were formed and named 'The Blue Train' for luxury land cruises; 'The Red Train', with a mix of first and standard class accommodation for 400 passengers; and 'The Green Train', for large crowds on day trips to sporting events or to the seaside.

Steam train excursions arranged by rail tour companies all over Britain continue to attract enthusiasts of all ages. Among several notable steam tours of 1997, A2 Pacific steam locomotive 'Blue Peter', hauling a 470 ton 'North Briton' excursion train of twelve immaculate coaches with 455 passengers aboard on the west coast main line over Shap,

achieved a speed of 64 mph at the summit during a thrilling run reminiscent of the heydays of LMS express trains between Glasgow and London. As the train raced southwards through the Lune Gorge towards Preston, passengers had the satisfaction of passing almost every vehicle on the adjacent M6 motorway

In October 1997, what was claimed as the world's first rail charter holiday package from sea to sea, titled 'The Cornish Experience', operated between Newcastle and Newquay. The train was formed of luxury Pullman-style coaches, and the excursion package included accommodation in high quality hotels at Newquay for a week, with full-day and half-day tours around Cornwall. To launch the venture, the diesel locomotive assigned to this luxury train was also named 'The Cornish Experience'.

On 9 August 1998, the annual Grampian Railtours 'Northern Belle' crossed the border south into England for the first time. Starting from Aberdeen, and calling at Stonehaven, Montrose, then over the Tay and Forth bridges, the train arrived at Berwick-upon-Tweed for a visit by its passengers to Bamburgh Castle. This tour re-traced part of the route of the LNER's legendary 'Northern Belle' of the 1930s, described in Chapter 7.

Over sixty main line steam tours were scheduled between 1 September and 31 December 1998, including visits to the sea at Weymouth, Penzance, Falmouth, Fort William, Broadstairs, Tywyn, Dover, Kyle of Lochalsh, Inverness, Holyhead, Wick, Thurso, Blackpool, Plymouth, Newquay, and Portsmouth.

The 'Royal Scotsman', operated by the Great Scottish & Western Railway, is the most exclusive and luxurious train running in Britain today, offering several tours of England, Scotland and Wales, with departures from Edinburgh (Waverley) or London (Paddington). The luxury nine- coach train carries a maximum of 32 passengers, with fourteen staff in attendance. Like the pre-war 'Northern Belle', the 'Royal Scotsman' is stationary at night, stabled at various locations, including near the sea at the Kyle of Lochalsh, or Llandudno, or Dunbar, depending on the selected itinerary.

'British Pullman' luxury excursions operated by VSOE have proved to be very popular in recent years. For the 1998 season, steam haulage included Merchant Navy class steam locomotive 'Clan Line', which holds a remarkable speed record for the 'Atlantic Coast Express' set near Axminster in the summer of 1961 among the hills of Devon, and described in Chapter 4.

To the coasts of Cornwall, Devon and Somerset

Heavens ! What a goodly prospect spreads around;
Island of bliss, amid the subject seas.

James Thomson, 1727

Of all railway journeys to the sea in Britain, those to Cornwall, Devon and Somerset are surely the most fondly remembered. And of the many titled trains that serve the southwest, the most famous is the 'Cornish Riviera' whose pedigree goes back to 1897 when the GWR ran its 'Cornishman' express to Penzance, with the longest non-stop journey in the world at that time, from London (Paddington) to Exeter (St David's), 194 miles in 223 minutes at an average speed of 52.2 mph.

This train was so popular that a new train, the 'Plymouth, Falmouth & Penzance Special' was introduced in 1904, departing from London daily at 1010 for Britain's most westerly terminus, setting a new record for the longest non-stop journey in the world, 245.7 miles from Paddington to Plymouth, on a route that was twenty miles longer than it is today. Such was the prestige of this train that a competition for a new name in the 1920s produced 1286 entries, with the prize of a first class return ticket to anywhere on the GWR network. An additional 700 suggestions were submitted to staff at local GWR stations.

The winner was 'The Riviera Express', but another entry 'The Cornish Riviera Limited' was subsequently adopted and then modified to 'The Cornish Riviera Express'. It was the combination of luxury, speed, dependability, and destination which made this train unique and so popular from the day of its first appearance. The same is true today

One GWR travel poster compared Cornwall to Italy by turning a map of the latter to align it with Cornwall, revealing a remarkable resemblance in the two coastlines, and by inference, climate. The wording on the poster urged rail travellers to "see your own country first: there is a great similarity in climate between Cornwall and Italy." Comparisons were also drawn between Cornwall and the northwest coast of France, with Cornwall identified as 'the Brittany of Britain' in GWR posters, which showed St Michael's Mount as seen from the train near Penzance. In a fanciful mood, the GWR also named Cornwall 'The Arcadian Coast'.

In 1935, the GWR celebrated its centennial year with a new set of luxurious coaches for the 'Cornish Riviera Express'. These were the longest and widest ever seen in Britain on regular scheduled service, making maximum use of wide spacing between GWR tracks, a legacy from Brunel's original broad gauge lines from Paddington to the southwest. Staff on the new coaches included a valet to serve the needs of gentlemen aboard, and a maid in nurse's uniform whose duties were "to constantly patrol the train, and especially watch over ladies travelling without an escort."

The 1930s were great years for the GWR, and on summer Saturdays several relief trains were needed to take holiday crowds to the eight seaside resorts in Cornwall, Devon and Somerset served by the 'Cornish Riviera Express'. Penzance and St Ives were the principal destinations, with through coaches detached en route for Newquay, Falmouth, Looe, Plymouth, Minehead, and Ilfracombe. The latter two resorts were served by 'slip coaches' detached at high speed from the train before it reached its first scheduled stop.

All these resorts except Ilfracombe and Minehead are served today by trains on Britain's rail network. The West Somerset Railway runs steam trains in season between Minehead and Bishop's Lydeard on Britain's longest (20

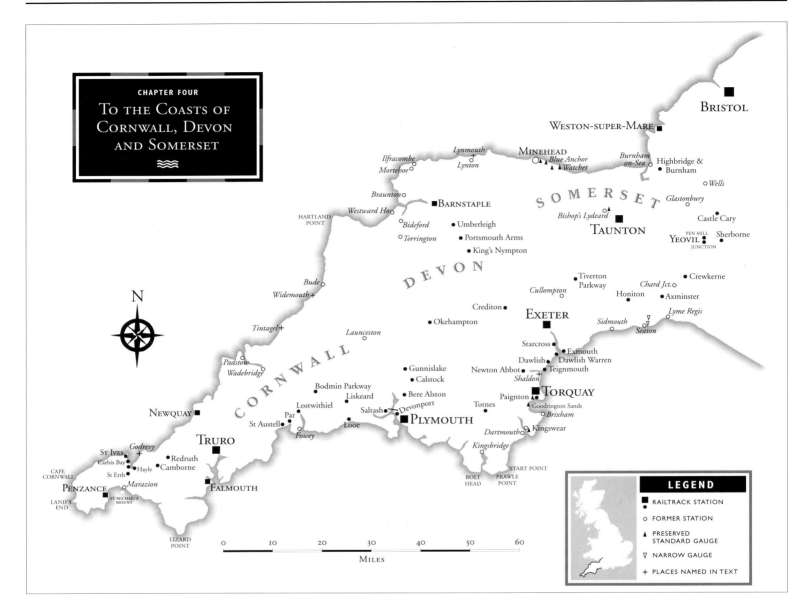

miles) preserved standard gauge railway, which may in due course restore daily passenger train service through to the main line station at Taunton.

In its new First Great Western green and ivory livery, the 'Cornish Riviera' departs on weekdays from Paddington at 1035, arriving Penzance at 1535. While this train has been through several changes in name, appearance and timings, it remains the premier year-round express to the sea. The number of holidaymakers it has carried is incalculable, as is the pleasure that they have enjoyed on its daily 305 mile journey from London to Penzance.

After leaving London, the train first meets the sea between Starcross and Dawlish Warren as it sprints along the coast to Teignmouth, after which there are only two brief glimpses of the coast before the train reaches Marazion, near Penzance. Shortly after leaving Plymouth, the train crosses the Royal Albert Bridge over tidewater, giving a view up the great

harbour; the other sighting of the sea is just west of Par, as the train passes close to St Austell Bay.

There are four branch lines served by the CR in Cornwall, all leading to the sea, and we shall visit the most westerly first, changing trains at St Erth for St Ives. A four-mile ride by train along the north Cornwall coast between Lelant and St Ives offers the finest panoramic views from high above the sea of any rail line in Britain. The Atlantic waters that sweep over a wide expanse of golden sands are Mediterranean blue in the sunshine, and in the distance St Ives basks in the radiance of light reflected from the sea, for which it is famous.

This view is best seen from the train, or by walking along the coastal path, since the approach to St Ives by road from Penzance or St Erth is inland. Some other outstanding sea views that may be seen from the train in Britain, a personal choice, are listed in Appendix 4.

The short branch line from St Erth to St Ives was the last

broad gauge line to be built by the GWR and was opened in 1877. It transformed a sleepy fishing village into a popular resort, with the train coming to rest beside Porthminster Beach, so that a walk straight from the train to the beach is very appealing at any time of year. One of the many delights of St Ives is that it offers beaches facing every point of the compass, and while it is not now an island, it has all the character of one. Here the sun may be followed round from beach to beach all day, with the sunset seen best from Porthmeor Beach.

High above the sea stands the Tregenna Castle Hotel, with its large grounds and splendid views of St Ives Bay. The hotel was built by the GWR, and is described in Oliver Carter's book on railway hotels as "a vehicle for the Great Western Railway's creation of the Cornish Riviera." It was said that von Ribbentrop, the German ambassador to Britain in the 1930s, so admired and coveted the Tregenna Castle with its commanding view of the north Cornwall coastline that he

Seaside rail travel personified. Until the 1960s it was the practice on summer Saturdays for the main portion of the 'Cornish Riviera Express' to terminate at St Ives rather than Penzance, its arrival being a major event at the small branch-line terminus. The shadows are lengthening as waiting cars meet passengers from the ten-coach train, but the beach is still packed with holiday-makers enjoying the sun, sand and sea.

sought from Hitler a promise that if Britain was invaded, the Tregenna Castle would be his. Guests visiting this great hotel today will understand why it is so admired in its serene setting overlooking the sea, town and harbour below.

St Ives has much to offer the visitor, and has become so popular in the summer that it is best to arrive by train and avoid the congestion of cars converging on the town, with its narrow streets and crowds of sightseers. For walkers, the four

mile coastal path from Lelant via Carbis Bay provides a splendid scenic approach to St Ives, whose shoreline extends around 'The Island' to Porthmeor Beach, where surfers ride the Atlantic swells that break on the shore. There are many interesting walks in St Ives along the lanes and passages lined with former fisherman's cottages leading to the beaches, which are easily reached on foot from any part of the town.

For over a century, artists have found inspiration at St Ives for their works, which are displayed in galleries along laneways which open up new vistas to the sea. Some finely restored buildings are tucked away in the maze of alleys that link beaches on each side of 'the island'. The conspicuous Tate St Ives, with its dazzling white facings and circular entrance facing Porthmeor Beach, contains a collection of past and present works of the St Ives school of artists.

Several famous writers came here to entice the muse, perhaps none more so than Virginia Woolf who wrote of the many blissful holidays she spent in childhood at Talland House, purchased from the GWR by her father Leslie Stephen in 1882. He had discovered this large residence overlooking the station on one of his walking tours of Cornwall in 1881, and it was here in the years from 1882 to 1894 that Virginia "found and fixed her idea of happiness."

Godrevy lighthouse at the northeast entrance to St Ives Bay inspired Virginia Woolf to write her novel 'To the Lighthouse', and in the early morning Godrevy Island appears in profile as a huge battleship against the horizon, best seen from near Porthminster Beach. A walk from this beach along the Warren to the harbour is always pleasing, especially at high and low tides, for

Cornwall has managed to retain its coastal branch lines to St Ives, Newquay, Falmouth and Looe, but a sad casualty was that from Lostwithiel alongside the estuary to Fowey, closed to passengers in 1965. Collett 0-4-2 tank engines could often be seen passing the hours at Fowey's attractive wooden station on the one-coach service. The branch is still open for china clay traffic. (NRM - RJS1752)

while the high tide conceals, the low tide reveals a small sheltered beach in the harbour, where fishing boats rest on their keels, and receding waves leave their signatures on the sand.

The first visit to a seaside resort is usually the most memorable, because first impressions are the strongest and most enduring. Yet places like St Ives never fail to captivate with each visit, when memories are enriched by its constant attraction, for it is the classic example of a small seaside community promoted by the GWR to become one of its most popular resorts. On summer Saturdays in the 1960s, a direct ten-coach 'Cornish Riviera Express' left Paddington for St Ives, where passengers would arrive with great excitement and depart with a touch of sadness.

Cornwall is the only place in Britain where four branch lines to the sea radiate from a main line that is never more than nine miles from the coast as the gull flies. The routes are: St Erth-St.Ives, Truro-Falmouth, Par-Newquay, and Liskeard-Looe. There are also three in Devon: Gunnislake-Plymouth, Exeter-Exmouth, and Exeter-Barnstaple, the closest station to Ilfracombe, Westward Ho!, and Clovelly.

Where the railways had first choice of access to the coast, the train still provides the best sea views, while the road goes inland, notably between Marazion and Penzance, Starcross and Teignmouth, Topsham and Exmouth, Lelant and St Ives. Across the water from Lelant is Hayle, where Cornwall's first steam railway was inaugurated in 1834.

A short train journey from St Ives to Penzance brings St Michael's Mount into view as the train rushes along the shore past the old Marazion station, with its five well-weathered Pullman coaches stabled there: Alicante, Floro, Juno, Calais and Mimosa. A scenic three-mile walk along the beach to Marazion brings us to the causeway leading to St Michael's Mount at low tide. At high tide the island may be reached by boat from the beach.

There are daily sailings from Penzance harbour to St Mary's, the largest of the 145 Scilly Islands and islets which lie about 28 miles from Land's End. When John Wesley ventured by small boat from St Ives to these islands in 1743, it took him seven hours in rough seas, and on arrival he found the isles to be "a paradise that could only be reached through purgatory." Wesley returned to Cornwall 32 times between 1743 and 1789, finding it fruitful ground, responsive to his great evangelical zeal.

Penzance is the furthest west of any rail terminus in Britain, but it is not Britain's most westerly railway station. That distinction is held by Arisaig, on the line to Mallaig in Scotland. Nor is Land's End the most westerly or most southerly point of mainland Britain, since the tilt of Scotland to the west places Ardnamurchan Point 20 miles further into the Atlantic than the tip of Cornwall, while the Lizard is further south.

However, Penzance station is the most southerly in Britain, and a good starting point to explore the coast of Cornwall, or for a visit to the Scillies. For walkers, the coastal path may be taken westwards from Penzance station to reach Land's End and Cape Cornwall, England's only cape, or eastwards to St Michael's Mount and beyond, using branch lines to access more distant resorts and sections of the coastline between Falmouth and Looe.

The next branch line south to the sea after leaving Penzance is from Truro to Falmouth, whose vast harbour, known as Carrick Roads, is guarded by Pendennis Castle at the western entrance and St Mawes to the east. For several centuries Falmouth handled more ships than any port in the land except London, and in 1815 over 300 vessels were counted here on a single day. The shoreline around Carrick Roads is so extensive that the best way to tour this historic harbour is by boat.

Falmouth was at one time the destination for many transatlantic steamships, since it provided the fastest sea and rail route for passengers and mail between New York and London. The GWR recorded some high speeds on the 292 mile run from Falmouth to Paddington, including the first 100 mph by a steam locomotive, recorded in May 1904 by the 'City of Truro' on Wellington Bank, between Exeter and Taunton.

Truro, situated on the upper reaches of the river Fal, is a cathedral city and administrative centre for Cornwall. As the train heads east from Truro station, the cathedral's three spires rise high in the sky near the railway viaduct. The cathedral was completed in 1910, the first to be built in England since Wren's famous St Paul's cathedral in the 17th century. While Durham, Salisbury, Exeter, Ely, Lincoln, Peterborough and York have cathedrals visible from the train, none is as close to a main railway line or seen as clearly as is Truro, where trains in both directions pass the cathedral slowly enough to give a good view from the high viaduct.

There are 34 railway viaducts between Truro and Plymouth, more than on any other main line of similar length in Britain, and it is while crossing these viaducts by train that some of the finest views are obtained. There are also several castles visible from the train, notably Restormel on top of a hill above the Fowey valley between Lostwithiel and Bodmin Parkway stations.

After leaving Truro, the next station is St Austell, two miles from the sea. Black's Guide to Cornwall (1879) lists 64 places in Cornwall which are named after saints, and there is no other area of Britain which contains such a heavenly host of communities within such a small region. St Austell has attracted many people to come and live here, the largest town in Cornwall to be named after a saint. In summer, the station has an almost Mediterranean air with sub-tropical trees and plants growing beside the platform.

Between St Austell and Par, some of the famous 'Cornish Alps' may be seen from the train, for we are now in the vicinity of Cornwall's china clay industry. Par is the junction for Newquay, on the only branch line to have direct cross-country HST service in the summer from the midlands and north of England, with 'Holidaymaker' trains travelling overnight to reach Newquay on Saturday mornings. The line from Par climbs up the steep Luxulyan valley, passing the 'Cornish Alps' near Bugle and Roche before descending to Newquay, Cornwall's largest seaside resort.

On arrival at the station high above the sea, the best places to admire Newquay's scenic setting are the headlands and cliffs that extend east and west of Great Western Beach, a short walk from the station. At low tide, the beaches become a huge expanse of sand, and there are pleasant walks along this section of the coast, with fine views along the coast. When the soaring Atlantic surf rolls in from the northwest, Newquay is paradise for surfers at any time of the year.

As early as 1849 a railway was built between Newquay harbour and St. Dennis, halfway to Par, but it was not until 1876 that the vital link to the main line was completed so that trains could cross Cornwall from Newquay to Fowey through the

TO THE GREAT WESTERN SEA

· SUMMER 1939 ·

LONDON Paddington		0730	0850	0900	0930			1025	CR 1030	1035		1040		1045	1100	1200
EXETER	XC 1125	1156		1240		XC 1255	XC 1305				XC 1330	XC 1335	1337	XC 1355	1358	
TORQUAY			1250	1347			1350					1435		1445		1530
PLYMOUTH	1315	1345			1350	1405		1440	1432	1447	1455	1500	1515		1525	
NEWQUAY					1545			1625							1735	
TRURO										1630		1638			1715	
FALMOUTH	1620				1620							1718			1750	
ST ERTH	1610								1641		1718				1803	
ST IVES	1648								1705		1755				1835	
PENZANCE	1630								1655	1710	1730			1750	1820	

THIS IS AN EXTRACT FROM THE GWR SATURDAY TIMETABLE

CR = CORNISH RIVIERA   **XC = CROSS-COUNTRY TRAIN**

Photo: St Ive's Harbour, 1999 (John Hadrill)

Luxulyan valley down to St Blazey, and through Cornwall's longest tunnel at St. Pinnock (1173 yards), to West Fowey.

Until 1934, Fowey was served by two branch lines, one from St. Blazey (near Par), and the other from Lostwithiel. The line from St Blazey came through Pinnock Tunnel, and was closed in 1934, while passenger services on the branch line to Fowey from Lostwithiel survived until the Beeching Axe fell in the 1960s.

Four miles by road from Par station, Fowey's dramatic setting is best seen from the gardens and woods above Ready-money Cove and St Catherine's Point. The deep narrow harbour lies below a steep hillside on which the town is built, and at night when lights are reflected in the water, or in the early morning when sunshine breaks through the summer haze, the yachts and fishing boats in Fowey's safe haven reveal picturesque Cornwall at its best.

From Par, the train climbs eastwards to Lostwithiel, past Restormel Castle to Bodmin Parkway station, where the preserved Bodmin & Wenford Steam Railway operates in season along the former GWR branch line to Bodmin General station, continuing alongside the River Camel to Boscarne Junction, 6.5 miles from Bodmin Parkway station.

Trains from Bodmin Parkway to Liskeard ascend the steep southern flank of the Fowey valley, crossing several viaducts and passing close to forested slopes, with the main road far below. Liskeard is the junction for the Looe train, which has its own station beside the main line, but at right angles to it. Unique among all rail routes in Britain, this branch line is part of the network, yet isolated from it for all scheduled passenger trains to Looe.

In a valley below Liskeard station is Coombe Junction, where Looe trains reverse down to the sea. The track below Coombe was built on an old canal bed, where granite blocks were placed to bear the weight of heavy freight trains that once passed through this junction carrying quarried stone from Bodmin Moor down to the coast.

The steep descent from Liskeard station to Coombe requires a 180 degree turn, enabling the train to pass beneath the viaduct carrying the main line between London and Penzance. It was said that if a traveller arriving at Liskeard on the main line had just missed the Looe train, it was possible to sprint down Lodge Hill and climb aboard the train as it reversed on the Coombe switchback, but that was only possible in the days of steam locomotive operations.

Descending from Coombe, the Looe train travels along the river valley through woods to St. Keyne, Causeland, and Sandplace, reaching the end of the line at East Looe, upstream from the town centre. At extreme high tide and river flood conditions, this line may be under water in places. Buses then replace the train service.

On the opposite bank across from the station is West Looe, rising above the estuary of the Looe river which flows through this historic port. With its narrow streets, busy harbour and beaches, Looe has much to attract the visitor, but like most resorts in Devon and Cornwall, it is very crowded in the summer. A carefree way to approach Looe is to take the train and enjoy a walk down to the beaches, avoiding traffic congestion on roads leading to the sea.

A mile offshore is Looe Island, the largest on the Cornish coast. It was mistaken for a warship in WW2 and attacked by the Luftwaffe, who claimed that they had sunk the 'Ark Royal' here, twelve miles west of the great naval base at Plymouth. This is one of several places where the famous aircraft carrier was reported to have been sunk during WW2.

From Looe station it is uphill by train all the way back to Liskeard, with the ritual of unlocking and locking the points at what was once busy Coombe Junction, and is now Britain's only standard-gauge switchback for the purpose of taking a train up or down a steep hillside. The main line eastwards from Liskeard passes over the Looe line, which may be seen from the first high viaduct (there are ten between Liskeard and Saltash), as the train accelerates towards Plymouth.

At Saltash, speed is reduced to 10 mph to cross Brunel's famous Royal Albert Bridge over the river Tamar, the boundary between Devon and Cornwall.This was the first railway suspension bridge in the world and when completed in 1859 formed the final section of track linking London to Penzance.

Cornwall, like the Isle of Wight, is proudly independent, for it is almost entirely surrounded by water, two sides by sea and the third side by the Tamar. When Brunel's bridge across the river was opened, a contemporary writer remarked that the railway finally "spanned the silver streak which separated the Briton from the Englishman," adding that expansion of the railway network into Cornwall would destroy "the isolation of the wild West."

On arrival at Plymouth (North Road) station, we change trains and travel along the branch line to Gunnislake. This is a surviving section of the Southern Railway's former main line between London (Waterloo) and Plymouth, on which coaches of the 'Atlantic Coast Express' came down from Devon's lofty hills to the sea, travelling around the western edge of Dartmoor to Tavistock, then across the Tavy and under the Royal Albert Bridge, followed by a steep climb to join the GWR line into Plymouth.

Today's train from Plymouth to Gunnislake follows the 'ACE' route as far as Bere Alston, where it reverses to cross the high Calstock viaduct, one of the last great railway viaducts to be built in the twentieth century (1908), an elegant structure in the classic tradition of the early railway builders, with its twelve tall arches 130ft above the Tamar. Trains do not linger long at Gunnislake station, so we will remain with the train to re-cross the Calstock viaduct, reverse again at Bere Alston, and follow the Tamar back to Plymouth.

The great harbour, fortress and naval base at Plymouth are linked with many of the most famous names in Britain's seafaring history. The Hoe, where Drake played his legendary game of bowls, is the focal point in Plymouth for visitors coming by sea or land, and from the high promenade there are fine views of Drake's Island and Plymouth Sound.

Four rivers, the Plym, Tavy, Tamar, and Lynher meet at Plymouth and flow through the harbour, scene of many ship arrivals and departures during the past four centuries, as well as popular 'Navy Days' when ships in the dockyard are open to visitors. Plymouth is an excellent centre for exploring Devon and Cornwall, and there is much to see and enjoy in this proud and pleasant city, heavily bombed in WW2 and rebuilt in the 1950s.

Plymouth North Road station is one of two (the other is Exeter St David's) where the GWR and SR trains departed in opposite directions for London. The GWR trains headed east, while the SR trains went west to the Tamar, then north via Tavistock and Okehampton before turning east to Exeter. The choice of two rail routes between Exeter and London remains: the slower scenic line of the former 'Atlantic Coast Express' through south Devon hills and lush Dorset vales to Waterloo, or the more northerly and faster route taken by the 'Cornish Riviera' to Paddington.

It was from the R.A.F. base at Cattewater on the outskirts of Plymouth that Aircraftman T.E.Shaw (Lawrence of Arabia) wrote on 16 April 1929 to Sir Hugh Trenchard, Chief of the Air Staff, claiming a record time of 4 hours 44 minutes on his motorcycle between London's Hyde Park Corner and Catte-

A Kingswear train crosses Churston viaduct in 1959. This attractive structure in a superb setting now forms part of the Paignton & Dartmouth Railway, on which restored GWR steam trains provide passengers with unforgettable sea views. (NRM - MWE23/59)

water. This, Lawrence observed, was only thirteen minutes more than the 'Cornish Riviera Express' from Paddington to Plymouth.

One can only marvel at his high speeds on the roads of 1929, more than thirty years before the first motorways were built. He also claimed to have achieved a maximum speed of 108 mph on his Brough motorcycle 'Boanerges', just short of the record of 109.5 mph set by the 'Cornish Riviera Express' between Lavington and Westbury.

Between Plymouth and Totnes the train climbs Hemerdon Bank to reach the southern flanks of Dartmoor, descending Rattery Bank into Totnes, where the South Devon Railway has its station nearby on the preserved line to Buckfastleigh. After a climb and descent of Dainton Bank, hardly noticeable in a powerful and smooth riding HST, we merge with the tracks from Paignton and Torquay just before Newton Abbot, a train spotter's paradise from the 1920s to the 1950s, when as many as 33 express trains to the sea could be counted on summer Saturday afternoons.

Torquay, together with Paignton, Goodrington and Brixham all grouped around Tor Bay, forms the largest resort area served by train on this part of the coast. It would be hard to find a greater variety of shoreline within one bay, for here are secluded wooded coves, long sandy beaches, and rocky outcrops with narrow crescents of sand revealed as the tide recedes.

The village of Torquay became a fashionable place to live during the Napoleonic Wars, when Royal Navy officers established elegant houses around the bay for their families to enjoy the temperate year-round climate. Since it was no longer possible to winter on the French Riviera, Tor Bay became the English Riviera, and so it has remained. With the wide sweep of its bay, its palm trees, Mediterranean atmosphere and many fine beaches it has been compared favourably to the Bay of Naples. Tennyson, who came here in 1838, called Torquay "the loveliest sea village in England."

A century later, Torquay had spread all around its rocky headland, with fine hotels, houses and gardens leading down to the sea. The town centre is in a valley leading down to the harbour, a good starting point for walks along the promenade beside Torre Abbey Sands, Corbyn Beach and Livermead Sands to reach the outskirts of Paignton, the end of the line for trains on the railway network.

Paignton is also the terminus of the Paignton and Dartmouth Railway, whose restored GWR steam trains link the two Devon resorts on a route that combines some of the most picturesque features one could find in a short railway excursion of seven miles. On departure from Paignton station, the train passes close to Goodrington Sands, followed by a climb through wooded hills and across viaducts at Hookhills and Broadsands, with views of the Devon and Dorset coasts.

Beyond Churston the train enters Greenway Tunnel, crosses another viaduct, and descends to the River Dart, with a stop at Britannia Crossing for those who wish to use the upper ferry. The last half mile of track is alongside the estuary to Kingswear station, with its landing stage for the ferry to cross over to Dartmouth, the only station in Britain never to receive a train since the day it opened on 16 August 1864. Eight miles upstream from Dartmouth, the South Devon Railway operates its steam trains between Totnes (Riverside) and Buckfastleigh.

Brixham had its own branch line from 1867 to 1963, with trains from Brixham Road (now Churston) on the Paignton-Kingswear route. In 1971, with the decline in passenger traffic, all through trains from London to Kingswear were withdrawn by BR. Local services survived until 1972, with BR operating under a subsidy from Devon County Council.

The coastline between the estuaries of the Dart and Exe has several attractive resorts offering visitors the benefits of a mild winter climate. This is what appealed to Jane Austen at Dawlish, John Keats at Teignmouth, and to Queen Charlotte, Disraeli, Tennyson, Elizabeth Barrett, Charles Kingsley and Arnold Bennett at Torquay.

Between Torquay and Teignmouth, the railway line heads inland to pass around the wide estuary of the Teign. On this part of the Devon coastline the beaches, coves, steep cliffs, and rocky headlands continue around Babbacombe Bay in a series of bays at Anstey's Cove, Redgate, Babbacombe, Oddicombe , Watcombe, Maidencombe, and Shaldon.

Shaldon stands on a steeply sloping cliff overlooking the Teign estuary, where trains on the main line from Newton Abbot speed towards Teignmouth and Dawlish, both popular holiday resorts. Watching trains near Dawlish remains a pastime for many people as they stroll along the sea front beside the railway tracks, where high tides and strong winds sometimes send sea spray from one side of the promenade, while HSTs thunder by on the other. The beach at Dawlish is a mixture of red sand, pebbles and rocks, overlooked by red cliffs through which the train passes in five short tunnels as it approaches Dawlish Warren.

Rounding the coast, we travel north along the wide estuary of the Exe to reach Exeter, a city in Roman times, once a busy port, and now a great hub of commerce, education and tourism. The nave of its great cathedral, completed in 1369, has the longest unbroken stretch of Gothic vaulting in the world. Other notable buildings include the Bishop's Palace, Guildhall, Customs House, Rougemont Castle with its moat, tower, and museum, as well as many attractive houses grouped around the cathedral. Exeter Central station, adjacent to Northernhay Gardens, is the closest station to the city centre and cathedral. This is a city to walk around and to enjoy at leisure.

It was at Exeter St David's station that Allen Lane conceived Penguin Books after a visit to the bookstall there and finding, like many before him, that there were no suitable modestly-priced books to read on the journey. Among writers who visited Exeter, Daniel Defoe found the city "full of gentry and good company" in 1726, and George Gissing lived here for two years, writing two books and saying: "Every morning when I awake, I thank heaven for silence." That was in 1891.

Exeter has three railway stations named for saints within a one mile radius: St David's, St Thomas (for Sainsburys), and St James Park. On weekdays, more than twenty trains from many parts of the country converge on Exeter St David's between 1130 and 1430, including the westbound and eastbound 'Cornish Riviera' expresses, and several long-distance cross-country trains travelling to or from resorts in Devon and Cornwall.

In order to continue by train to south coast resorts served by the former Southern Railway, we will travel by HST from Exeter to Paddington, then follow the route of the 'Atlantic Coast Express' from Waterloo down to Devon, visiting seaside destinations that were once served by this famous train. We will also visit some of the interesting places en route.

On leaving Exeter for the 174-mile run to London, the train follows the rivers Exe and Culm to pass the ancient town of Cullompton (fourteen miles from St David's), whose archives show over 40 spellings of the town's name since Domesday. In 1858, the timetable of the Bristol and Exeter Railway printed in the Tiverton Gazette showed the 'down' train stopping at Cullompton, and the 'up' train stopping at Collumpton. The Post Office, Ordnance Survey, and countless others used a rich mixture of variants.

This was the only town in Britain that could not settle its orthography for centuries, and even today the name is often mis-spelled. In his appeal for contributions to help restoration of the parish church, the late Sir John Betjeman chose the spelling 'Cullumpton'. The impressive tower of the church can be seen on the hillside north of the tracks as the train speeds towards Tiverton Parkway station.

Between Tiverton Parkway and Taunton is Wellington Bank, down which GWR ocean mail trains from Falmouth and Plymouth speeded to beat rival trains of the Southern Railway, whose main line to London was more challenging, via Okehampton, Exeter, and Salisbury. Travelling on a HST today one hardly notices the climb or descent of Wellington Bank, where the Royal Train carrying King Edward VII and Queen Alexandra sprinted on its way to the Devon coast in March 1902, setting a record for the longest non-stop journey to the sea, 229 miles from Paddington to Kingswear via Bristol in 263 minutes.

After this exhilarating royal progress, the GWR decided to name its most powerful class of steam locomotives 'Kings', and these were assigned to haul the 'Cornish Riviera' as far as Plymouth each day. They were too heavy for the Royal Albert Bridge over the Tamar, so the lighter 'Castle' class was used in Cornwall for the remaining coaches of a train that had left Paddington with fourteen or more, weighing over 600 tons including locomotive.

In the final decade of steam there were several high-speed runs by the 'Cornish Riviera', whose men on the footplate were determined to show the power and speed these locomotives could achieve in hauling fourteen coaches, before all the 'Kings' were withdrawn from service in 1962. Several trains on the Western Region reached the magic 100 mph, and the highest recorded post-WW2 speed by the CR was 108 mph in the autumn of 1955, set by 'King Richard III' near milepost 88 between Lavington and Westbury, en route to Exeter.

While faster speeds had been recorded by LNER and LMS locomotives, a new GWR 'King' or 'Castle' class locomotive was judged by O.S.Nock to be "the nearest thing to a railway Rolls Royce that I have ever encountered."

We now hasten to London (Paddington) via Taunton, Westbury, and Reading to continue our journeys by train around Britain's coasts on another rail route from London to Devon and Cornwall. We will travel on the main line of the former Southern Railway, whose trains from Waterloo ventured as far west as Padstow in Cornwall, territory that the GWR regarded as its own fiefdom.

Not only did the SR claim the north Cornwall coastline from Padstow to Bude, it also served the north and south Devon coasts, in addition to a huge stretch of the south coast of England from Exmouth in Devon to resorts all along the Kent coast.

Rivalry in the 1920s between the GWR and SR for west country passengers resulted in a new train, the 'Atlantic Coast Express', bright jewel in the SR crown, with by far the longest route of all its trains, titled or otherwise. It had a younger pedigree, and its life (1926-1964) was brief compared to the 'Cornish Riviera', yet this one train provided more through coaches to more seaside destinations on its 260 mile run from London (Waterloo) to Padstow than any other train in Britain.

The daily ACE service from Waterloo served nine destinations in Cornwall and Devon, namely Padstow, Bude, Ilfracombe, Sidmouth, Seaton, Exeter, Torrington, Plymouth and Exmouth. On summer Saturdays, seven relief ACE trains were needed to take the holiday crowds from Waterloo to the coast, and on some occasions two extra trains were assigned exclusively for Ilfracombe passengers. A total of eight restaurant car trains left Waterloo between 1024 and 1205, heading to resorts in Devon and Cornwall, along tracks that flashed in summer sunshine like the silverware on white linen table-cloths in SR dining cars.

Only the Waterloo-Exeter, Exeter-Okehampton and Bere Alston-Plymouth sections of the former SR main line to Plymouth survive today, and of the ACE branch lines to the coast, only Exeter-Exmouth, and Exeter-Barnstaple operate throughout the year. In travelling along former ACE routes to the sea from London we shall pass through some of the most spectacular slices of countryside in England.

After leaving Basingstoke and Salisbury behind, the train enters Somerset near Templecombe, where the famous 'Pines Express', southbound on the Somerset & Dorset line to the sea at Bournemouth, crossed beneath the tracks of the 'Atlantic Coast Express' heading west on the SR main line into Devon and Cornwall. It was said that people went to Templecombe, 112 miles from London, for two reasons only. One was to visit St Mary's Church, with its controversial medieval painting of the Christ head; the other was to change trains, which ran from this railway crossroads into Dorset, Devon, Wiltshire and beyond - to the north, south, east, and west.

At one time over 200 trains passed through Templecombe every 24 hours, and in 1910 over 200,000 wagons were transferred between the two lines which met here in the small peaceful village that was known as 'the Crewe' of Somerset.

Following closure of all S&D lines in 1966, the ruins of Templecombe station were passed by every train between Waterloo and Exeter, and the prospects for survival of this former SR main line serving so many towns and villages in the west country looked dim. Having lost their station, and faced with the possible loss of their line, the local inhabitants campaigned for retention of the line and restoration of the station that they and their ancestors had used for generations.

In the railway renaissance of the 1980s, when local councils worked together with British Rail to revive railway facilities in towns and villages around Britain, Templecombe station was rebuilt and returned to the timetables on 3 October 1983. It now has a unique sculpture garden beside the platform to greet passengers, though there is little time for those in the train to admire the artistry and humour inspired by railway timekeeping. Some of the inscriptions on the sculptures, alluding to the old S&D railway, are used as chapter headings in this book.

No other railway in Britain was held in such affection and ridicule as the Somerset & Dorset, always struggling to survive. Robert Read, General Manager of the S&D, certainly fulfilled his family motto: 'res non verba', for he personified those qualities that contributed to the greatness of Victorian England: vision, courage, vigour, integrity and utter devotion to duty. He would surely smile if he were to see the railway sculptures rising like a phoenix today from the ruins of Templecombe, named Britain's best small station in 1987.

The 'Flying Scotsman' has called here, posing for photogra-

CLASSIC
WEST COUNTRY

Watching trains at Dawlish has long been a favourite pastime, especially when high tides and strong winds send sea spray hurtling over the tracks. The waves are breaking in tremendous style as 37101 passes with a Sunday relief from Leeds to Plymouth in August 1985. (P.Underhay/Colour-Rail DE1035)

I.K. Brunel's magnificent Royal Albert Bridge over the Tamar estuary remains a highspot of the journey from Paddington to Cornwall, although it has never seemed quite the same since completion of the parallel road bridge. This view from the sixth coach of the up 'Cornish Riviera' was taken in April 1959 when it still existed in glorious isolation. (Colour-Rail BRW586)

The 'Atlantic Coast Express' was unique in conveying through carriages for no less than eight different destinations: Seaton, Sidmouth, Exmouth, Ilfracombe, Torrington, Plymouth, Bude and Padstow. Only four of these were actually on the Atlantic coast! A Merchant Navy class locomotive, complete with headboard, is waiting at Exeter for the various pieces of the jigsaw to be put together before it begins the run up to London Waterloo. (NRM - SR/173)

phers, and several steam excursions have passed this way. In 1988, British Rail named one of their Class 33 locomotives after this historic village station in tribute to the determination of its inhabitants in restoring scheduled services to this delightful part of the west country, where names of ancient villages such as Kington Magna, Fifehead Magdalen, Purse Caundle and Abbas Combe resonate with memories of village life that has changed little over the past centuries in and around Templecombe.

When the S&D line closed in 1966 it seemed inconceivable that a steam-hauled 'Pines Express' would ever run again near Templecombe. Today, the Gartell Light Railway operates a narrow-gauge version of this train on part of the old S&D trackbed between Yenston and Templecombe, with stations at Common Lane, Pinesway Junction, and Park Lane which houses a museum with local railway memorabilia. In this quiet corner of Blackmore Vale, a small railway miracle has taken place.

As the train from Waterloo to Exeter nears Sherborne, the old castle given to Sir Walter Raleigh by Queen Elizabeth I in 1599 is seen close to the line on the left. The new castle, about a mile away, is not visible from the train, but is mentioned in Hardy's 'The Woodlanders', where Sherborne appears as 'Sherton Abbas'. Two Saxon kings are buried in Sherborne Abbey, which for over three centuries had its own bishop. The famous school, founded in 1550, forms part of the Abbey precinct, and was the location for the 1969 remake of 'Goodbye Mr Chips' with Sherborne station featuring in the film.

One branch line through Dorset to the sea that has survived

is west of Sherborne and near Yeovil, which has two stations, neither in the town. The Exeter train stops at Yeovil Junction, whereas trains heading south to the sea at Weymouth come from Castle Cary and stop at Yeovil Pen Mill, over a mile away by road from Yeovil Junction. We shall travel along this scenic route through Dorset in Chapter 5.

From Yeovil Junction, the train to Exeter climbs to Crewkerne, then descends past the former Chard Junction to Axminster, where on a summer's day in 1961 a remarkable speed record of 104 mph was set by the 'Atlantic Coast Express' hauled by Merchant Navy Class locomotive 35028 'Clan Line', which fortunately has been preserved. When details of this record run were published in 1962, it was thought advisable to conceal both the name of the locomotive and the date, in case the speed achieved near milepost 146 should land the driver in trouble, for it was far in excess of the posted maximum on this section of the line.

Travelling by diesel train along the sinuous single track today, we can only marvel at a magnificent achievement by driver and fireman of a scheduled passenger train as it charged downhill from milepost 133 west of Crewkerne, through Chard and Axminster, before slowing in the climb up to Honiton tunnel entrance at milepost 152.

Leaving Axminster the train climbs past the former Seaton Junction, where a branch line served the resort town of Seaton. Part of the former trackbed has been restored as a tramway, so that once again the pleasure of going down towards the sea by rail can be enjoyed in the comfort of immaculately-restored double-decker trams of the Seaton & District Electric Tramway. It is planned to extend the present three-mile line all the way to the sea front. One mile west of Seaton is Beer, with its model railway centre.

After climbing to Honiton, it is seventeen miles mostly downhill to Exeter Central, passing the site of Sidmouth Junction (now Feniton), where a branch line once meandered down the Otter valley to Sidmouth, Budleigh Salterton, and around the coast to Exmouth. Trains today travel from Exeter along the east shore of the Exe via Topsham, Exton and Lympston to the terminus at Exmouth. A short walk from the station to the sea front is rewarded with fine views across the Exe to the south Devon coast where trains travel on the main line between Exeter and Penzance.

Some trains from Exmouth travel all the way to Barnstaple via Exeter Central and St David's stations, on the only railway route with daily through trains between Devon's south and north coasts. The line from Exeter to Barnstaple is named the 'Tarka Line' and runs for 39 miles near the rivers Exe and Taw, crossing the Yeo between Morchard Road and Lapford stations.

This is the longest branch line in the West Country, noted for its route through a soft and mellow landscape, with well-preserved stations where great express trains from London to the Devon and north Cornwall coasts once thundered through stations with names such as Kings Nympton, Portsmouth Arms, and Umberleigh, the latter station having the most gentle gradient marker of any station in Britain, 1 in 5400.

Train service has been revived along part of this former route of the 'Atlantic Coast Express' to resorts in Devon and Cornwall. On 24 May 1997 the Exeter to Okehampton line was re-opened to passenger trains, another welcome sign of a renaissance on Britain's privatized railway network. This line opens up a wonderful area of the west country to rail travellers, including Dartmoor and the north Cornwall coast.

Barnstaple was once the hub for five railway lines radiating to Taunton, Ilfracombe, Lynton, Bideford and Exeter. From 1901 to 1914 Bideford also had a line running to Appledore and Westward Ho!, with eleven stations in seven miles. The narrow gauge (1.96ft) line to Lynton was sponsored by publisher Sir George Newnes, and opened in 1898, with nine stations along its 19 mile route to the north Devon coast, where the terminus was 700ft above the sea, and 250ft above

the town, not far from Sir George's house.

The Lynton & Barnstaple Railway was taken over by the SR in 1923, and closed in 1935, but fortunately the station buildings at Woody Bay (four miles from the sea) have been acquired by the L&BR Association. There is one unique feature of this railway that still survives: Chelfham viaduct, a massive structure built by Devon stonemasons, and the largest narrow gauge railway viaduct in Britain. In March 1996, planning permission was granted to re-lay part of the line, with a long-term aim of linking Barnstaple with Lynton by railway once more.

Although operational for only 37 years, the old L&BR, with its little green trains labouring up steep gradients to a line summit of 980ft near Woody Bay, was one of the most admired of all England's narrow-gauge lines, and it is remembered with affection by railway enthusiasts. The line traversed the western fringes of Exmoor, and depended on local traffic and tourism in the face of strong competition from buses, which were faster and more convenient.

The Lynton & Lynmouth cliff railway, also a legacy from Sir George Newnes, remains in service today, providing a useful link between the two towns, as it did when L&BR locomotives known locally as 'Exmoor Ponies' steamed in and out of Lynton station. The cliffs on this part of the coast are very steep, and Countisbury Hill near Lynton is England's highest sea cliff (1,000ft).

Barnstaple station, at the end of the line from Exeter, is a quiet and rather sad place when one recalls all the trains crowded with holidaymakers that used to converge here. The former line between Barnstaple and Ilfracombe hugged the tidal estuary of the Taw, turning inland through rich Devon pastures and hills to reach the coast. It was a popular country railway, and operated 'rabbit specials', with staff at each wayside station loading consignments brought in by local farmers. A bus now links Barnstaple station to the town and continues westwards to Braunton and Ilfracombe.

Hills around Ilfracombe gave trains a difficult start on departure from the coast, for they had to climb a gradient of 1 in 36, the steepest at any seaside resort in Britain, to reach the line summit (633ft above sea level) at Mortehoe. The road from Ilfracombe to Barnstaple runs close to the old trackbed, and the first six miles from the former Barnstaple Quay station now provide a pathway for walkers and cyclists as far as Braunton.

Ilfracombe was well served by the 'Atlantic Coast Express' and the equally famous 'Devon Belle', with its luxury Pullman coaches and unique beaver tail observation car. It was the last Pullman express to be introduced by the SR to serve the seaside, and the first to be withdrawn from service in 1954, after only eight summer seasons.

When inaugurated in 1947, the 'Devon Belle' attracted a great deal of interest, for a Pullman observation car was a rare sight

A local service from Newton Abbot to Kingswear climbs away from Goodrington sands behind 'Castle' 5059 Earl St Aldwyn in June 1961. Today this picturesque stretch of line forms part of the preserved Paignton and Dartmouth Railway.
(P.W. Gray/Colour-Rail BRW182)

The 1 in 36 climb away from Ilfracombe to a summit over 600ft above sea level at Mortehoe was the steepest at any seaside resort in Britain. Operating conditions could sometimes be very difficult, but the bank presents no problems to a 'Battle of Britain' class locomotive on an afternoon local in September 1961.
(J.F.W. Paige/ Colour-Rail BRS51)

The bridge over Little Petherick Creek once signified that the 260 mile journey from Waterloo to the Southern Railway's extremity at Padstow was almost over. Like most of the company's 'Withered Arm' west of Exeter, this stretch of line closed in the Beeching era. It is now a popular footpath offering sweeping views over the Camel estuary.
(Derek Cross/Colour-Rail BRS257)

Cornwall is unique in retaining four attractive branch lines to the sea. That to Looe runs close to the tidal estuary as seen in this 1959 view of Terras Crossing.   Trains have to be replaced by buses at times of extreme high tide and river flood conditions.
(P.W. Gray/Colour-Rail BRW265)

anywhere in Britain, and had never before been seen in Devon or Cornwall. The elegant cream and brown Pullman livery was much more striking than the SR dark green, and attracted much attention as the DB headed westwards from London's Waterloo station on its 227 mile journey to Ilfracombe.

Operating on Fridays to Mondays in the summer of 1947, the DB departed at noon from Waterloo for Ilfracombe and Plymouth with fourteen heavy Pullman coaches, a total weight of over 600 tons including locomotive and tender. It was the only train to pass through Salisbury station without stopping, and was booked to reach Ilfracombe at 1733, in time to enjoy a late afternoon stroll along the beach of this delightful Devon resort, while the locomotive, tender, and observation car were turned round for the return journey. At times, strong Atlantic gales blowing on the exposed high turntable at Ilfracombe station (257ft above sea level) would do the turning, making it difficult to align the tracks.

All trace of the once great terminus of Ilfracombe, with its long platforms high above the town, has disappeared, and its final years were sad ones for railway travellers. After the last DB left at the end of the 1954 summer season, the ACE survived for another ten years, then left forever. The station was closed to all passenger trains on 3 October 1970, and the track remained until 1975, but all attempts to preserve this scenic line failed.

A path has been built along part of the trackbed, giving fine views from the site of the former station, where so many holidaymakers had climbed up from the town, at the end of their holidays, loaded with souvenirs and happy memories. The former station at Mortehoe is now part of a tourist attraction whose theme, apt yet sad for railway enthusiasts, is 'Once upon a time'.

Although the railway that served it so well has gone, Ilfra-combe remains a popular seaside resort, an amiable place in a spectacular setting. For many years, the ocean-going paddle steamer 'Waverley' would come into Ilfracombe to take holidaymakers across the sea to Tenby, on the Pembrokeshire coast, a journey of 42 miles by sea, compared to a train journey of about some 240 miles.

Ilfracombe proudly retains much Victorian charm and beauty in its floral displays, gardens, coastal walks, beaches, harbour, and entertainments for all ages. Surrounded by rich green hills that tumble down to the sea, it is a delightful place to visit and explore the local beaches or those nearby at Woolacombe, Lee Bay, and Combe Martin. After all the summer tourists have left, Ilfracombe once again becomes a peaceful haven for its inhabitants, noted for their longevity in its temperate climate.

From Ilfracombe there is a pleasant four-mile walk along the South-west Coast Path through Lee Bay to Bull Point from where on a fine day, Lundy may be seen on the skyline 20

miles away. Three miles to the south are Woolacombe Sands, over two miles long and facing the full force of mighty Atlantic rollers, making this a popular beach for surfers.

Bude is the most northerly resort in Cornwall served by the ACE until withdrawal of service in 1964. The train that left London (Waterloo) at 1055 with its own restaurant car reached Bude (228 miles) at 1635, with plenty of daylight left in midsummer to enjoy the three miles of golden sands, and the Atlantic surf for which Bude, and Widemouth to the south, are famous. At low tide the sands extend far out to sea, and along the coast as far north as Duckpool, with its spectacular rocky cove.

Before the railway came to this part of Cornwall, huge quantities of beach sand were transported on the Bude Canal to Launceston, 30 miles away. Today there is little left of this waterway, or of the railway that replaced it, and was in turn closed down in the 1960s. With the re-opening of the Exeter-Okehampton section of the former ACE line to Bude, it is now possible to get closer by train to Bude on this restored line than from the other 'end of line' at Barnstaple to the north.

It was a long journey of 260 miles from Waterloo station to Padstow in Cornwall, the furthest west that the ACE travelled to the sea, through Exeter, Okehampton (near the line summit of 650ft), Halwill Junction (for Bude), Launceston, and Wadebridge, reaching Padstow in the late afternoon. No other train has been so eulogised by a poet laureate, for to John Betjeman this was the most wonderful train in the railway firmament, traversing the hills of north Devon and Cornwall to reach the Camel river at Wadebridge, and the sea at Padstow.

One of the largest medieval towns in Cornwall, Padstow was a busy port where sailing vessels had to navigate the treacherous Doom Bar at the entrance of the harbour to reach the safety of the docks. The shifting sands were dreaded by sailors, whose ships were helpless in the grip of fast-flowing tides and fierce gales that swept many to their death in the wide estuary.

It is worth staying several days in Padstow in order to enjoy some fine walks around the Camel shoreline at extreme low and high tides, for each reveals or conceals interesting sandy beaches, sandbanks, rocks, and marine life along the estuary. When the tide comes in, walkers should remain on footpaths above the beaches, for the flood tide can quickly trap those who linger too long on rocky ledges or sandbanks.

There are probably more railway archaeological sites along former ACE routes than anywhere else in southern England. There are also some excellent pathways to the sea along old trackbeds, for example between Wadebridge and Padstow on the south bank of the Camel. In 1996, the line from Bodmin General station to Boscarne Junction was re-opened, with access to the Camel Trail, affording a journey back in time by train and on foot for walkers who come to this attractive part

TO THE SOUTHERN SEA

ATLANTIC COAST EXPRESS	
·S U M M E R 1 9 3 9·	
LONDON (Waterloo)	1100
EXETER	1412
ILFRACOMBE	1606
BUDE	1639
PADSTOW	1737

Introduced in 1926. At the height of the summer season, eight complete restaurant car trains left Waterloo between 1024 and 1205 on the ACE service.

WITHDRAWN IN 1964

DEVON BELLE	
·S U M M E R 1 9 5 0·	
LONDON (Waterloo)	1200
EXETER	1536
ILFRACOMBE	1733

Introduced in 1947, the only all-Pullman service between London and Devon, and the longest Pullman route to the sea in Britain, with connecting service to Sidmouth Junction for Sidmouth and Budleigh Salterton.

WITHDRAWN IN 1954

BOURNEMOUTH BELLE	
·S U M M E R 1 9 6 4·	
LONDON (Waterloo)	1030
SOUTHAMPTON	1155
BOURNEMOUTH	1235

Introduced in 1931, with up to twelve Pullman coaches in peak summer service, the heaviest passenger train to the sea on western routes of the Southern Railway.

WITHDRAWN IN 1967

Photo: Sea front at Combe Martin, near Ilfracombe (John Hadrill)

of the north Cornwall coast.

Abandoned railway routes in Britain's countryside now provide corridors for the movement of wild animals, and support a greater variety of species than adjoining cultivated land. Covered by wildflowers in Spring, rich with blackberries in summer, and invaded by butterflies on sunny days, nowhere is this more evident than along former railway routes in the west country. The views from embankments beside the Camel, and on crossing Petherick bridge, where murmurs and memories of former journeys linger quietly in the air, are well worth the six-mile walk from Wadebridge to Padstow.

While many old railway trackbeds have been built over to form new roads or industrial estates, over a thousand miles of abandoned railway lines all over Britain have now been converted to footpaths open to the public, and the West Country has a good share of these. The great appeal of 'rails-to-trails' conversions is that they are level, or nearly so, and easy for people of all ages to walk along.

This legacy from the heydays of railway travel, which came to an end with the closure of more than 8,000 route miles between 1947 and 1969, has passed to us largely through the work of countryside preservation groups. The Camel Trail that runs beside river and estuary to the sea is a fine example of transformation of a former main line to a scenic pathway. For nearly forty years the ACE served the Devon and Cornwall coasts, until its final journey to London from Padstow and other coastal resorts on 5 September 1964, headed appropriately by West Country class 34023 'Blackmoor Vale'.

In his book titled 'The Withered Arm', T.W.E. Roche described the 'Atlantic Coast Express' thus: "The ACE shunned the great tourist resorts of the south and sought out the high places and the lonely places; no other main line could look up directly to the towering peak of Yes Tor; it was the Dartmoor main line; it penetrated more deeply into King Arthur's land, and two of its north Cornwall stations are immortalized in Betjeman poetry."

Fifty years ago, rural Somerset had an extensive network of railway lines serving the county and its seaside from hubs at

Blue Anchor station on the 20-mile West Somerset line, the longest preserved coastal railway route in Britain. Steam services began in 1976, five years after British Rail closed this once busy branch. (John Hadrill)

Somerset & Dorset outpost. Burnham-on-Sea was developed as the railhead for an unsuccessful 'Channel to Channel' service from Bournemouth to Cardiff using train and ferry. 3F 43427 had arrived on an excursion in 1959, eight years after the withdrawal of regular passenger traffic. (R.E. Toop/Colour-Rail SD109)

POSTERS OF
DISTINCTION

Great Western centenary poster of 1935 by Murray Secretan. 'King' 6009 King Charles II is emerging from one of the tunnels between Dawlish and Teignmouth with the 'Cornish Riviera Express'.

With its special observation car, the all-Pullman 'Devon Belle' caused something of a sensation when introduced by the Southern Railway in 1947. As can be seen from the timetable, it made only one advertised stop between Waterloo and Exeter, where it divided into portions for Ilfracombe and Plymouth.
(NRM/Science & Society -2)

Taunton, Yeovil, Templecombe, Bath and Bristol. There is now only one major seaside resort in Somerset on the rail network, and that is Weston-super-Mare, a popular destination for holidaymakers, with its miles of golden sands which stretch far out to sea as the tide recedes along Weston Bay.

Weston-super-Mare's Birnbeck Pier, built in 1867, was one of the most popular in the country, and included among its attractions a water chute and switchback, while the Grand Pier (1904) with its massive glass-roofed pavilion claimed to have the largest covered space in one building of any pier in Britain.

The promenade faces due west towards Bridgewater Bay and is flanked by hills on each side, with Burnham-on-Sea to the south and Sand Point to the north. In a 1947 railway poster, Weston-super-Mare was described as "blessed with a happy, comfortable atmosphere in smiling Somerset."

Seven miles north of Weston-super-Mare is Clevedon, with its tree-shaded gardens and bowling greens close to the pebbled shore of Ladye Bay. The best viewpoint over the town and the wide sweep of the Bristol Channel is from Dial Hill (290ft), a mile north of the original village that developed into a popular resort served by a branch line from Yatton.

Clevedon's pier was completed in 1869, a masterpiece of Victorian design and engineering, delicately poised on elegant slender legs. One section collapsed during load-bearing trials in 1970, and today only the far end of the pier with its pavilion remains, like an abandoned island out to sea.

For nearly a century, steamers would take holidaymakers from Clevedon's pier to Ilfracombe, Tenby, Swansea, Lynmouth, and Chepstow (for Tintern Abbey). Clevedon has lost its railway and most of its pier but retains much of its Victorian architectural heritage, and is within easy commuting distance for those who work in Bristol and enjoy living by the sea.

South of Weston-super-Mare, where the estuaries of the rivers Parrett and Brue converge in Bridgewater Bay, is Burnham-on-Sea, a modest Victorian resort once served by the Somerset & Dorset Railway, which in 1863 established a 'Channel-to-Channel' rail service between Burnham and Bournemouth. This was to provide a direct link from South Wales to the English Channel, since Cardiff, Burnham, Templecombe and Bournemouth are almost on a straight line. There were four through trains a day each way, and the railway timetable included the ferry services between Burnham and Cardiff, but the S&DR was in financial difficulties from the start, and the 'Channel-to-Channel' services were withdrawn shortly afterwards.

On 29 October 1951, the Highbridge-Burnham line was closed to daily passenger traffic, but occasional excursion trains to the sea were permitted to use the track until 8 September 1962. The last passenger train on the proud but impecunious S&DR that once covered the West Country from Bath to Bournemouth, from Wells and Glastonbury to Bridgewater and Burnham, ran on 7 March 1966.

It was all part of the sad litany of rail closures around Britain, and there is now only one station between Weston-super-Mare and Bridgewater. This lone station is named Highbridge and Burnham, on the main line from Bristol to Taunton, but few trains stop here, for most are cross-country expresses that hurtle through at 80 mph.

Down the coast along Bridgewater Bay one can travel back in time to the great days of steam on the West Somerset Railway to recapture the pleasures of branch line operations on the longest preserved coastal railway route in Britain. After British Rail closed this line on 4 January 1971, the West Somerset Railway Company was formed, and on 28 March 1976 the first steam train since closure was given the 'right away' to travel from Minehead to Blue Anchor station by Lord Montague of Beaulieu

There are nine stations on this 20-mile line between Minehead and Bishops Lydeard, near Taunton. Four of these are near the sea, and in recent years some main line charter trains have come to Minehead from Taunton and elsewhere on the network. In high season, the 'Quantock Belle' dining train provides passengers with light lunches, cream teas, dinners and bar service as they travel by steam train beside the sea.

The station at Watchet is close to the sea front, and a century ago the sand in the harbour was so clean and firm that cricket was played there in the summer. To the west, cliffs rise to 250ft, giving fine panoramas along the coast, and in places there are small caves hollowed out by the sea. Coleridge was inspired to write his poem 'The Ancient Mariner' here after meeting an old sailor and learning how albatrosses were caught at sea.

Minehead's railway terminus has been well preserved in its fine location beside the promenade, where sands are sheltered from west winds by the great mass of North Hill which rises above the town. The opening of Butlin's Holiday Camp near the station in 1962 brought a welcome influx of holidaymakers to Minehead in summer seasons, but they were unable to convince BR to continue year-round service, and a closure notice was issued for this branch line on 6 January 1969. The holiday camp survived.

The harbour at Minehead is more than one thousand years old and in Saxon times belonged to the son of Lady Godiva. As we approach the new millennium, let us hope that the planned expansion of several preserved railways in Britain will include the restoration of scheduled steam trains between Minehead and the rail network at Taunton, along this delightful part of the Somerset coast.

The south coast: Dorset to Kent

The Mid-Day Pullman will leave at 1.0 pm
All change at the Equinox
Seasonal Tickets.

Sculpture 'Tempus Fugit' at Templecombe Station by
Sioban Coppinger, Alec and Fiona Peever, 1990.

Dorset has lost several of its railways to the sea, notably the Somerset & Dorset line through Templecombe, where the famous 'Pines Express', en route from Manchester and Liverpool to Bournemouth, crossed the tracks of the 'Atlantic Coast Express' to Devon and Cornwall. From 1910 to 1967 the 'Pines Express' was one of the most popular cross-country trains from the north of England to the south coast, with up to twelve coaches double-headed for the steep gradients south from Bath to the line summit at Masbury, 811ft above sea level, then to Templecombe and through Dorset to Blandford Forum and Bournemouth.

A rail journey between Bath and Bournemouth was so idyllic that one could hardly complain of the time that it took to travel the 71 miles, with the Mendips facing the train on departure from Bath, involving an almost continous climb for the first eighteen miles. The 'Pines Express' was the fastest train on this line to the Dorset coast, taking 2h 17min, and stopping at four stations en route. The slowest train took 4h 10min, stopping at all 26 stations, crossing five main lines and two branch lines in the process, averaging 17 mph from Bournemouth to Bath.

On the Saturday before August Bank Holiday in 1951, nine cross-country 'expresses' passed through Midford station (4 miles south of Bath) between 1422 and 1550, which required precise timekeeping on the single line at each end of the station, often with only one minute allowed between passage of trains in opposite directions. With single track along most of the route from Bath to Bournemouth, the line was used to capacity on summer Saturdays, and delays of an hour or more were common, more frustrating for those eager to reach the coast than for those leaving.

The western boundary of Dorset meets the sea just outside Lyme Regis, and until 7 March 1966, passengers on S&DR trains would change at Templecombe and Axminster to travel on the meandering branch line down to the medieval port and historic town of Lyme Regis. The Duke of Monmouth landed here in 1685 on the pebble beach just west of the Cobb in his ill-fated attempt to capture the throne from his uncle, James II. The town, with its fine panorama of Lyme Bay, became a fashionable watering place for the gentry of Bath in the 18th century, and has remained a popular holiday retreat on this part of the Dorset coast. The nearest station to Lyme Regis is now Axminster, five miles to the north, on the Waterloo-Exeter main line.

Charmouth, two miles east of Lyme Regis, was the favourite Dorset seaside village for Jane Austen, who wrote that it was "the happiest spot for watching the flow of the tide, for sitting in unwearied contemplation." This small village certainly did not lack royal visitors, who also came for privacy and the healthy climate. King Henry VIII's first wife, Catherine of Aragon, came to Charmouth in 1501, and Charles II stayed here in 1651 as a fugitive.

All the coastline around Lyme Bay is pleasing, with Golden Cap (617ft) plunging down to the sea from the fertile lands above. The former railway line to Bridport and West Bay via stations with quaint names like Toller Porcorum has gone, but sections of the old trackbed have been converted into a public walkway passing close to historic Eggardon Hill on the way to the sea.

SOUTHERN CASUALTIES

Rame Head forms a splendid backdrop to a bird's eye view of Seaton, terminus of a branch from Seaton Junction on the main line from Waterloo to Exeter. Part of the former trackbed has now been restored as the Seaton & District Electric Tramway.
(T.B. Owen/Colour-Rail BRS369)

Sunset on the Hayling Island branch. The state of the timber bridge across the Langstone Channel meant that the line became the last haunt of the famous 'Terrier' tanks, which were well able to cope with the severe weight restrictions. Closure came just a week after this photograph was taken on 26 October 1963. (B.R. Oliver)

QUAYSIDE LINES

Lymington Pier, a basic station providing easy transfer from train to ferries for the Isle of Wight. It is the terminus of a five-mile branch from Brockenhurst which skirts the southern fringes of the New Forest. (John Hadrill)

Weymouth Quay, the last place in Britain where one could encounter the unlikely sight of a main-line train creeping along streets crowded with cars and pedestrians. Flagmen precede the passage of a Channel Islands Boat Express in July 1976. (Brian Davis)

Lyme Regis terminus, with one of the three veteran Adams radial tanks which for many years provided the entire motive power on the branch from Axminster. Although the line once carried 60,000 passengers a year, closure took place in 1965. (J.S. Gilks)

Maiden Newton is now the closest station to this section of the coast, and also to such Dorset treasures as the Cerne Giant and the village of Cerne Abbas. From Maiden Newton, trains continue south to Dorchester and down to the seaside at Weymouth. In the summer, some Bristol to Weymouth trains are locomotive-hauled with extra coaches and large guard's vans, ideal for cyclists, whose bicycles are carried free. These trains are shown in rail timetables as 'Weymouth Sand & Cycle Explorer' services.

The journey south from Yeovil (Pen Mill) through Thornford, Yetminster, Chetnole, Maiden Newton, and Dorchester is as close as one can get to rail travel through Wessex at the time of Thomas Hardy's novels. This is perhaps the most pastoral branch line in Britain, a journey through an ancient landscape that has changed little since arrival of the railways in Dorset. Each station leads to villages and country lanes where Hardy and his characters once walked.

Between Thornford and Maiden Newton the train passes close to Dorset farmyards, thatched cottages and rich dairy meadows, before arriving at Dorchester West station on the former GWR line from Castle Cary to Weymouth. The main SR line from London to Weymouth comes into Dorchester South station, half a mile away, and then joins the branch line from Yeovil, climbing up and through the last range of hills before

descending to the sea.

Thomas Hardy travelled by train on many occasions, and wrote during his journeys, when speed was slow and changes of carriage were frequent. He was an early riser too, and at 4 a.m. on a Spring day in 1870 he set off from Bockhampton in Dorset for St Juliot in Cornwall, changing trains at Dorchester, Yeovil, Exeter, Plymouth and Launceston. On such journeys such as this he had plenty of time to jot down thoughts and ideas for his novels and poems, when the privacy of a compartment was far more agreeable than today's open seating with cellular phones intruding everywhere.

Weymouth boasts one of Britain's cleanest and safest sandy beaches, sheltered from westerly gales by the massive Isle of Portland, whose solid block of limestone is the Gibraltar of Dorset. Chesil Beach to the west forms an 18-mile breakwater for Abbotsbury, enclosing the largest seawater lake in England. The port of Weymouth became famous as a resort in 1789, when George III was the first reigning monarch to use a bathing

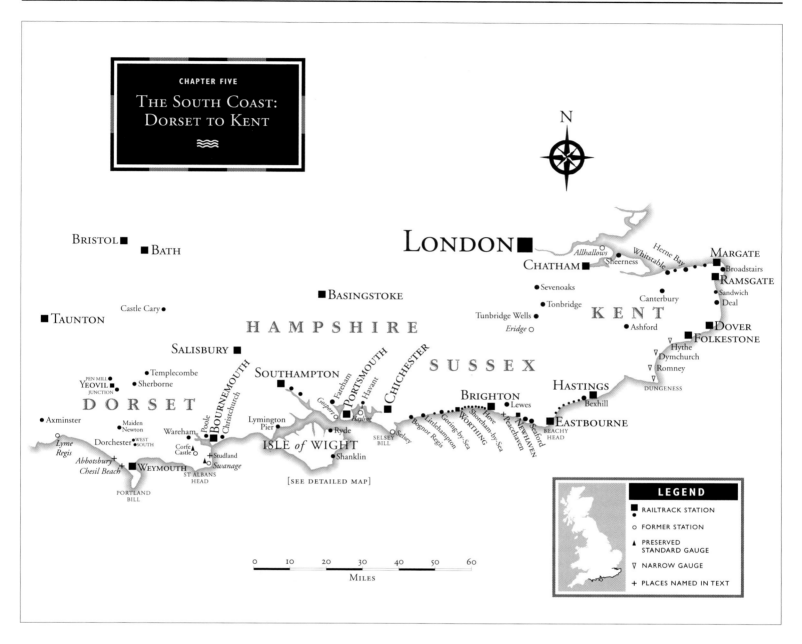

CHAPTER FIVE

THE SOUTH COAST: DORSET TO KENT

≋

N

BRISTOL ■ ■ BATH

LONDON ■
Allhallows ○   *Whitstable*   *Herne Bay*   MARGATE
CHATHAM ■   Sheerness   ● Broadstairs
                              RAMSGATE
● Sevenoaks   Canterbury ●   ● Sandwich
● BASINGSTOKE   ● Tonbridge   K E N T   ● Deal
Castle Cary ●   Tunbridge Wells ●   ● Ashford   DOVER
■ TAUNTON   *Eridge* ○   FOLKESTONE
H A M P S H I R E   ▽ Hythe
SALISBURY ■   Dymchurch
                    SOUTHAMPTON PORTSMOUTH CHICHESTER S U S S E X ▽ Romney
● Templecombe   HASTINGS   DUNGENESS
PEN MILL   Fareham   ● Bexhill
YEOVIL ■ ● Sherborne   Gosport ○ Havant   BRIGHTON ● Lewes
JUNCTION   BOURNEMOUTH   Hove   EASTBOURNE
D O R S E T   Lymington *Hayling* Worthing Shoreham-by-Sea BEACHY
● Axminster   Maiden   Pier   ● Ryde Goring-by-Sea Peacehaven HEAD
           Newton   Wareham Poole Christchurch SELSEY Selsey Bognor Regis Newhaven
Lyme   Dorchester ● WEST   BILL   Littlehampton Seaford
Regis   SOUTH   Corfe ▲ ISLE of WIGHT
Abbotsbury +   Castle ○ + Studland
Chesil Beach + ■ WEYMOUTH   Swanage   ● Shanklin
           ST ALBANS
PORTLAND   HEAD   [SEE DETAILED MAP]
BILL

0   10   20   30   40   50   60
              MILES

LEGEND
■ RAILTRACK STATION
○ FORMER STATION
▲ PRESERVED STANDARD GAUGE
▽ NARROW GAUGE
+ PLACES NAMED IN TEXT

machine here, and in the Wessex novels of Thomas Hardy, this resort was named Budmouth. In a letter to Vanessa Bell in May 1936, Virginia Woolf wrote: "I rather think Weymouth is the most beautiful seaside town in Europe, combining the grace of Naples with the sobriety of George the Third."

The railway station is close to the sea front, whose promenade provides fine views extending from the Isle of Portland to St Alban's Head. Weymouth is Britain's closest port to the Channel Islands, and ferries sail regularly to Guernsey and Jersey from the quay. After the demise of the 'Brighton Belle' in 1972, the only titled train to run on BR's Southern Region was the 'Channel Islands Boat Express' from Waterloo, with its distinctive coach destination boards, the last survivors of their kind to be seen on British Rail.

On arrival at Weymouth, the boat train was fitted with a

flashing light and bell so that it could continue its journey through the town to Weymouth Quay station. This was the only place in Britain where one could come across a main line train creeping along streets crowded with cars and pedestrians, a scene that disappeared in the late 1980s.

Nine miles east of Weymouth is Durdle Door, with its arch of white limestone rock at the tip of a headland which plunges steeply to a shelving beach of pebbles. Two miles further east is Lulworth Cove, an oyster-shaped natural harbour between high chalk cliffs. This part of the Dorset coast is beautifully sculpted with coves and headlands, heaths and downs, forming one of the most geologically and scenically varied segments of coastline in Europe.

Swanage is the seaside terminus of the preserved Swanage Railway, which runs steam trains across the Isle of Purbeck to

ISLE OF
WIGHT

Ryde Pier, unique in that it still carries trains of Britain's railway network. This nostalgic scene from 1961 shows 'O2' 33 Bembridge *on a Ventnor service with the paddle-steamer* Ryde *alongside.*
(J.P. Mullett/Colour-Rail BRS884)

Period scene from 1963 at Newport, once the junction for lines to Ryde, Cowes, Freshwater and Ventnor. The cars include a Morris 8 ragtop, Standard 9, Austin 55 and a Wolseley 1500.(J.S. Gilks collection/Colour-Rail BRS762)

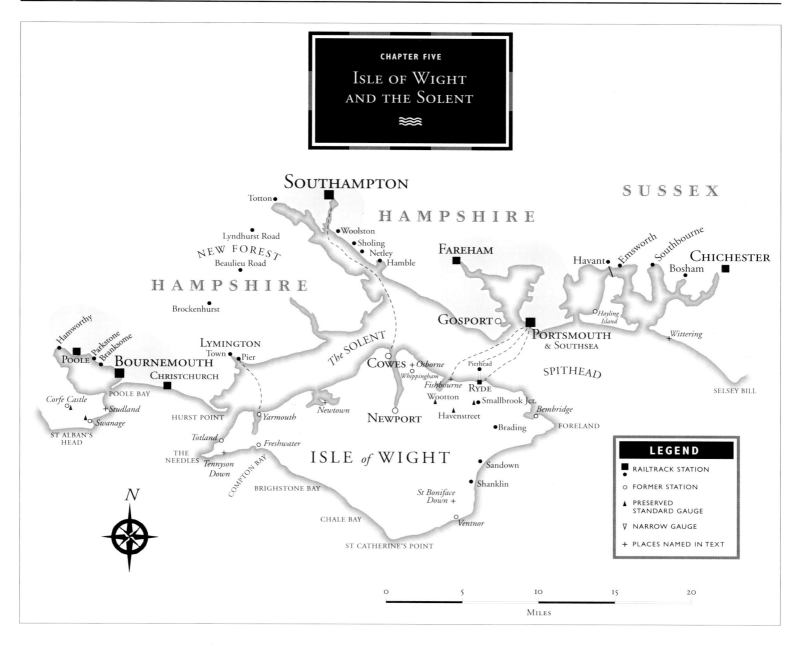

Corfe Castle and Norden, not far from the main line at Wareham. A luxury Pullman dining train, the 'Wessex Belle' travels the six-mile line in season, and in 1997 the 'Dorset Coast Express' special was revived, thirty years after its last run from Waterloo to Swanage, just two months before the end of steam services on this Dorset branch line.

Two miles along the coast from Swanage is Studland Bay, whose gently shelving white sandy beach attracts many visitors in summer months. There are sweeping views of earth, sea and sky between Ringstead Bay and Studland and the double high tides which occur between Lulworth Cove and Portsmouth mean that beaches at Swanage and Studland usually have high water for much of the day.

Poole has the largest and finest natural harbour for yachts and small vessels between Tor Bay and the Hamble. The rivers, creeks, estuaries and islands that provide moorings around Poole have a combined perimeter of 98 miles at low tide. Bournemouth and Poole are well served by fast electric trains from Waterloo, and also by cross-country trains from the north, including the 'Dorset Scot' and a re-routed 'Pines Express', via Oxford, Reading and Southampton.

At Bournemouth, the blending of sea airs and richly scented pine trees is said to be the prime reason for the wonderfully healthy atmosphere. Disraeli came here for a visit in December 1874 on Queen Victoria's recommendation of "the very salubrious air", and he completed his New Year's Honours list during his stay at the seaside. He made sure to include her favourite poet Tennyson on the list he submitted for Her Majesty's approval.

While the 'Devon Belle' was by far the longest Pullman

journey to the sea from London, the 'Bournemouth Belle', introduced in 1931, offered what many considered the finest moving restaurant in the country, with a wine list to rival that other famous Pullman train, the 'Brighton Belle'.

The large and luxurious Pullman coaches of the 'Bournemouth Belle' glided smoothly along for 108 miles, allowing plenty of time to enjoy a delicious meal in comfort. For many years, connoisseurs of good food and wine would invite friends to meet them in Waterloo station at noon to board the 1230 Pullman for luncheon en route to Southampton, where they either continued on to Bournemouth, or boarded a return train to London.

From seven to ten Pullman coaches were assigned to the 'Bournemouth Belle', and two hours were allowed for the run to Bournemouth, including a stop at Southampton. The train was taken out of service at the outbreak of WW2, and restored on 7 October 1946 with a more powerful 'Merchant Navy' steam locomotive hauling 12 Pullman coaches for the summer season. When the line was electrified all the way to Bournemouth in 1967, this elegant train to the southern sea was withdrawn.

The beaches in the Bournemouth area extend for seven miles from Sandbanks to Christchurch Bay. Cliffs of golden sandstone are intersected by a series of steep valleys called 'chines' down to the sea front. It is a dignified resort with acres of beautiful parks and floral gardens, pine trees, and delightful walks along the promenade and seashore. In Thomas Hardy's novel 'Tess of the d'Urbervilles', Bournemouth was named 'Sandbourne', and described by him in 1891 as "a fashionable watering-place, with its eastern and western stations, its piers, its groves of pines, its promenades, and its covered gardens."

From Bournemouth we head east to Brockenhurst, the junction for a five-mile journey by train along southern fringes of the New Forest to Lymington Pier station, where train passengers may, with good timing, walk straight on to a ferry for the Isle of Wight.

The Lymington-Yarmouth ferry is one of several operating between the mainland and the IOW. Ferries also cross the Solent to Ryde from Portsmouth or Southsea, and also to Cowes from Southampton, whose great port was developed by the London & South Western Railway and its successor, the Southern Railway.

With the IOW shielding this part of the coast from the open sea, and double tides providing deep water for 17 hours out of 24, Southampton has been a port and haven for nearly 2,000 years. Today it is Britain's premier ocean-liner port. To continue our journey along the south coast from west to east, we shall take the Lymington-Yarmouth ferry with the shortest and most enjoyable crossing to the IOW,

It was to Osborne House on the Isle of Wight that Queen Victoria came for peace and rest from the stress and strain of a monarch's life in London and Windsor. As on any island, there is a different way of life here and the residents are proud and protective of their geographic isolation, regarding the mainland as a different country across the water. This was echoed by the ferryman at Yarmouth who called out: "This way for England" to all those leaving the island.

Nowhere on the IOW is more than seven miles from the sea, making it an ideal place for walking or cycling, using ferries from Lymington, Portsmouth or Southampton to cross the Solent. Ryde pier was opened in 1814 and the first railway line was completed in 1862 from Cowes to Newport, followed in 1866 by the line from Ryde Pierhead to Ventnor. Much of the impetus to build these lines came from the large numbers of visitors to the island where their Queen lived in seclusion after the death of her beloved consort Albert in December 1861.

Tennyson moved to Farringford House near Freshwater Bay in 1853 for privacy and inspiration. His fame preceded him, and with the railways bringing so many admirers to Freshwater, he was obliged to move in high season to a more secluded location near Haslemere. His monument stands 482ft above the sea at Tennyson Down overlooking the Channel, and it was here that he described the sea air as "worth sixpence a pint." It certainly is, perhaps even more so at the top of St Boniface Down (785 ft), the highest point on the island.

Among the many visitors to the IOW, with its thatched cottages and fresh sea air, was Karl Marx, who came here in July 1874, and wrote exuberantly to Friedrich Engels: "This island is a little paradise." For Queen Victoria's visits to her regal paradise at Osborne, a station was built at Whippingham so that she could travel in the comfort and privacy to which she was accustomed. Her first train journey on the Isle of Wight was made on 11 February 1888, for a royal visit to the hospital at Ventnor, and her final departure was on her death here in 1901. Shortly afterwards, her son King Edward VII gave Osborne House to the nation.

In the 1880s the most expensive rail journey in the world was said to be on this island, priced at one shilling and two pence for the two miles from Ryde Pierhead station to Ryde St Johns. Most of the ticket price was to help pay for the high cost of rebuilding the pier and installing rail tracks that required a strong foundation to support the heavy weight of steam trains that ran along the pier to and from the ferries.

By the turn of the century, six independent railway companies were operating and competing for business on the island. These were merged into the Southern Railway in 1923 and nationalized in 1948 as part of British Rail's network, which totalled 55 route miles on the island.

Between 1952 and 1966, the branch lines radiating from Newport gradually withered away as car traffic increased. The only line to survive, between Ryde and Shanklin, was electrified in 1967 using vintage 1938 Piccadilly Line trains

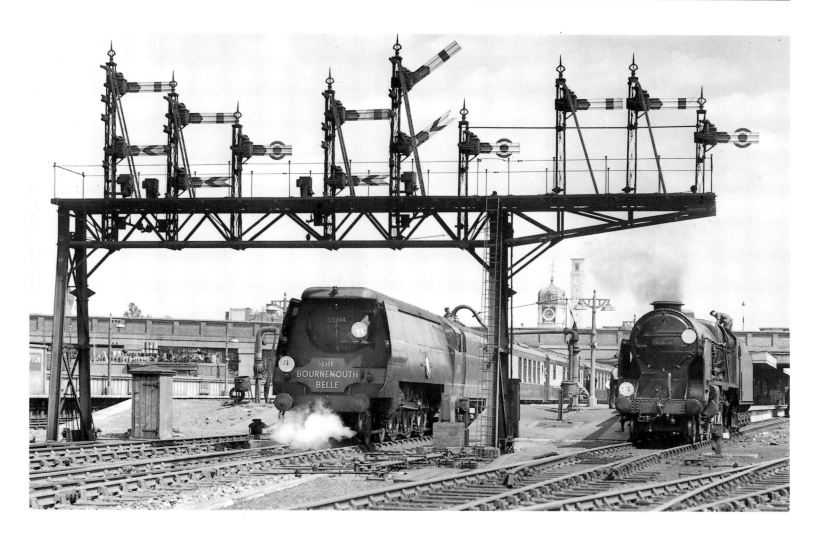

retired from London's Underground system and put out to pasture on this green and pleasant island. The trains were refurbished in the 1990s and provide fast and frequent service between Ryde Pierhead and Shanklin, with six intermediate stations, including the restored Smallbrook Junction, where the IOW Steam Railway operates seasonally.

The first steam trains to be revived on the island ran between Havenstreet and Wootton in 1971, until the line was extended eastwards from Havenstreet to complete a vital link with trains at Smallbrook Junction on the Ryde-Shanklin line, so that passengers could once again travel by train all the way from Wootton to Ryde Pierhead. New transport proposals for the IOW foresee an extension of steam operations from Smallbrook Junction into Ryde, and a re-opening of the former line from Wootton into Newport, the island capital.

Locomotives and coaches of the IOW Steam Railway have been meticulously restored to their original configuration, and are as close to museum display quality as will be found on any preserved railway in Britain. This is the true paradigm of railway revival, where dedicated and hard-working preservation groups have succeeded in restoring steam railways to a standard of excellence far higher than they ever reached

A Merchant Navy class locomotive takes water at Southampton in 1949 before passing under the fine signal gantry with the 'Bournemouth Belle'. For many years this train boasted what was widely considered to be the finest moving restaurant in the country, much frequented by connoisseurs of good food and wine. (NRM - SR249)

under British Rail. As someone was heard to utter: "God save our gracious steam."

It is unfortunate that so many piers around Britain's coastline have disappeared or closed down during the past fifty years. Of the hundred or so that were built in the Victorian and Edwardian eras, less than half have survived, and many of these are at resorts covered in this chapter. Ryde pier is unique in that it carries trains of Britain's railway network, connecting with ferries to Portsmouth Harbour station. In 1895 the Isle of Wight bristled with seven piers, all prompted by and benefiting from arrival of the railway.

From the pierhead at Ryde there is an excellent panorama of the Solent and Spithead, scenes of so much maritime history, royal reviews of the fleet at Spithead, passages of huge ocean

liners, and countless yacht races during the past century. To the west is Cowes, whose annual regatta is held during the first week of August. As we leave the train at Ryde Pierhead station and board the ferry to Portsmouth, let Jane Austen express the sentiments of so many fortunate inhabitants and visitors who have found peace and pleasure here:

"She thinks of nothing else but the Isle of Wight, and she calls it *the Island*, as if there were no other island in the world."

Portsmouth Harbour station is built upon the sea, with platforms supported by piers scoured by the tides. Ferries leave from their respective jetties beside the station to cross the Solent to the Isle of Wight, or to cross the harbour to Gosport, the largest town in Britain without a railway station. Three great ships, HMS Victory, HMS Warrior, and the Mary Rose are only a short walk away from Portsmouth Harbour station, and offer excellent guided tours.

There is much to see and do in and around Portsmouth and Southsea, whose seafronts face the IOW, Spithead, and the Solent. It was here that Sherlock Holmes was conceived, Dickens was born, Charles II was married, and Rudyard Kipling lived. This is a delightful part of the coast on which to reside or to take a holiday, only 90 minutes by train from

Period view of Brighton station about 1885. Its dramatically curved and lofty arched roofs reflected the town's status as a celebrated and fashionable resort, transformed by the railway and known by the 1860s as 'the greatest watering-place in the world'. One of Henry James' characters observed in 1892: 'He's always splendid, as your morning bath is splendid, or a sirloin of beef, or the railway service to Brighton.'
(NRM - 716/20/63)

Waterloo to the sea, where beaches of sand and shingle extend from Lee-on-Solent to Eastney and Hayling Island, with principal harbour entrances at Portsmouth, Langstone, and Chichester.

The train from Portsmouth to Brighton runs near the coast in places, giving brief glimpses of the sea at high tide as we head eastwards towards Chichester. The old Hayling Island line closed long ago; however there are several stations within a mile or two of the sea, notably at Bosham, scene of King Canute's legendary attempt to defy the tides, and whose Saxon church is shown on the Bayeux tapestry. The next station is Fishbourne, with extensive ancient ruins of the largest Roman settlement in northern Europe. From

Fishbourne it is six miles down the estuary to the open sea, where at low tide a sand and shingle beach extends from the entrance of Chichester Harbour to Selsey Bill.

On the main line between Portsmouth and Brighton, two lines branch to the sea. The first is to Bognor Regis, a pleasant seaside resort and retirement area within easy reach of London by train. The 'Regis' was added after King George V recuperated at Queen Victoria's "dear little Bognor" in 1928 after a serious illness. The king had less affectionate words for Bognor, but at least he recovered enough during his convalescence here beside the sea to reign for another seven years.

The second rail line serves Littlehampton at the mouth of the Arun, with beaches to the east and west extending for several miles at low tide. There are pleasant walks westwards to Middleton-on-Sea and Felpham, where William Blake lived from 1800 to 1803, the only part of his life not spent in London. He said of Felpham: "Heaven opens here on all sides her golden gates."

From Littlehampton to Brighton the coastline is heavily populated, and the train stops at twelve stations in eighteen miles as it travels through Goring, Worthing, Lancing, Shoreham-by-Sea and Hove. From Bournemouth in the west to Margate in the east, a distance of 160 miles, no equal length of coastline in Britain can claim such a high proportion of senior citizens enjoying the pleasures of living beside the sea.

At Brighton there are so many attractions and entertainments for residents and visitors that it has been called "London by the sea." It all started in 1753 when Dr Richard Russell of Lewes settled here and published a book on the virtues of sea bathing and the drinking of sea water at what was then a small fishing village named Brighthelmstone.

The Prince Regent came here in 1783, and after secretly marrying Mrs Fitzherbert in 1785, he commissioned the building of a Royal Stables, for his love of horses equalled his love of women. The Royal Pavilion, built between 1815 and 1822, with its domes, minarets, columns, parapets, and delicate tracery, has given the town its most distinctive symbol and air of fantasy, attracting visitors to this fashionable resort for over 175 years.

When the railway from London to Brighton was completed in 1841, a train ride of 51 miles to this health spa by the sea became one of the most popular excursions in Britain at that time, taking two hours by train, compared to five uncomfortable hours by the fastest stage coach from Piccadilly Circus. In the first six months of 1844, over 360,000 visitors came by rail to enjoy the sea air and other delights that Brighton offered.

In 1883, Magnus Volk built the world's first electric railway on the beach between the Palace Pier and Black Rock, and it is still running. In that same year, the London, Brighton & South Coast Railway ran a 'semi-fast' steam train from Brighton to London, which took 5h 24min to get from sea to city, surely one of the slowest and most eccentric journeys in Britain, yet worth recalling, for it illustrates how some trains meandered at that time.

The train left Brighton at 0620 and headed west to Chichester, where it stopped for 40 minutes to allow another train to connect. At 0818 it set off via the South Downs to Midhurst, joining yet another train, now with the signboard 'Through train to London Victoria', the only one of the day. It left Midhurst at 0915, stopping at Selham, Petworth, and Fittleworth before joining the mid-Sussex line at Hardham Junction, just south of Pulborough, and close to the old Wey-Arun canal.

By 1017 it had reached Horsham, after which it called at Ockley, Holmwood and Dorking, where it finally became a 'semi-fast', stopping only at Epsom, Sutton, and Clapham Junction, arriving in Victoria station at 1144. It is hard to believe that such a train existed, or that anyone would take it, but they did, for this was the LB&SCR in 1883, when both life and travel were more serene and civilized.

In 1899, a 'Brighton in an hour' service was established with the 'Brighton Sunday Pullman Limited', which in 1903 covered the 51 miles in 48min 41sec, reaching a top speed of 90mph. This train was so popular that in 1908 it became a daily service, and was given the name 'Southern Belle', equipped with the first Pullman coaches made in Britain, for which the return fare was twelve shillings to travel in "the most luxurious train in the world."

Two years later it made two return trips each day, and in 1933 when the line was electrified, the world's first and only all-electric Pullman train, named the 'Brighton Belle', carried as many as four hundred passengers in luxury on each trip to the sea and back three times a day.

By 1904, cross-country excursion trains were coming to Brighton and other coastal resorts in the south from all over Britain, on routes such as Birkenhead-Brighton; Manchester-Dover & Brighton; Newcastle-Bournemouth; and Bradford/Leeds-Poole & Paignton. Today there are good cross-country services from Scotland and the north of England to Brighton and other south coast resorts, with through trains crossing the Thames in London en route to or from Brighton, bypassing all London termini.

The huge growth of Brighton in recent years has changed the celebrated Edwardian resort that greeted visitors and residents arriving in luxurious Pullman trains. In one of his songs, Noel Coward regretted that "Brighton is Brighton no more", yet there is still much to enjoy in this great resort, especially the sea vistas, the beaches, promenades and gardens, the variety of entertainments, the joie de vivre, and the conviction that it is the sea with its power to heal that can cure all ills. In his novel 'Clayhanger', Arnold Bennett wrote that in Edwin Clayhanger's opinion, Brighton "was vaster than the imagining of it.... he had not conceived what wealth would do when it organized itself for the purposes of distraction."

The 'Brighton Belle' was withdrawn at the outbreak of WW2 and reinstated in October 1946. By the mid-1960s there were four daily journeys each way and the travel time had been reduced to 55 minutes. This was an immensely popular train with its speed, comfort, service, good food and wine, and promise of punctuality. Over thirty million miles were clocked up by the electric Pullmans, and countless passengers who lived in Brighton and commuted to London enjoyed the pleasure of luxury travel to the sea in good company after a hard day's work in the city.

From some stations between London and the south coast, a railway journey to Brighton in the 1950s was not as fast or convenient as that by the 'Brighton Belle'. For example, a person in Otford, Kent, wishing to travel by train on the shortest route to the sea, 38 miles away, would have to change trains at Sevenoaks, Tonbridge, Tunbridge Wells, Eridge, and Lewes. But it was a wonderful excursion through the Kent and Sussex countryside on a summer's day, and when the connecting trains met, which they usually did, getting there and back on twelve trains in a day was all part of the adventure for an enthusiastic railway traveller.

By 1972 the 'Brighton Belle' Pullmans were almost forty years old and needed replacement. To the dismay of its loyal patrons, British Rail announced withdrawal of this famous train, the last survivor of the much-loved Southern 'Belles', with effect from 30 April 1972. Powerful voices were raised in protest, Sir Laurence Olivier's the most compelling, but tradition lost out to economics, and the last 'Belle' left Brighton at 2230 for Victoria. It was reported that Sir Laurence did succeed in having kippers restored to the breakfast menu for a brief reprieve before this veteran of British Pullman trains to the sea was retired from service.

Some of the Pullman coaches from the 'Southern Belles' have been restored and are back in service on such trains as the 'Venice Simplon Orient Express' and on preserved lines in Britain. In 1996, the VSOE Pullman car 'Zena' was completely overhauled and returned to service at a cost of £125,000. In 1997 a new 'Brighton Belle' emerged, using modified Class 319 coaches with a lounge area and more spacious first-class seating, but the ambience had gone, as had the Pullman livery, replaced by trendier colours of the 1990s.

Newhaven is a ferry port, and even though Eurostar trains have taken away some of its traffic, there are those who prefer the Channel funnel to the Channel tunnel. The harbour here is usually busy with fishing boats and freighters, as well as small craft moored in the relatively sheltered estuary of the Ouse, as the coast near Seaford is more exposed to storms. On a clear day at Seaford Head (282ft) it is possible to see the Portsdown hills above Portsmouth, 36 miles away.

Just west of Newhaven is Peacehaven, where the Greenwich meridian of zero degrees longitude leaves the south coast of England, and a monument on top of the cliffs marks the precise spot. The only other seaside resorts in Britain with this distinction are Cleethorpes and Withernsea in Lincolnshire, where the zero degree meridian heads out to sea with only water and ice between Withernsea and the North Pole. The Greenwich meridian also passes through Sheffield Park station on the preserved 'Bluebell Railway' line and is marked on one of the platform pillars.

Eastbourne is an elegant resort which became popular in 1780 when four of the children of King George III spent their summers here. The first trains arrived in 1847, and Pullman coaches were introduced in 1875, followed by the first all-Pullman service in 1881, described in its brochure as "a train of vestibuled luxury." During the many years of Southern Railway Pullman services to south coast resorts, the 'Eastbourne Pullman' enabled business men to live here and work in London, as many did elsewhere on the Southern network, which had more Pullman trains to more coastal resorts than any other railway company in Britain.

In 1923, when King George V and his household concluded that the old royal train was no longer suitable for his style of travel, some of the carriages were transferred to the SR, who assigned them to one of the morning first-class business trains from Eastbourne to London Bridge. In the afternoon, this unique set of coaches formed the business special back to the sea, a delightful and comfortable journey after a hard day in the City.

The coaches came to the SR complete with royal upholstery and fittings, but these were eventually replaced with more conventional railway carriage furnishings. For years, first-class passengers on this service could claim they had occupied seats where royalty, or its household, had once sat, if not slept.

An even older royal saloon, one of two originals built for Queen Victoria's diamond jubilee was found in 1982 on a cliff-top caravan site on the coast of Wales. It had served as a holiday home for almost fifty years, and after restoration to its former glory is now on display at the Windsor station exhibition hall.

Today, Eastbourne retains its popularity as a fashionable holiday destination and place to retire, with its elegant Georgian and Victorian buildings, fine promenades, band concerts, and variety of cultural events throughout the year. Beachy Head is nearby, cradling Eastbourne among one of the most spectacular stretches of cliff scenery in Europe, and in bright sunshine the steep ramparts of turf-topped chalk are almost dazzling, for they usually break up the cloud cover, placing Eastbourne high on the list of Britain's sunniest seaside resorts.

The railway station at Normans Bay is only a pebble's throw from the historic beach where William the Conqueror landed on 28th September 1066 to fight and defeat Harold at Battle, whose railway station is on the main line from London to Hastings. One of the railway junctions just west of Hastings is called Bo-Peep after the rhyme written in the 18th century for the local innkeeper's daughter, alluding to smugglers (sheep), barrels of French brandy (tails), and the searches of the local excisemen in pursuit, all part of railway lore along this coast.

Hastings, St Leonards, and Bexhill form an eight-mile resort shoreline with a wide range of attractions for the visitor. There is fast train service from London to St Leonards and Hastings, as well as a coast line running west from Hastings to Bexhill, Eastbourne, Brighton, and beyond. The old part of Hastings snuggles below the ruined Norman castle built in 1068, and the beach provides a safe mooring for small fishing vessels, whose nets hang from lofts clustered around a maze of narrow

Eastbourne in the immediate post-war era when cars had yet to swamp the surrounding streets. The town, developed as a resort by the seventh Duke of Devonshire, is noted for its elegant Georgian and Victorian buildings, although the station is an architectural muddle with its turret clock, pagoda-like lantern and profusion of ornamental ironwork. (NRM - 665/2/63)

twisting streets leading up to the old part of the town.

Rye was once a busy port and is now an inland citadel over two miles from the sea. The '1066 Walk', a 30 mile footpath, was opened in 1997 to link Rye in the east with Pevensey in the west, so that walkers may now follow in the footsteps of William the Conqueror and his Norman army when they invaded England. The new path completes a continuous walkway from Winchester to Dover, and via Channel ferry to a network of European footpaths.

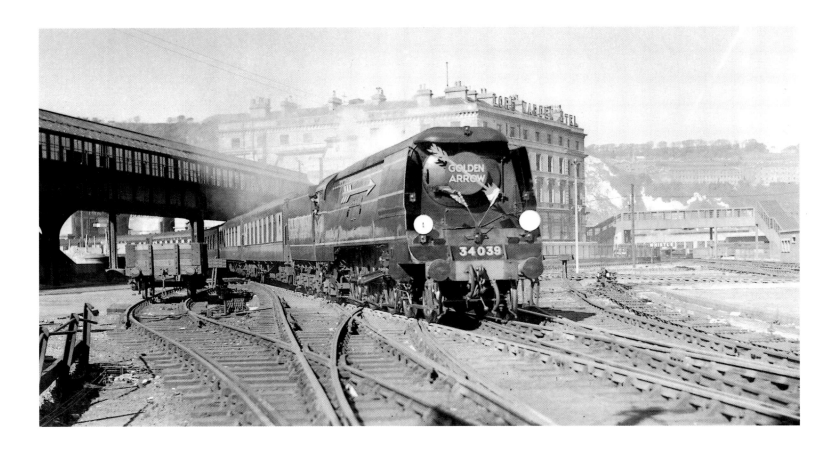

The 'Golden Arrow' in all its glory leaves Dover Marine behind a West Country class locomotive in 1948. Few titled trains have captured the imagination in the same way as this once magnificent service run in conjunction with the 'Fleche d'Or' from Calais to Paris. (NRM - SR/137)

East of Rye and Lydd is Dungeness, turning point for the narrow-gauge Romney, Hythe and Dymchurch Railway, which opened in 1927 with fourteen miles of track across Kent's historic Romney Marsh, and steam locomotives scaled down from famous prototypes. The RH&DR is the only railway serving communities from Dungeness to Hythe, and celebrations to mark seventy years of service in peace and war by the world's only fifteen inch "main line in miniature" were held here in 1997.

With chalk cliffs towering above its harbour, Folkestone is on the Eurostar rail route from London to the Channel tunnel. It is also a ferry port where fast Seacat ferries leave for Boulogne, crossing the Channel in 55 minutes. The harbour's newest attraction is a former Russian submarine, the only one open to the public in a British port. East of the harbour is the first of 74 Martello towers which are found along this coast as far west as Seaford.

A new segment of England, called Samphire Hoe, was created from the debris excavated during construction of the Channel tunnel. The sixty-acre site, owned by Eurotunnel, sits at the base of Shakespeare Cliff, one of the famous white cliffs of Dover. Its one-mile sea frontage has been landscaped and sown with wildflowers, protected from Channel storms by a sea wall, so that visitors may safely walk along the footpaths built upon the thousands of tons of clay and marl that once lay far below the waves.

For over two hundred years, a tunnel under the Channel had been proposed and debated. A start was made in 1880, not far from the present site, when a deep shaft was dug at the foot of the cliffs, and a tunnel driven for over a mile out to sea. More than a century later, Britain was linked to the continent by Eurostar trains, which commenced scheduled passenger services in 1995. For those who prefer fast scenic travel over the sea rather than below it, there is also a hovercraft service from Dover to Calais.

Dover has been a main entry point for travellers coming by sea to Britain ever since the Romans built a lighthouse in 43AD on top of the cliffs. No other geographic feature of Britain is regarded with such sentiment as the famous white cliffs of Dover, whose chalk bastions tower 300 ft above the sea, with a castle nearby to guard this traditional "gateway to England."

For over 35 years two famous trains from London (Victoria) brought passengers to Dover for the ferries to France. One was the 'Golden Arrow', whose luxury service to Paris started on 15 May 1929. The other train, introduced seven years later and which outlived the 'Golden Arrow', was the 'Night Ferry', Britain's only daily cross-channel train before the tunnel was completed.

Few titled trains in Britain captured the imagination to the same extent as the 'Golden Arrow' to Dover, where passengers left the train to board the ferry to Calais, then to Paris on the 'Fleche d'Or' to connect with the Blue Train, the Sud Express, the Rome Express, or the Simplon-Orient Express. At the outbreak of WW2, all services ceased and were not resumed until 15 April 1946, when nine Pullman coaches left Victoria for Dover, headed by Merchant Navy locomotive 'Channel Packet', gaily decorated with golden arrows, national flags and colourful headboard.

The last steam-hauled 'Golden Arrow' left London on 11 June 1961, and the last all-Pullman service was withdrawn in May 1965. After this, ordinary second-class coaches far outnumbered the few remaining first class Pullman coaches, and the inevitable last journey of a sadly austere 'Golden Arrow' was made on 30 September 1972. One can only regret the disappearance of this great train, which provided such outstanding service and comfort to passengers between London and Dover for over three decades.

After withdrawal of 'Golden Arrow' services, the 'Night Ferry' continued to provide the only through train from London to Paris via Dover. Twenty coaches were built for this service, which was inaugurated in 1936, and for the first time it was possible to travel all the way from London to Paris in one train. This was real luxury, for passengers on the 'Golden Arrow' were obliged to walk from the train to the ferry at Dover, whereas those on the 'Night Ferry' could usually be assured of a comfortable night's sleep all the way from London to Paris, with gentle handling of the wagons-lits on and off the ship, and a calm sea in the Channel.

The 'Night Ferry' was one of the longest passenger trains running nightly in Britain. It included up to ten wagons-lits, several baggage coaches, and up to five coaches providing dining and lounge services, kitchens, and accommodation for train staff . From 1957, the 'Night Ferry' also carried cars to Paris and Brussels, hard work for 'Merchant Navy' class locomotives until the 1960s, when electric traction took over.

From his home at Chartwell in Kent, Prime Minister Winston Churchill arranged to have the 'Night Ferry' stop at Sevenoaks station en route to Dover whenever he had to travel to Paris, for he preferred the comfort, privacy, service, and first-class sleeping facilities on this train. During their long years of exile from Britain, the Duke and Duchess of Windsor also travelled aboard the 'Night Ferry' between Paris and London on several occasions, appreciating the incognito that an overnight journey in a wagon-lit compartment provided.

By 1980, the luxurious wagons-lits were 44 years old and had reached the end of their useful life. The airlines had lured many former 'Night Ferry' passengers from what was a far more spacious, civilized and comfortable mode of travel. British

Rail's final 'Night Ferry' left London for Dover and Paris on 31 October 1980, the locomotive carrying its distinctive midnight blue and gold headboard for that sad All Hallow's evening.

From Dover to Deal the rail line is forced inland, returning to the coast at Deal before turning inland again towards Sandwich, one of the old cinque ports, now two miles from the sea. At low tide, a huge triangle of sand almost a mile wide extends to Pegwell Bay, where the world's first international hoverport was established in 1968.

When Julius Caesar landed near Deal in 55 BC, this part of the coastline was geographically very different from today. What is now Ramsgate was an island, with the Goodwin Sands clustered five miles away. Today, Ramsgate's station is conveniently close to the beach and inner harbour, where colourful yachts and pleasure craft are moored safely and snugly inside. High above the beach are elegant buildings, giving the resort an almost Mediterranean appearance, especially at night when lit by thousands of coloured lights.

An all-Pullman express train titled the 'Thanet Belle' was introduced in 1921, travelling non-stop from London to Margate en route to Ramsgate. This luxury train was so popular that in 1930 the Southern Railway added some third-class coaches and more station stops along the coast in order to increase revenue. This more cosmopolitan 'Belle' ran until WW2, when it was withdrawn, as were all other Southern 'Belles'.

'Thanet Belle' service was restored in the summer of 1948, calling at Whitstable, Herne Bay, Margate, Broadstairs and Ramsgate. Its title was changed to 'Kentish Belle' in 1951 during the 'Festival of Britain', and it survived until electrification of the Kent coast lines in 1959. Paddle steamers sailing from London's Tower Pier to Margate and Ramsgate offered an enjoyable day trip by sea, with an optional return by train to London. Fast ferries from Ramsgate now provide frequent services to Ostend, with a crossing time of 100 minutes.

Broadstairs is a popular yachting centre, and was described by Charles Dickens, who travelled widely abroad, as "one of the freshest, freest watering places in the world." The town still retains much of the attraction that brought him back year after year to the narrow twisting streets featured in his writings. In November 1998, Britain's last lighthouse keeper handed over his lonely vigil at Broadstairs to remote computer control, ending a tradition of manned lighthouses that had started here in 1499.

From Broadstairs, trains cut across the North Foreland, a major coastal turning point in Britain, to reach Margate. This part of the Kent coast, extending for twenty miles from Herne Bay to Ramsgate and easily accessible by train, is a favourite playground for Londoners.

Margate has Kent's most popular beaches, extending for nearly three miles in a series of bays, with clean sands and

Ramsgate Harbour terminus in 1924, two years before it closed. Cramped and approached by a tunnel almost a mile long on a gradient of 1 in 75, it was notoriously difficult to operate. Among major stations, it nevertheless had few equals in terms of proximity to the sea shore. (NRM - HPR/SE268)

rock pools. The marine parade, with its cafes and entertainments facing the harbour, pier, sands and rocks, is lively throughout summer, especially when the illuminations are switched on. Every traditional amusement and activity of a large British seaside resort is here, attracting huge crowds of visitors to this mecca of pleasure on the Kent coast.

Westwards now, with the train stopping at Westgate-on-Sea, Birchington, Herne Bay, and Whitstable, famous for its oysters since Roman times, and a visiting port in the 1990s for the last ocean going paddle-steamer, the 'Waverley'. Whitstable welcomed the first steam train to travel to the Kent coast on the six mile Canterbury and Whitstable Railway in 1830. On today's rail network, the distance by electric train is eighteen miles via Faversham.

We are now heading into the Thames estuary, so we will take a train from Whitstable to Sittingbourne, the junction for Sheerness-on-Sea, where the Thames estuary is still wide enough to give a sense of the sea. From the time of Samuel Pepys (1633-1703) until 1959 Sheerness was a naval dockyard; now it is a commercial port on the Isle of Sheppey, separated from the mainland by muddy waters of the Swale.

Continuing towards London by train we stop at Gillingham, Chatham and Rochester on the Medway, taking the train northwards from Rochester to Gravesend, formerly the junction for a branch line to Allhallows-on-Sea, the last station to be opened by the Southern Railway (in 1932), and the nearest place for Londoners to take a day trip to the sea.

Allhallows has an extensive parkland of holiday houses and caravans, well-spaced along green fields rising gently from the estuary, where the tide goes out a long way from the muddy river shore. We follow the Thames upstream into London via Gravesend, Dartford, Woolwich, and Greenwich, crossing the river on the busy railway line between Waterloo (East) and Charing Cross stations.

Our next coastal destination is Southend in Essex, so we will leave from London's Fenchurch Street station to continue our journey along the north bank of the Thames and up the coasts of Essex, Suffolk and Norfolk.

To the coasts of Essex, Suffolk and Norfolk

"If an Englishman wishes to have a patriotic feeling, it must be about the sea."

Robert Louis Stevenson

Southend-on-Sea, 36 miles from London, is the largest seaside resort in Essex, and is served by trains on two routes from the city. The shorter line, closer to the Thames, is from Fenchurch St station to Southend Central via Leigh-on-Sea and Westcliff-on-Sea. The longer and faster line is from Liverpool St station to Southend Victoria, a distance of 41 miles. With frequent electric train services, and its proximity to London, Southend welcomes more day visitors than either Margate on the Kent coast or Brighton on the Sussex coast.

Pleasure boat excursions along the Thames from London also bring day trippers to Southend's pier. It is over a hundred years old and the world's longest pleasure pier, with a railway to take passengers 1.3 miles over sand, shingle, and sea to and from the pierhead, for at low tide the sea is a mile from the promenade. Fun and frivolity extend most of the way along Southend's sea front which links Leigh-on-Sea to Thorpe Bay, a distance of six miles.

High above Southend stands Cliff Town, whose terraces were built in the 1790s, and are now part of a heritage area. There is still a touch of Georgian character here, and fine views of the Thames estuary on a clear day. Beyond Southend, the railway line continues to Thorpe Bay, and ends at Shoeburyness, where the Maplin Sands extend for ten miles to Foulness Point and the estuary of the Crouch.

To reach Burnham-on-Crouch we return to Southend Central station and walk to Southend Victoria, taking a train to Wickford, then the Southminster train to Burnham, on the north bank of the River Crouch. Before the railway came, Burnham was a busy port, but frequent fast train services to

and from London took away most of the coastal trade. However, local oysters, cockles, and whelks from nearby east coast grounds still find a ready market here.

The estuaries of the Crouch and Roach form an ideal sailing area along this tranquil part of the Essex coast which is indented with several river estuaries, forcing the railway line inland to Chelmsford, Witham, and Colchester, before returning to the coast at Clacton-on-Sea. On the line from Colchester to Clacton, stations at Alresford and Great Bentley are equidistant from Brightlingsea on the Colne estuary. This small port is the only one of the historic cinque ports outside Kent or Sussex.

Clacton has fast electric train services from London, bringing crowds of visitors to its sea front and beaches, whose sands extend for seven miles to Frinton and Walton-on-the-Naze, both well served by train. Before the railway arrived in 1881, steamboats from Woolwich pier in London brought visitors to Clacton to enjoy the sea air, and for walks along the sands, promenade and gardens. The 'Eastern Belle' Pullman train, which ran from London to several east coast resorts in the 1930s, visited Clacton more than any other destination along the coast. There were also daily cruises in the summer to Clacton from Tower Pier on the Thames until the 1960s.

Beyond Walton-on-the Naze is Harwich, reached by train via Colchester. The railway line to Harwich was completed in the 1860s, bringing passengers to the packet-boat service for Holland, and to the resort area of Dovercourt, whose beach extends southwards for three miles to Pennyhole Bay. Ferries leave Harwich daily for the continent from Parkeston Quay station, named after a former chairman of the Great Eastern

CHAPTER SIX

To the Coasts of Essex, Suffolk & Norfolk

≈≈

The **WASH**

Wells *Stiffkey* *Cley* *Weybourne* *Sheringham*
Walsingham *Blakeney* *Holt* ▲ *West Runton* **Cromer**
+ *Overstrand*
Hunstanton ○ ○ *Mundesley*
○ *Heacham*
Melton Constable *North Walsham*
Wolferton ○
+ *Sandringham* *Worstead* ● + *Hickling*
Hoveton & Wroxham ○ *Potter Heigham* ○ *Caister-on-Sea*
■ **KING'S LYNN** **GREAT YARMOUTH** ■
○ *North Elmham* *Berney Arms* ● ○ *Gorleston-on-Sea*
COUNTY BOUNDARY ○ *Hopton-on-Sea*
○ *Dereham* ■ **NORWICH**

NORFOLK *Reedham* ● **LOWESTOFT** ■
○ *Wymondham* *Oulton Broad*
Beccles ●

Diss ●

○ *Southwold*

SUFFOLK *Saxmundham* ●

○ *Aldeburgh* **N**

Woodbridge ●
IPSWICH ■ *DEBEN*
ORWELL
FELIXSTOWE ■
COLCHESTER *STOUR* **HARWICH** ■
■ *Walton-on-the-Naze* ●
Frinton ●

CHELMSFORD *MERSEA ISLAND*
■ **CLACTON** ■

ESSEX

Southminster ●
Burnham-on-Crouch ●
Leigh-on-Sea ● **SOUTHEND**
■ ● *Shoeburyness*
Westcliff
THAMES ESTUARY

LEGEND

■ RAILTRACK STATION
●
○ FORMER STATION
▲ PRESERVED STANDARD GAUGE
▽ NARROW GAUGE
+ PLACES NAMED IN TEXT

0   10   20   30   40   50
MILES

Railway. The port was first settled in medieval times, and in 1340 this was the assembly point for Edward III's fleet which defeated the French in the first great sea battle of the Hundred Years War.

The River Orwell from Ipswich, and the wider River Stour from Manningtree meet at Harwich, the busiest port in Essex, whose border with Suffolk follows the River Stour to the sea. The famous diarist Samuel Pepys was a Member of Parliament for the town, and Secretary of the Navy when the dockyard was built here in 1666. It is now used as a passenger terminal for ferries to continental ports. In 1997, the Great Eastern Railway named its Manningtree-Harwich route the 'Mayflower Line' in recognition of the port from which the famous 'Mayflower' originally set sail for the New World, captained by a Harwich man, Christopher Jones.

Two of the town's museums are in its lighthouses: the 'High' contains the National Museum of Wireless and Television, while the 'Low' one houses the Maritime Museum. The lighthouses, Customs House, dockyard, and former home of Mayflower's Captain Jones form part of the Harwich Maritime Trail.

The port and resort of Felixstowe owe their development to the vision and enterprise of Colonel George Tomline, Lord of the Manor, who campaigned for a railway line from Ipswich to

Harwich Town station in 1949 with a Manningtree train simmering at the platform. The arrival of the railway at the town's fine natural harbour stimulated the development of nearby Parkeston Quay and the resort area of Dovercourt. (T.J. Edgington)

The narrow-gauge Southwold Railway, running through tranquil Suffolk countryside, closed as early as 1929. Never noted for its speed, the line was the but of a local humorist Reg Carter, whose comic postcards have long outlived the trains he depicted.

THE SOUTHWOLD EXPRESS   A COW ON THE LINE IS LUCKILY SEEN BY THE GUARD - IN HIS EAGERNESS TO STOP THE TRAIN HE PUTS THE BRAKES ON TOO SUDDENLY !

Changing times at Lowestoft.   An ex Great Eastern 2-4-2 tank is on a Yarmouth service in 1954 (top)
Just over forty years later much has been swept away in this 1995 scene of a two-car diesel unit waiting among the weeds (left).
(T.J. Edgington - 2)

the Beach Station, where the first train arrived in 1877. Tomline then constructed a large commercial dock with railway jetties in 1885 in order to attract business to the port. The site of the town was well chosen on the low cliff of Red Crag, with a flat expanse of land for the streets, and a broad strand below on which to build this resort, where cliffs have been transformed into hanging gardens, a pleasant backdrop to the promenade below.

On the railway line from Ipswich to Lowestoft, at the head of the River Deben, is Woodbridge, a popular sailing centre with its boatyard conveniently located beside the station platform. Across the harbour is an ancient tide mill, the last of its type in the country when it ceased operating in 1957. There has been a tide mill here for over 700 years, and the old mill pond is now a yacht basin. Woodbridge is an interesting town, with picturesque buildings of mellow brick, and streets that are busy with visitors in the summer.

Saxmundham is the nearest railway station to the historic seaside town of Aldeburgh, where the annual music festival attracts many of the world's greatest musicians. Along this part of the Suffolk coast the railway line runs six miles inland, bypassing Southwold with its church tower and lighthouse forming prominent landmarks above the roofs of the town.

This delightful Suffolk resort was at one time served by the Southwold Light Railway, whose trains ran on a nine-mile branch line from Halesworth, with intermediate stations at Wenhaston, Blythburgh, and Walberswick. The line was opened in 1879 and closed in 1929. All that remains is part of the former trackbed near the River Blyth, offering pleasant walks along a route that once carried over 100,000 passengers a year.

During its half-century of service to Southwold, the railway operated four locomotives, each named after a village on its eight-mile route to the sea. The steam trains meandered along to the coast through a countryside where the speed limit was set at 16 mph in order not to disturb the tranquil rural life of Suffolk. In its present-day isolation from the rail network, Southwold has retained a delightfully relaxed atmosphere that other resorts with frequent trains from large centres of population have lost during the past century.

Lowestoft is served by two rail lines, one from Ipswich, the other from Norwich. Its fortunes were founded on its proximity to North Sea fishing grounds since Lowestoft Ness is the most easterly point on mainland Britain, making it 'The Sunrise Coast'. The town is linked by rivers and canals to the Norfolk Broads, Britain's newest National Park, where popular sailing centres are connected to an extensive area of waterways from Hickling Broad, north of Great Yarmouth, to Oulton Broad not far from Lowestoft station which was awarded the 1998 title of 'Best Railtrack Station in the East Anglia Zone.'

The railway line northwards from Lowestoft goes inland to Reedham, the junction for trains to Great Yarmouth. On this branch line to the coast stands Berney Arms station, the most isolated in England. There is no road anywhere near this station on the Halvergate Marshes, four miles from Reedham, and five miles from Great Yarmouth. In 1844, supported by a Norfolk brewer (of whom there were many), the Yarmouth & Norwich Railway opened this line under an agreement with the brewer that every station would have a public house nearby to benefit both railway and brewery, and that all trains would stop at each station.

In its lonely location on the marshes with no road access, very few passengers used this station, and some trains did not stop, so the publican took the railway to court, and won his case. All trains had to stop here, and a few still do, upon request to the conductor. Even Rannoch station on its desolate moor in Scotland has good road access. To catch a train at Berney Arms involves either a hike across marshes, or a sail along Breydon Water and the River Yare or one of its tributaries, then a walk to reach the station platform. The pub, about half a mile away, remains open for business.

The 1998/99 winter timetable of Anglia Railways shows two trains each weekday to the sea via Berney Arms, and four trains on Sundays, no doubt to provide more opportunities for a hike to the pub and plenty of time to enjoy a drink before returning home across a landscape that is dotted with windmills on fields and flat marshland.

The meandering River Waveney forms the county boundary between Suffolk and Norfolk until it reaches Breydon Water, where the boundary line runs south along the fringe of Great Yarmouth, the largest port and seaside resort in Norfolk. The River Yare also flows into Breydon Water, all that remains of a huge estuary that once reached inland as far as Norwich and

Beccles. Between them, Suffolk and Norfolk have the driest regional climate in the country.

When the railway reached this part of the coast in 1859, it changed a small watering place into a popular seaside town and established Great Yarmouth as principal entry point to the Norfolk Broads from the North Sea. In a Victorian guide to health resorts of Britain, Great Yarmouth was recommended because "the air is dry and bracing, and favourable to people of weakly habit," adding that visitors who stayed for several weeks "would benefit from inhaling the smoke of oak chips burnt to prepare bloaters."

Prior to WW2, the LNER's fast and luxurious 'Eastern Belle' Pullman train brought crowds of visitors to Great Yarmouth on day trips from London, allowing plenty of time to enjoy the sea front, fine sands and amusements on its two patriotic piers, Britannia and Wellington.

Until widespread rail closures from 1959 onwards, Norfolk was well served by trains on branch lines of the former Midland & Great Northern Joint Railway. Regarded in its time as an intruder into Great Eastern territory, the M&GNJR inspired respect and even affection among its many local passengers in Norfolk and Suffolk. The terrain was relatively easy for railway construction, except where rivers had to be crossed, or access to the sea had to be gained, and thus Norfolk was well-endowed with a railway network in which no village in the county was more than ten miles from a station.

An important railway hub was built by the M&GNJR at Melton Constable in 1881, turning a small hamlet with few cottages into an industrial workshop and locomotive building centre, much admired as Norfolk's small-scale Swindon or Crewe. Today, Melton Constable is an archaeological site of ambitious Victorian railway enterprise, while not far away there are signs of a railway renaissance in which the Mid-Norfolk Preservation Trust is proceeding with restoration of the former line from Wymondham to Dereham and North Elmham.

Among branch lines through Norfolk to the sea in the 1950s was one to Great Yarmouth from the LNER main line at Little Bytham via Spalding, King's Lynn, Melton Constable, and Norwich. Its closure was earlier than other branch lines around Britain, and the last train left Yarmouth South Town station on 28 February 1959, bound for Melton Constable on the same day that passenger trains were withdrawn by BR on most lines of the former M&GNJR.

The Norwich-Great Yarmouth route is one of the few that survived from a rail network that once included over 180 route miles in Norfolk and Lincolnshire. Fortunately, a short section of the 'Muddle-and-Get-Nowhere' line westwards from Sheringham has been restored, with steam trains on the preserved North Norfolk Railway travelling through an area of outstanding natural beauty close to the coast. Great Yarmouth's former Beach Station is now a bus terminus, and although the next railway station along the coast is only 23 miles away by sea, a journey by rail from Great Yarmouth to Cromer involves changing trains at Norwich, followed by fifty miles of travel via North Walsham.

On 1 July 1896, the Great Eastern Railway inaugurated its 'Norfolk Coast Express', which ran daily non-stop from London to the Norfolk village of North Walsham, 131 miles in 156 minutes, a good timing when one considers the fifteen miles mostly uphill from Liverpool Street to beyond Brentwood en route to the seaside at Cromer and Sheringham.

In the summer of 1951, when the Festival of Britain proclaimed 'Britain Can Make It', three titled trains from Liverpool St to the north Norfolk coast were hauled by locomotives of the new 'Britannia' class, and for the summer season all three went to the coast, the 'East Anglian' to Great Yarmouth, the 'Norfolkman' to Cromer, and the 'Broadsman' to Cromer and Sheringham. Some high speeds were recorded by these handsome and powerful locomotives, notably 94 mph at Diss, and an average speed of 85 mph for 26 miles by 70035 'Rudyard Kipling' between Ipswich and Norwich.

By the late 1960s, Norfolk had lost most of its branch railways and its titled trains. Cromer lost two of its three railway lines and one of its two stations, so the only trains to this seaside resort now come from Norwich via North Walsham, which was once the hub for five lines. It is hard to believe that trains once ran to places such as Potter Heigham, one of many Norfolk Broads sailing centres that were served by the railways.

In May 1980, the title 'East Anglian' was restored to the London-Ipswich-Norwich-Great Yarmouth service. Perhaps executives of British Rail had noted the results of a question-naire circulated by the German Federal Railways to 4600 of their passengers, of whom 87 percent voted for retention of their titled trains.

Trains from Norwich to Cromer and Sheringham pass through Norfolk Broad country, with a brief glimpse of boats near Hoveton & Wroxham station. In February 1997 this line was officially named 'The Bittern Line', in recognition of a bird found near the only surviving railway line from Norwich to the north Norfolk coast. A century earlier this route might have been called the 'Worsted Line', for the station at Worstead once served a thriving woollen industry here, which dates back to medieval times. In the 1998 Railtrack 'Best Station Awards', Worstead won the award for 'most passenger-friendly unstaffed station' - an oxymoron for today's rail traveller to digest.

After passing near the southern fringe of Cromer, the train turns east and reaches what is left of Cromer Beach station, which has suffered the indignity of many grand railway stations, having been stripped down to a single platform, with a supermarket occupying most of the old station precinct. A

short walk down through the lower part of the town brings us to the pier, promenade, and beach.

Miles of sand and shingle extend along the North Norfolk coast on both sides of Cromer. The branch railway that ran from Cromer down the coast to Mundesley has long gone, but there is a footpath from Cromer to Mundesley and onwards to Happisburgh, whose fortunes for centuries were founded upon its hazardous sands, several miles offshore and nine miles wide. This part of the coastline is littered with skeletons of countless ships beneath the waves, and many vessels that foundered near Happisburgh during fierce northeast gales have yielded a rich bounty for villagers patrolling the beach for treasures thrown up by rough seas.

Cromer is recorded in the Domesday Book, when it was known as Shipden, with two churches, one of which was lost through sea erosion in the fourteenth century, its ruins now in the vicinity of Church Rocks. Because of its commanding position on the coast, and offshore sandbanks which are constantly shifting, Cromer is an important lifeboat and light-house station.

The conspicuous 160ft church tower, the tallest in Norfolk, is girdled by old fishermen's houses and quaint streets, giving the visitor a taste of the Victorian charm which has attracted so many visitors by train to this resort during the past century. In Jane Austen's novel 'Emma', she wrote "You should have gone to Cromer, my dear, if you went anywhere. Perry was a week at Cromer once, and he holds it to be the best of all sea-bathing places. A fine open sea, and very pure air."

At Cromer, the train reverses to continue westwards along the coast to Sheringham, whose main street down to the sea front separates its two railway stations. A single platform open to the weather has to suffice for passengers to and from Norwich, while across the road is the elegantly restored station of the North Norfolk Railway, where steam locomotives and carriages recapture the great era of train travel along this coast from the 1920s to the 1950s. The NNR trains run on the 'Poppy Line' for six miles from Sheringham to Weybourne and Holt, on what was once an important rural line linking Cromer with Melton Constable, until closure in 1964.

Of the many attractions in and around Sheringham, the most nostalgic is surely a visit to the preserved railway, where a journey back in time begins with a ride on a NNR steam train, passing through some of the prettiest coastal scenery in East Anglia. On certain weekends there is an 'East Coast Pullman' with dining in a Pullman coach from the former 'Brighton Belle'.

The popularity of Sheringham and Cromer as east coast railway destinations was confirmed by Anglia Railways in September 1997, when through trains between London and Sheringham were reinstated after a long absence, with one train in each direction during winter weekdays. This required an early start at 0623 from Liverpool St. and a late return to

THE LMS INFLUENCE

The Fenchurch Street to Southend line gave the London, Midland & Scottish Railway an important presence on the Essex Coast. Chalkwell, just to the west of Southend, has a beach sandwiched between the railway and the lower reaches of the Thames estuary. The tide is in and space is especially cramped as a train from Shoeburyness passes in 1959.
(A. Morris/Colour-Rail BRM1678)

The other line which took the LMS to the East Coast of England was the now largely-closed Midland & Great Northern. 4MT 43160 is leaving Caister-on-Sea in April 1957 with an afternoon stopping service from Yarmouth Beach to North Walsham.
(E. Alger/Colour-Rail BRE752)

Cromer Beach station in happier times, complete with ridge-and-furrow overall roof and much pseudo half-timbering on the main building. Today a supermarket occupies most of the precinct. It was partly the desire to be free of the 'curse' of excursionists that kept Cromer from being served by any railway until 1877. (NRM - LGRP/8246)

London, departing from Sheringham at 1954. But it did allow plenty of time to enjoy some bracing North Sea air, and brisk walks along the promenades at both Sheringham and Cromer.

Following the success of these weekday trains, Anglia Railways introduced through trains on Sundays in their 1998/99 winter timetable, with departure from London at 0820, and return from Sheringham at 1954.

Sheringham is a delightful seaside town, noted for the longevity of its inhabitants. There is no harbour here, and recently there has been major re-construction of the sea front to improve access to the beach and promenade. Since 1780, the town has been noted for its lobsters, and the fishing boats seen on the beach today go out for lobsters, whelks and crabs. Some of the old cottages with their flint facings and pantiles remain, and the town has a fresh and friendly air at any time of year. Two miles southeast stands Beacon Hill (329 ft) the highest point in Norfolk, offering fine panoramic views from its summit.

West of Sheringham, large amounts of sand and shingle swept down by storms on the coasts of Lincolnshire and Yorkshire are deposited on the shoreline between Hunstanton and Stiffkey with every tide, so that places such as

Cley-next-the-Sea are now separated from the sea by half a mile of marsh and sand.

In the battle against erosion around Britain's coastline, this is one of the few places where the land is slowly advancing out to sea. Nature reserves abound in Norfolk, notably on this part of the coast, where Cley and Blakeney marshes and sands are among the best in Britain for rare bird sightings. There are some fine walks starting from Cley around Britain's first local nature reserve, established in 1926.

Cley was at one time ranked second only to King's Lynn in importance on this coast. The most notable feature today is the 18th century windmill with its brick tower, white sails, and conical wooden cap, often photographed. Cley has many attractive houses of flint and red brick, and the Church of St Margaret is one of Norfolk's finest in a county that is endowed with many beautiful churches and civic buildings.

Blakeney village has a small quay beside a channel which almost dries out at low tide, while near to the quay is a marker showing the height of floodwaters that inundated Blakeney in 1953. The parish church is visible for miles around, and has a second tower which was built as a lighthouse to guide boats along the channel into the harbour. A stroll around the quayside reveals the charm and tranquillity of this well-preserved village. A small ferry takes passengers to Blakeney Point only when the tide is in, for the harbour is not navigable at low water.

Wells-next-the-Sea is the largest of the harbours on this part of the north Norfolk coastline. It was linked by rail in 1857 to Dereham, and to Heacham in 1866. Both lines are gone, but Wells with its two narrow-gauge railways is as popular as ever with visitors.

The Wells & Walsingham Light Railway, four miles long, is the world's longest 10.25 inch gauge steam railway. It was built by Captain Francis and opened in 1982 with a finely modelled locomotive named 'Norfolk Hero', after Lord Nelson who was born near here. The second rail line is that of the Wells Harbour Railway, running for one mile from the harbour to Pinewoods Caravan Park in season. Two narrow-gauge railways serving the public in one village must be unique in Britain.

Walsingham, terminus of the light railway, is a place of pilgrimage for thousands from all over Europe who have worshipped at the shrine of Our Lady of Walsingham since the 11th century. An ancient track known as the Walsingham Way extends from the restored 'Slipper' chapel at nearby Houghton to this shrine, and it is said that Henry VIII walked barefoot along the pathway to pay homage to the Virgin Mary.

At low tide the sea retreats for over a mile from Wells, and it comes in quickly across the sands of Holkham Bay. The channel into the harbour is called 'The Run', and in rough weather the crossing of Wells Bar by fishermen with a boatload of whelks is worth watching. The Norfolk coast is famous for its great variety and quality of locally caught seafoods, and there is no better souvenir for visitors to this coast than a taste of the sea.

The only resort on England's east coast that faces west, Hunstanton has a fine sandy beach and is a favourite spot for sailing and waterskiing. The Great Eastern Railway arrived here in 1862, promoted by the Lestrange family who for generations had lived in nearby Hunstanton Hall. The railway terminus at Hunstanton served villages along this part of Norfolk's coast until the line from King's Lynn was closed on 5 May 1969.

There is a large gap on the railway network map of Norfolk between Sheringham and King's Lynn, the next station along the coast. Three train journeys totalling 87 miles are necessary, via Cromer, Norwich, Thetford and Ely. Buses provide a road link from King's Lynn to Hunstanton, a distance of fifteen miles.

For over one hundred years the railway brought visitors to this popular resort on the Wash. The writer of Murray's Guide in 1892 wondered whether he could recommend it to the genteel visitor because "It must be remembered that Hunstanton during the summer is exposed to constant forays of excursionists, who are brought here hundreds at a time from Cambridgeshire, Lincolnshire and elsewhere. Their visits do not lead to an increase in the comfort of the inns or of the beach."

Norfolk's north coast ends as it began, with red and white stripes. Hunstanton has its red and white striped cliffs, banded with red Carstone and white chalk, as well as red brick houses and white caravans. Happisburgh (pronounced Haisboro) at the southern fringe of the north Norfolk coast has a gaily painted red and white striped lighthouse for identification of the dangerous lee shore when strong northeasterlies are blowing.

King's Lynn, northern terminus of the railway line from London via Cambridge and Ely, is the agricultural and business centre for much of Fenland and north Norfolk, and its name continues to be associated with the monarchy. It was formerly known as Bishop's Lynn until Henry VIII confiscated it from the Bishop of Norwich.

Seven miles away is Sandringham House and its large estate, the personal possession of the reigning monarch. Wolferton was the royal railway station for Sandringham estate, but it was unable to survive the Beeching axe which severed so many lines in Norfolk, including this royal one. Wolferton station is now a museum.

The old part of King's Lynn is elegant and well preserved, and the port was ranked fourth in the realm in the 14th century. It is still active, despite heavy silting of the Wash, 300 square miles of shallow, muddy sea, into which hundreds of tons of silt are deposited each year by the four rivers which drain the Fens: the Ouse, Nene, Welland, and Witham. Long ago, the Fens were the home of fiercely independent people. Boadicea fought the Romans in Fen country; Hereward the Wake led a force against the Normans, and King John came to King's Lynn en route to Newark Castle, losing his baggage and regal treasures in the Wash. Searches for royal relics continue to this day.

The best way to see the historic centre of King's Lynn is on foot. There are many fine buildings here, including the churches of St Margaret and All Saints; The Guildhall (1421); the Red Mount Chapel for pilgrims (1485); the Greenland Fishery house (1605); and the Customs House (1683).

Lynn (as it is often called) has an interesting centre core, compact, dignified, and gracious, with tangible proof of its continuing prosperity in the recent restoration of its 12th century Norman house. The town also has well-endowed museums, two market places, and lively associations with the arts.

One of the world's greatest navigators, Captain George Vancouver was born in King's Lynn in 1757, and died in Petersham near London in 1798. From 1791 to1795 he circumnavigated the world, charting the northwest coast of North America, generally agreed to be the most intricate 10,000 miles of coastline on this planet - a far cry from the muddy shores around King's Lynn at low tide.

The county boundary between Norfolk and Lincolnshire runs across Terrington Marsh, six miles west of King's Lynn, crossing the coastline at Breast Sand, turning west to follow the channel of the River Nene, which flows into the Wash. To the north, seaside resorts are reached via the east coast main line from King's Cross, so we return to London in order to travel in one of the fast GNER electrics as we continue our journey up the coast.

The swing bridge taking the line from Ipswich to Lowestoft Central across Oulton Broad, which forms part of an extensive waterways network connecting many popular sailing centres. L1 67704 brings a two-coach local onto the iron girders in May 1958. (E. Alger/Colour-Rail BRE1488)

Hunstanton, the only resort on England's east coast that faces west, was served by the Great Eastern Railway from 1862. The terminus is still busy in August 1959 but the branch from King's Lynn closed ten years later. (T.J. Edgington)

Railways greatly helped the development of seaside holiday camps as suggested by this advertisement hoarding at Hopton-on-Sea. The ultra-respectable cyclist adds to the 1950s' flavour as D16 62511 crosses with a train from Liverpool Street to Gorleston. (E. Alger/Colour-Rail BRE375)

The elegantly restored station at Sheringham, where steam trains of the North Norfolk Railway begin their six-mile journey to Weybourne and Holt. Once part of the Midland & Great Northern route linking Cromer with Melton Constable, this stretch was nicknamed the 'Poppy Line'. (John Hadrill)

East coast main line routes to the Sea

Eclectic trains
Frequent excursions
The company cannot be held responsible for the departure of the time.

Sculpture 'Tempus Fugit' at Templecombe Station
by Sioban Coppinger, Alec and·Fiona Peever 1990
Commissioned by British Rail Community Unit.

The most eclectic train ever to run in Britain left King's Cross on the east coast main line each Friday evening in June from 1933 to 1939, when the sun hovered around the summer solstice to give maximum daylight for a week of land cruising in England and Scotland. This train was the 'Northern Belle', a truly luxurious LNER hotel on wheels, which roamed over both LMS and LNER tracks on an itinerary which can never be repeated, since several of the lines no longer exist. Certainly this was a journey to the sea worth recalling.

It was first class all the way, and the fare for a week's travel and accommodation was twenty pounds for an 1800 mile cruise, including a tour of the Lake District, a trip by steamer on Loch Lomond, a tour on the West Highland line to Mallaig and a sail down Loch Long to the Firth of Clyde. Such was the fame of the 'Northern Belle' that it was always fully-booked in anticipation of enjoying the pleasures of good company, fine food, and all the comforts that the LNER could devise for its unique and legendary train.

Fourteen coaches were provided for the sixty passengers, in what could be compared favourably to a royal train, as it pulled out of King's Cross at 2100 heading up the east coast main line. The locomotive from 1938 onwards was one of the streamlined A4 Class Pacifics, and the first two coaches behind the tender were for train staff. Next came an all-electric kitchen car with a master chef in charge; then two restaurant cars, each seating thirty. The next coach included a cocktail bar, ladies' retiring room, hairdressing salon, smoking saloon, and purser's office.

Coach seven contained a large lounge, writing room, library, and a lounge reserved exclusively for the ladies. The next six coaches were sleeping cars, each with bedrooms, baths and showers for ten passengers. At the rear was a baggage coach equipped with individual wardrobes for all on board. This was as close to a cruise ship as one could conceive for land travel, except that the train did not travel through the night, but was stabled in a quiet country siding or coastal location to ensure that passengers enjoyed a good night's sleep.

The itinerary for each cruise varied, and with such a long train it was necessary at times to divide it into day and night sections on scenic branch lines, so that passengers could go sightseeing in the day section, or take a coach tour, or loch cruise, while the rest of the train proceeded to the next rendezvous point. A typical itinerary for a week of railway cruising on board the 'Northern Belle' was as follows:

After travelling north to Darlington, the train left the main line, heading west through Teesdale to Barnard Castle for the night. Breakfast was served at 0930 on Saturday as the train climbed up and over the moorlands of the Pennines until the highest railway summit in England was reached near Stainmore, 1,370 ft above sea level. On its long descent, the 'Northern Belle' glided through Barras station, where one could gaze at the finest landscape to be seen from any station in Britain, with the Eden valley spread out below, the Pennines soaring to the east, and the fells of Lakeland to the west, with peaks of Helvellyn, Skiddaw and Saddleback on the distant skyline.

Continuing its journey down from Barras to Kirkby Stephen,

CHAPTER SEVEN

**EAST COAST
MAIN LINE ROUTES
TO THE SEA**
≈≈≈

SCOTLAND

ENGLAND

N

BERWICK-UPON-TWEED

Beal ○
HOLY ISLAND
(Lindisfarne)

Bamburgh + FARNE ISLANDS
+ *Seahouses*

Alnwick ○ ● Alnmouth

● Whitley Bay

■ CARLISLE

NEWCASTLE ■

● Seaburn

Cockermouth ○
● Workington *Bassenthwaite* ○

■ SUNDERLAND

● Seaham

Keswick ○ ● Penrith

● Whitehaven

● Appleby

HARTLEPOOL ■ Redcar Marske Saltburn
Staithes

Kirkby Stephen ●

MIDDLESBROUGH ■ ○ ○ + *Runswick Bay*
Hinderwell ○ *Sandsend*

Stainmore
(1370 ft) +

DARLINGTON Gt Ayton ● ■ WHITBY

Battersby Danby Lealholm Glaisdale Grosmont
● ● ● ● ● ● ● ● ▲

Robin Hood's Bay ○

Ravenscar ○

▲

SCARBOROUGH ■

Pickering ○ ▲

● Filey

■ LANCASTER

Bempton ●

Castle Howard + ● Malton

Bridlington

+ *Barmston*
+ *Skipsea*
+ *Atwick*

YORK ■

○ *Hornsea*
+ *Mappleton*
+ *Cowden*

■ PRESTON

HULL ■

○ *Withernsea*

SPURN HEAD

GRIMSBY ■ Cleethorpes
▽

○ *Mablethorpe*
○ *Sutton-on-Sea*

LINCOLN ■

Skegness ●

● Wainfleet ●

Sleaford ●

Boston ●
The WASH

Spalding ●

KING'S LYNN ■

PETERBOROUGH ■

LEGEND
■ RAILTRACK STATION
○ FORMER STATION
▲ PRESERVED
STANDARD GAUGE
▽ NARROW GAUGE
+ PLACES NAMED IN TEXT

0 10 20 30 40 50 60
MILES

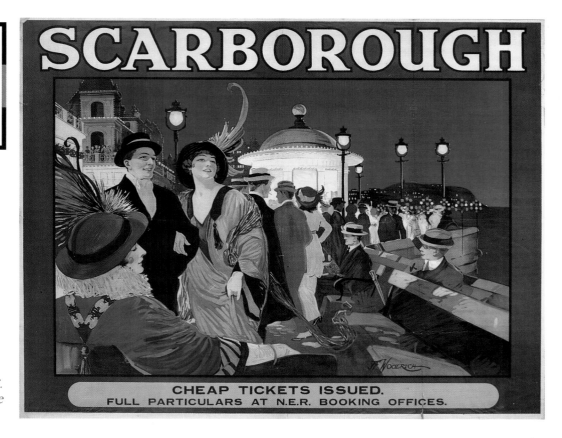

A North Eastern Railway poster by F. Woolrich, well capturing the elegance of Scarborough in its heyday.

Another striking poster by Tom Purvis, this time showing the famous LNER named train 'The Coronation' crossing the Royal Border Bridge at Berwick. (NRM/Science & Society - 3)

Left: Skegness, as depicted by Tom Purvis - once described as 'the man who invented the great English poster with a totally original style'. This imaginative and dramatic study was inspired by a Japanese print of Yokohama which Purvis owned.

EAST COAST POSTERS

The 'Northern Belle' and what today would be called its 'on-train team', photographed in 1934. This truly luxurious LNER hotel on wheels, conveying just sixty passengers in its fourteen coaches, visited several coastal destinations in its travels as far afield as Aberdeen and Mallaig.
(NRM - 646/91)

the train joined the famous Settle-Carlisle line, travelling north as far as Appleby, where it branched off down Edendale to Clifton, on the west coast main line south of Penrith, arriving at 1120. Passengers boarded motor coaches at Clifton station, while the train continued on to Penrith.

Most of Saturday was spent touring the Lake District, with lunch at Keswick, then south to Thirlmere, Grasmere, Ambleside and Windermere, where tea was taken. In the late afternoon, motor coaches took passengers over the Kirkstone Pass to Patterdale, and along the western shores of Ullswater to Penrith, where the train was waiting. In the evening while dinner was served, the 'Northern Belle' proceeded via Carlisle

and the Waverley route through Edinburgh, then over the Forth and Tay bridges to Dundee and Montrose for a quiet night on the Inverbervie branch line beside the sea.

On Sunday the train made an early start for Aberdeen, and breakast was served at the Palace Hotel before leaving for Grantown-on-Spey, where the train stayed while passengers took a coach tour of Aviemore and the Spey valley. During the afternoon the train continued its scenic journey through Morayshire and Banffshire, reaching furthest north on the cruise at Elgin, before returning to Aberdeen for dinner at the Palace Hotel. After dinner the train headed westwards up the valley of the Dee to Ballater, which was reached at 2330. Passengers were assured of a quiet Sunday night among the Grampian mountains, six miles from Balmoral Castle.

From Ballater, a Monday morning coach tour of upper Deeside included Balmoral, Braemar and Linn o'Dee, with lunch and tea served at hotels along the way, before returning to Aberdeen for a tour of the granite city. The train then headed southwards across the Tay and Forth bridges to Dalmeny for the Monday night.

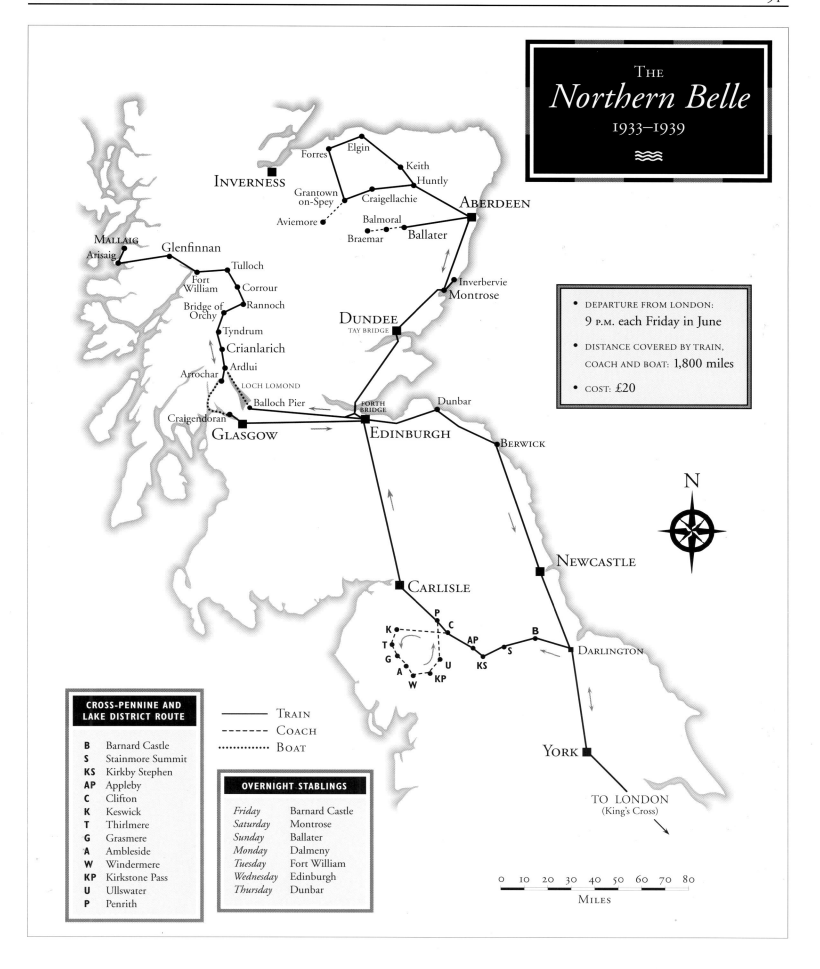

THE
Northern Belle
1933–1939

- DEPARTURE FROM LONDON:
  9 P.M. each Friday in June

- DISTANCE COVERED BY TRAIN,
  COACH AND BOAT: 1,800 miles

- COST: £20

INVERNESS

Forres   Elgin
Keith
Huntly
Grantown   Craigellachie
on-Spey   ABERDEEN
Aviemore   Balmoral
Braemar   Ballater

MALLAIG
Arisaig   Glenfinnan
Tulloch
Fort   Corrour
William
Bridge of   Rannoch
Orchy
Tyndrum
Crianlarich   Inverbervie
Ardlui   Montrose
Arrochar   DUNDEE
LOCH LOMOND   TAY BRIDGE
Balloch Pier
Craigendoran   FORTH   Dunbar
BRIDGE
GLASGOW   EDINBURGH
Berwick

N

NEWCASTLE

CARLISLE
P
C
K
T   AP   B
G   KS   S
A   U
W   KP   DARLINGTON

YORK

TO LONDON
(King's Cross)

**CROSS-PENNINE AND
LAKE DISTRICT ROUTE**

——— TRAIN
- - - - COACH
············· BOAT

B	Barnard Castle
S	Stainmore Summit
KS	Kirkby Stephen
AP	Appleby
C	Clifton
K	Keswick
T	Thirlmere
G	Grasmere
A	Ambleside
W	Windermere
KP	Kirkstone Pass
U	Ullswater
P	Penrith

OVERNIGHT STABLINGS

Friday	Barnard Castle
Saturday	Montrose
Sunday	Ballater
Monday	Dalmeny
Tuesday	Fort William
Wednesday	Edinburgh
Thursday	Dunbar

0 10 20 30 40 50 60 70 80
MILES

CHANGING
TIMES

Pre-war days at Scarborough in August 1938. The two locomotives in LNER apple-green livery have coupled to the stock of returning excursion trains to Leeds and York. (Colour-Rail NE14)

Diesel units revived the line from Scarborough to Whitby in the late 1950s but unfortunately failed to save it from closure. The result was the loss of some of the most outstanding coastal views to be seen from a train, as instanced by this panorama of Robin Hood's Bay on the descent from Ravenscar. (David Sutcliffe)

The steam-hauled local passenger service linking coastal resorts had largely become a thing of the past by the early 1960s. L1 67764 captures the spirit of a bygone era as it pauses at Whitby West Cliff on its way to Middlesbrough via Sandsend and Staithes in May 1958, just prior to the line's closure. (J.C.W. Halliday/Colour-Rail BRE877)

Steam revival, as instanced by the North Yorkshire Moors Railway which provides Whitby holiday-makers with a delightful journey through the nearby National Park. Goathland station, closely associated with the television series Heartbeat, retains many features from the time it opened in 1865. (David Joy)

Early next morning the 'Northern Belle' proceeded to Balloch Pier station on Loch Lomond, where a steamer was waiting to take passengers for a cruise to Ardlui at the far end of the loch. The train meanwhile climbed along the shores of Gare Loch, Loch Long and Loch Lomond to await the passengers at Ardlui station.

All of the following route taken by the 'Northern Belle' may be explored by train today. Current timetables of the respective train operating companies should be consulted in planning journeys based on this retrospective celebration of the pre-war 'Northern Belle' cruises.

Leaving Ardlui, the train passed through Crianlarich where the tracks divide, either to climb to Tyndrum Upper station for Rannoch Moor, Fort William and Mallaig, or to descend to Tyndrum Lower station on the line which runs beside Loch Awe to Oban, ferry terminal for the western isles. Tyndrum, with a population of approximately one hundred, is probably the smallest community in Britain to boast two railway stations, each on a different line passing through some of the country's most scenic mountain landscapes.

The 'Northern Belle', all fourteen coaches, took the high road through Bridge of Orchy station up to and across Rannoch Moor, before the dramatic descent beside Loch Treig and down Glen Spean to Atlantic waters at Fort William. Here the six sleeping cars were detached, and the day section set off on the scenic West Highland line to Glenfinnan, Arisaig (furthest west of any station in Britain), then northwards beside the sands of Morar, with their dramatic seascapes of Rhum and Eigg, to reach Mallaig at 1620.

Daylight lingers long in June at this high latitude, and there was plenty of time for a stroll along the shore to admire the coastal panorama bounded by islands of the Inner Hebrides, before the train set off at 1700 for Glenfinnan, where a stop was made on the famous viaduct. The 'Northern Belle' then returned along the shores of Loch Eil, Loch Linnhe to Fort William where it remained overnight.

Early on Wednesday morning the train climbed once more above Loch Treig to Corrour on Rannoch moor, then down past the Bridge of Orchy, Tyndrum, Crianlarich and Ardlui to Arrochar and Tarbet station, which stands between Loch Lomond and Loch Long. At Arrochar pier a steamer was waiting to take passengers for a sea cruise down Loch Long to the Firth of Clyde at Craigendoran, where the train was waiting for departure to Edinburgh. Dinner was served at the North British Hotel and after passengers had re-boarded the train it was stabled at Corstorphine on the outskirts of Edinburgh for a quiet night.

All day Thursday was spent in and around Edinburgh, visiting the famous Castle, touring the Royal Mile, museums and galleries, with short sightseeing excursions, and meals at the hotel. At midnight, the train left Waverley station for Dunbar on the coast, where it stayed for the night. Early on Friday morning, while passengers slept, the fourteen coaches were eased gently on to the southbound main line for London. A leisurely breakfast was enjoyed as the train passed through Durham with its magnificent cathedral and castle, York with its Minster, Peterborough and its cathedral, to arrive at King's Cross at 1045.

For those fortunate to have cruised on the 'Northern Belle' this was a superlative experience, and we can only regret that there is no train in Britain to equal this in terms of itinerary, variety of landscapes, on-board services, loch and sea cruises, coach tours, and cost, even allowing for inflation. This was what the railways of Britain did so well in those golden pre-war summers,. when twenty pounds certainly went a long way, and it is hard to believe that a rail cruise could offer so much variety of travel by land, lake, and sea in such a short space of time.

From 1928 to 1961, the capitals of England and Scotland were linked by a steam-hauled train which did not stop anywhere on the 393-mile journey from King's Cross to Edinburgh. This was the famous 'Flying Scotsman', with a change of crew en route at high speed, in which the relief crew came through a passage in the tender to reach the footplate.

Before WW2 this train offered a wide range of services and facilities, including a lounge for reading and writing letters using unique 'FS' letterhead, a ladies' retiring room, a spacious cocktail bar, barber's shop, bookstall, library, and a steward to serve passengers, which included posting their mail on arrival at Edinburgh or King's Cross.

Throughout the great years of high speed steam services on the east coast main line from 1930 to 1939, the best moment for train spotters to be at the end of a platform at King's Cross was 1000, when five expresses departed in quick succession for the north, an impressive sight as firemen on the footplates heaved coal to develop enough power in each locomotive for high speeds to be maintained for hours on end between London and Edinburgh, or other destinations served on LNER routes from King's Cross.

In the great floods of 1948 on the east coast main line, trains between London and Scotland had to be diverted, so the FS ran for 409 miles non-stop, a new British record. At that time, top-link drivers were paid £27 every two weeks. Today, when passengers leave King's Cross on board the all-electric 'Flying Scotsman' or other fast trains to the north, it is hard to appreciate the asphyxiating climbs in firing and driving a 500-ton express train to Scotland uphill through seven tunnels in the first twelve miles after departure from King's Cross in those exciting days of steam haulage.

Several titled trains of the Great North Eastern Railway leave King's Cross each weekday on the east coast main line to Scotland, including the 'Flying Scotsman', the 'Scottish

Grimsby station as it looked in 1855, before traffic was greatly increased from the 1860s when the Manchester, Sheffield & Lincolnshire Railway started to develop nearby Cleethorpes as a major resort. One of the oldest towns in Britain, Grimsby is still a major port. (NRM - 2258/58)

Pullman', the 'Aberdonian', and the 'Highland Chieftain'. These high-speed trains give only brief glimpses of the North Sea as they speed towards Edinburgh, with the first good view occurring as the train approaches Alnmouth. We will therefore change trains at various stations along the route in order to reach the coast as we head north towards Scotland.

The first seaside resort served by the railway north of King's Lynn is Skegness, which may be reached from Peterborough, via Spalding and Sleaford, or from Grantham, via Ancaster and Sleaford. Both trains go through Boston, Lincolnshire, an ancient port with strong links to its namesake in New England. The conspicuous 272 ft tower of the church, the 'Boston Stump', is a landmark for miles around, and a navigational aid for ships negotiating the five-mile channel into the harbour.

Boston is an attractive town, with a large market place and handsome buildings dating back several centuries, when it was one of Britain's busiest ports. There are pleasant walks along the banks of the River Witham, and small boats may be seen travelling up the Witham canal to Lincoln and the Trent waterway, a gateway to Britain's extensive canal system

which pre-dated the railways.

Like many seaside resorts in Britain that offer miles of golden sands, promenades and a wide variety of entertainments, Skegness was created and nurtured by the Great Northern Railway in 1863. Most visitors came from Lincolnshire and the industrial midlands for day trips and summer holidays. There are over six miles of beach here, graphically depicted in the exuberant 'Jolly Fisherman' poster, first issued by the GNR in 1908.

Skegness was also the furthest north that the 'Eastern Belle Pullman' ventured from London for a day excursion. A brief visit to the attractions before the train departed southwards in the late afternoon was more than compensated by travelling in the

HANDLING
THE TRAFFIC

The concourse at Skegness, complete with modest floral decoration. A former fishing hamlet, the resort was created and nurtured by the Great Northern Railway and soon became famous for its miles of golden sands, promenades and a wide variety of entertainments. (John S. Gilks)

Interior of the signal box at Cleethorpes in 1985. Only 36 miles from Skegness by sea, rail closures of the 1960s now necessitate a journey of no less than 125 miles by train via Boston, Sleaford, Lincoln and Grimsby! (John S. Gilks)

luxury of a Pullman restaurant car, where a three-course meal could be enjoyed at leisure during the 160-mile journey home.

Wainfleet, once a port, was the intended terminus for this branch line, but the estate agent of the Earl of Scarborough, who owned land on the coast, persuaded the GNR to extend the line for a further five miles to the fishing hamlet of Skegness. The resort we see today is very much a Victorian creation, with the town's spacious streets set back from the sea front. Three miles south of the pier is the nature reserve of Gibraltar Point where, on a clear day, the north Norfolk coast may be seen across the waters of the Wash. Twelve miles up the coast is Sutton-on-Sea, a pleasant resort formerly served by trains on a branch line between Boston and Grimsby.

By sea it is 36 miles from Skegness to Cleethorpes, the next railway station along the coast. By train it is 125 miles, heading south to Boston, west to Sleaford, north to Lincoln, and finally east to Grimsby and Cleethorpes. This roundabout route, like many in Britain today, is a legacy of the railway closures of the 1960s, and on this journey we will enjoy a brief stopover at Lincoln, a great city whose cathedral and castle high on the hill are well worth a visit. The Romans chose Lincoln as the junction of two major roads, Ermine Street (A15), and Fosse Way (A46), both examples of Roman obsession with the straight line.

The massive central tower of Lincoln Cathedral was once capped by a tall spire, whose height reached 524ft above street level, making this cathedral (c.1350) the first man-made structure in the world to exceed the height of the Great Pyramid of Egypt (481ft). A fierce gale in 1548 brought the soaring spire down, so all we see today are three towers. Many people consider this cathedral to be the finest in Britain, even without its lofty spire.

After leaving Lincoln, the train to Cleethorpes first reaches the coast at Grimsby, a major fishing port, and one of the oldest towns in Britain, having been granted its charter by King John in 1201. Grimsby has two stations: Town, and Docks. It is not surprising that when the train doors open at the Town station, a tempting aroma of fish and chips usually pervades Platform 1, where the 'Mariner' buffet is conveniently located for the benefit of hungry passengers.

The development of Cleethorpes dates from the 1860s, when the Great Northern Railway built rail links with industrial towns of Lincolnshire and south Yorkshire, bringing visitors to this popular seaside town, with its fine promenade, sea wall and pier, all built by the GNR. The pier, dating from 1875, was twice as long as it is now, having been partially demolished in WW2 for military reasons.

Long before the spread of motorways around Britain, Cleethorpes welcomed thousands of visitors arriving each day by train in the holiday season. The station is close to the beach, whose area of sand triples at low tide, but the sea comes in quickly and landmarks can be lost in misty weather.

There is also a small railway here, operated by the Cleethorpes Coast Light Railway, the only narrow-gauge railway in Lincolnshire open to the public. It celebrated its fiftieth anniversary in 1998.

When the marine embankment was built in the 1930s between the boating lake and the dunes at Humberston Fitties, a stainless steel plate presented by a Sheffield foundry was set into the pathway, about a mile from the railway station, to mark the spot where the meridian of zero degrees longitude (the Greenwich meridian) heads northwards across the Humber estuary towards the North Pole.

In 1981 the great Humber Bridge was opened, joining Barton-upon-Humber with the western suburbs of Hull. The central span (4,626 ft) of this road bridge is one of the longest in the world, and the estuary near Cleethorpes is seven miles wide. Across the Humber from Cleethorpes is Spurn Head and the clay cliffs of Holderness, which extend thirty miles north to Bridlington.

To reach coastal resorts on the Holderness peninsula by train from Cleethorpes involves both rail and road journeys. The quickest route is to take the train to Barton-on-Humber, then bus across the great bridge to reach Hull, and another bus to Withernsea. Another route to Hull is to take the train to Stainforth and Hatfield junction, eight miles northeast of Doncaster, changing trains and travelling via Goole and Gilberdyke to Hull, the nearest station to Withernsea.

The Holderness coast has a long history of almost continuous retreat. During the past 750 years, much of this coastline has disappeared into the sea. More than thirty communities listed in the Domesday Book no longer exist, and even large towns such as Withernsea and Hornsea have predecessors which now lie beneath the waters of the North Sea.

After widespread flooding in 1953, the shoreline at Kilnsea near Spurn Head was strengthened by a massive concrete promenade, groynes, and boulders to protect the clay cliffs. Twenty years later, most of the structure had been reduced to a mass of rubble. Six miles north at Holmpton, a major slip of cliff face in 1978 resulted in a loss of more than twenty feet overnight, giving Yorkshire's Holderness peninsula the dubious distinction of having one of the fastest eroding coastlines in the world.

Withernsea, 15 miles by road from Hull, has a sand and shingle beach protected from erosion by a series of wooden groynes. A Hull businessman, Anthony Bennett, brought the railway here in 1854 and built the imposing Queen's Hotel, followed by a pier, the hallmark of a fashionable Victorian resort. A replica of Conwy castle, known as the Pier Towers, was built in 1875 to form the entrance gates to the pier, which was destroyed in 1882 by a fierce storm. The land around the resort is as flat as the proverbial pancake, dotted with caravans and holiday chalets.

Pullman service from London to Hull started in 1935 as part of the 'Yorkshire Pullman' train, giving citizens of Hull and visitors to the coast the fastest travel they had ever enjoyed between these two cities, until WW2 intervened. After the war, services were restored, and in 1967 a new 'Hull Pullman' was introduced with faster timings, reaching Hull in under three hours from London. The Pullman service remained popular until the mid-1970s, and survived relentless competition from road traffic until 1978, when it was withdrawn at the end of the summer season. For a short while thereafter, the 'Hull Executive' became the fastest locomotive-hauled train in Britain until HSTs took over the service on 3 January 1982.

The river Hull meanders south from Driffield into Hull, while the railway takes a straight line further inland, ten miles or more from the sea. Arram is the closest station to Hornsea, but Beverley provides the best approach by main road across the river, which acts as a huge moat to other smaller roads heading eastwards.

Hornsea grew into a resort largely due to the efforts of Joseph Wade, a Hull timber merchant who encouraged the railway to come here in 1864. The main street follows the eastern shore of Hornsea Mere, a huge freshwater lake two miles long and one mile wide. It is the largest lake in Yorkshire, home to large numbers of wildfowl and a popular sailing centre, less than a mile from the sea. To the south of Hornsea are beaches at Mappleton, Cowden, and Aldbrough, while to the north are more beaches at Atwick, Skipsea, and Barmston.

Heading northwards from Hull to Scarborough, the train reaches the sea at Bridlington, a popular Yorkshire resort situated at a break in the almost continuous line of cliffs, and sheltered from strong north winds by Flamborough Head. The first train reached this part of the coast in 1846, and the harbour was expanded in the 1850s, replacing a small medieval port. Charlotte Bronte came here in 1839, and was so overcome at her first sight of the sea that she burst into tears and had to sit down to recover. She stayed at Easton House Farm, and spent many hours writing her novel 'Shirley' (1849) in the summer house at the farm.

Four miles north of Bridlington, on the railway line between Filey and Scarborough, is Bempton, near Flamborough Head, where the Royal Society for the Protection of Birds has a coastal reserve on top of almost vertical cliffs, famous for their sea-bird colonies.

Filey developed into a resort during the nineteenth century on the site of a small fishing village, which consisted of two Victorian streets named Church and Queen, on the south side of a deep ravine. The railway line to Filey was completed in 1847, bringing day-trippers as well as those who wished to retire beside the sea, away from the big cities of industrial Yorkshire. The ravine kept the town small and compact, and it prides itself as an ideal family resort, with sands extending north to Filey Brigg and south for several miles at low tide.

The rail line north from Filey meets the main line from York to Scarborough at Seamer, three miles from Yorkshire's largest and oldest seaside resort, with a history extending back over a thousand years. A Roman signal station was sited on the rocky headland which dominates the town to the north, and on warm summer days Scarborough's two bays have an almost Mediterranean aspect, if not the same climate.

In 1626 a medicinal spring was discovered at a cliff near the harbour, immediately attracting health seekers who at that time relied mostly on natural cures. Thus Scarborough developed into a coastal spa to rival Bath and Harrogate. When Dr Robert Wittie claimed in 1667 that the spring waters could cure at least thirty diseases and that these same waters were "a most Sovereign remedy against Hypochondria, Melancholly, and Windiness", Scarborough's future was assured.

Fine hotels with their terraced balconies and gardens stand high above the south beach, and Scarborough today exemplifies the great building surge resulting from arrival of the railway in 1845. The Grand Hotel, towering above the beach, is symbolic of the great confidence of Victorian builders, whether of railways, factories, stations, hotels or monuments. Sir Joseph Paxton, architect of the Great Exhibition of 1851, notably its Crystal Palace, was commissioned to design a splendid new pavilion above the south beach, but this was destroyed by fire in 1876.

The title 'Queen of Northern Watering Places' was conferred upon Scarborough by early railway posters, and from 1923 until WW2 the LNER ran an express service called the 'Scarborough Flyer' from King's Cross in under four hours for the 230 miles, including a stop at York, the largest railway station in the world when completed in 1877.

The 'Scarborough Flyer' was one of the fastest and heaviest long-distance trains to the seaside, with through coaches to Whitby, and two restaurant cars to serve its passengers en route. Today, like other former titled trains to the coast, the 'Flyer' is but a memory, refreshed by restoration of a steam-hauled 'Scarborough Spa Express' in the 1980s on the Leeds-York-Scarborough route. This revival was greatly aided by an enlightened Scarborough town council who, with many supporters, ensured that passengers who came on a scenic journey by steam train could also enjoy a pleasant day by the sea before returning home.

Prior to the Beeching cuts, Scarborough had two stations: Central, and Londesborough Road, the latter used almost exclusively by summer Saturday holiday traffic. Much of this traffic came from the north and, to avoid reversal at York, trains travelled on a branch line between Pilmoor and Malton, where they rejoined the main line from York to the coast. All trains now use Scarborough Central station, one of over 400 stations in Britain that Railtrack has renovated since privatization.

Until 1958, trains ran along the coast from Scarborough to Redcar, through Robin Hood's Bay, Whitby, Sandsend, Hinderwell (for Runswick Bay), Staithes and Saltburn. On this line there were outstanding views from the train as it meandered close to the Yorkshire coastline and across viaducts near to the sea at Whitby, Sandsend, and Staithes. A 'Rail Trail' now links Scarborough and Whitby, using parts of the old trackbed along its route.

It is eighteen miles by sea from Scarborough to Whitby, and it used to be a similar distance by train, but it is now 160 miles by rail, and requires four trains to complete the journey. First, westwards from Scarborough to York via Malton (for Castle Howard); then north to Darlington, east to Middlesbrough, and finally south, stopping at every station in a delightful journey through villages and dales of North Yorkshire before reaching the sea again at Whitby.

The rail route from Middlesbrough to Whitby provides a good sampling of this varied landscape through Captain Cook country. Before leaving Middlesbrough, a visit to the

A holiday express pulls away from Scarborough, 'Queen of Northern Watering Places'. On the left under the canopy is the famous 'longest station seat', while in the background can be seen the station's overpowering clock tower and the Grand Hotel. (J.S. Gilks)

Cleveland Centre is recommended to see the fine 23ft replica of Cook's famous ship 'Endeavour', built by Whitby craftsmen whose predecessors built the original ship.

The first station after Middlesborough is Marton, the village where James Cook was born. A mile from Great Ayton station, overlooked by the prominent landmark 'Roseberry Topping' (1,051 ft) is the school where the world's greatest navigator was educated. The Captain Cook monument, an obelisk high on a hill to the east, may be seen between Great Ayton and Battersby, where the train reverses to head north, then east through the Cleveland Hills to reach the Esk valley at Castleton Moor.

Danby is an attractive village with its medieval bridge, fine church, ruined castle, and old mill, all near the station; it is also the home of the North York Moors National Park Centre. At Lealholm, the most scenic section of the line begins as the train follows the meandering Esk to the sea, with woods and streams, and in the distance a skyline of moors with their stone walls enclosing sheep pastures.

The station at Glaisdale is near the ancient stone Beggar's Bridge which dates back to 1619. All roads from the station climb steeply out of the valley, while the railway follows the River Esk all the way to Whitby. At Grosmont we reach the terminus of the North Yorkshire Moors Railway, where steam trains set off on a scenic eighteen-mile journey to Pickering.

This railway was built by George Stephenson in 1836, closed by BR in 1965, and restored by the NYMR in 1973. The line passes through the North Yorkshire Moors National Park, which is archaeologically rich with medieval guiding crosses, a paved Roman road, stone circles, long barrows, trackways, and dykes. Nowhere else in England have the remains left by prehistoric man on desolate moorland been less disturbed.

There are stations on the NYMR at Goathland, Newtondale Halt, and Levisham, with a steep climb of 1 in 49 between Grosmont and Goathland, after which the valley opens out. For trainspotters there are good vantage points as the line twists beneath Northdale Scar, and also through Newtondale near Levisham.

Less than a mile from the NYMR line between Goathland and Levisham is the Saltergate Inn, whose fire to welcome and warm travellers is said to have been burning continuously for over a century. The famous Lyke Wake Walk crosses the line north of Newtondale Halt, and there are several paths worth exploring from this station. The terminus at Pickering has no other rail connection, so we return to Grosmont to take a Northern Spirit train along the Esk valley into Whitby.

In November 1998, the NYMR operated the first of its new steam specials 'The Captain Cook Pullman', taking a steam train from its heritage line on to the Northern Spirit line from Grosmont into Whitby. This was the first steam train since 1987 to reach the sea by this route.

Between Grosmont and Sleights, the train crosses the Esk eight times on the approach to Whitby, passing under the high Larpool viaduct which once carried the coast line from Scarborough to Saltburn and Middlesbrough. In Whitby station a large tiled map shows the great network of railways that served Yorkshire until the 1960s. From the entrance of the station, and high above the harbour, can be seen the arches of Whitby Abbey, through which fierce gales have blown during the past six centuries.

Whitby is one of the most interesting and historic ports on the east coast, nestling under steep cliffs on either side of the harbour. For centuries fishermen and boatbuilders have toiled alongside the quay where the whaling ships unloaded their catch. One whaling captain, William Scoresby, built the first 'crowsnest' for his ship at Whitby, and used it to capture over 500 whales. Captain Cook (1728-1779) lived here when home from the sea, and a plaque on a house in Grape Lane marks the spot. Cook's ships were all built at Whitby and their names give us an understanding of his character and determination: Endeavour, Resolution, Adventure, and Discovery.

The town owes its development as a seaside resort to the railway schemes of George Hudson, railway entrepreneur and promoter of many rail routes in Britain. In 1835 he met George Stephenson at Whitby and learned of plans to build the North Midland Railway, which under Hudson's drive and enthusiasm was extended as the York & North Midland. This led to a decade of almost uncontrolled railway mania, with Hudson negotiating the amalgamation of several railways to form the Midland Railway, with himself as Chairman.

By 1846 he controlled nearly half of England's railways, had risen to become Lord Mayor of York and, on paper at least, the first railway millionaire in Britain. In the process of building his empire as undisputed 'railway king' at York, his devious tactics so tarnished his reputation that he was forced to resign his chairmanship.

Hudson is remembered today more for his great achievements than for his manipulations, and his native city of York has named a street after him, while Hudson House is part of the railway headquarters, and there is also a Hudson's Hotel near the Minster. A glance at the tiled railway map in Whitby or York stations will give some idea of the network that George Hudson masterminded, for he built more railways in Britain than any other man.

Apart from Captain James Cook and George Hudson, Whitby has several other claims to fame. Prime Minister Gladstone was Member of Parliament for Whitby. Lewis Carroll stayed here in 1854, and the sandy beaches below West Cliff are said to have inspired him to write 'The Walrus and the Carpenter'. John Wesley, founder of Methodism, wrote in his diary for 1761: "In all England I have not seen a more affectionate people than those of Whitby."

The harbour is usually busy, with a swing bridge to carry road traffic and pedestrians across the Esk to the old town on the east side, with its shops, quaint alleys, pubs and old cottages. On the heights above are the remains of the Abbey, built on the site of a Celtic monastery founded by St Hilda in 657. Nearby is the parish church of St Mary with its Norman tower, reached from the old part of the town by climbing a steep flight of steps. The famous 'Whitby Jet' ornaments made from hard black pebbles found on the beach here once supported a flourishing industry in the town.

On the west side of the harbour are more shops, cafes, entertainments, and a promenade leading to a massive stone

breakwater topped by an elegant lighthouse. Whitby Sands are popular at all times of the year and extend several miles westward to Sandsend. High above the harbour are hotels and residences with fine sea views, and on the upper promenade is an arch formed by a whalebone jaw to show the source of much of Whitby's earlier prosperity.

A memorial to Captain Cook, "an able, astute and humane commander, a prudent explorer, a meticulous cartographer, and a remarkable leader of men", stands on the East Terrace, but little remains of the railway line that threaded its way up the coast to Saltburn, as it was closed to passenger traffic in 1958. The southern section from Whitby to Scarborough survived until 1965.

Before closure of this scenic line along the Yorkshire coast, it was possible to travel from sea to sea by steam train across the highest railway summit in England, starting at Whitby and ending at Whitehaven on the west coast. There are now large gaps along the way, but let us recall this journey, since the trains travelled along one of the most challenging and spectacular routes joining England's east and west coasts.

From Whitby, passengers took the coastal line through

The abbey and church dominate the skyline across the harbour in this busy scene at Whitby in early BR days. The town then boasted four outstandingly scenic railway routes - through Robin Hood's Bay to Scarborough, along the coast to Middlesbrough, inland to Malton and up the Esk Valley to Battersby. Today only the latter remains.

Sandsend, Staithes, Saltburn and Redcar to Middlesbrough and Darlington. Crossing the main line from London to Edinburgh, trains headed west to the Pennines, through Barnard Castle and across Bowes Moor to Stainmore summit (1,370ft). Descending the Westmorland fells, trains called at Kirkby Stephen, then at Appleby, crossing the Settle-Carlisle line to reach Penrith. Here a Cockermouth and Whitehaven locomotive took over, meandering through the northern part of the Lake District, stopping at Troutbeck, Threlkeld, Keswick, and Bassenthwaite Lake on its way to Cockermouth, Workington and Whitehaven.

On the Cumbrian section of this sea-to-sea rail route there were six trains each weekday between Penrith and Whitehaven (47 miles), and the fastest took 2h 10 min. This was the only railway line that went across the Lake District, and the journey along the western shore of Bassenthwaite Lake was particularly delightful, giving fine views of Skiddaw and Saddleback (Blencathra) across the waters of the Lake District's only 'Lake'. Tennyson (1809-1892) chose Bassenthwaite for his honeymoon, and perhaps was thinking of it in writing 'Morte d'Arthur', when Excalibur was thrown into the depths of a lake on which sailboats cruise and race today.

This former scenic line near Bassenthwaite is difficult to find, as a widened A66 has been built over part of the old trackbed. Threlkeld station survives as a County Council building, and the station yard is now a car park for those who wish to walk westwards along the old rail route to Keswick.

To return from Whitehaven on the Cumbrian coast to Whitby on the north Yorkshire coast today requires changes of train at Carlisle, Newcastle, and Middlesbrough. The next station along the coast north of Whitby is Saltburn, reached via Middlesbrough, Redcar and Marske.

Before 1860, Saltburn was described as "a small hamlet with sixteen houses situated upon the sea and under a mountain, with quaint villagers engaged in fishing and seal catching, but mainly smuggling." The initial impetus to build a resort at Saltburn came from a Quaker ironmaster, Henry Pease who intended this to be a 'celestial city' with streets named after precious jewels, for rest and recuperation of ironworkers from Teesside.

The railway reached Saltburn in 1861, combining the station with its own Zetland Hotel, whose private platform enabled patrons to alight from their carriages under awnings leading directly into the Zetland. In building this magnificent hotel the railway company was determined to develop a seaside resort to rival all other Victorian watering places, adding a pier in 1868 and a water-operated cliff hoist in 1870. This was rebuilt in 1884 as an inclined tramway which is still in use today, with the ascending and descending cars moved by filling or draining the 20,000 gallon water tanks according to the passenger load in each car, with cables connecting the two cars.

Saltburn's impressive station building is now mostly occupied by shops, offices, and a tourist centre. The former Zetland Hotel has been converted into flats, with a walkway where the tracks once led to the rear entrance. The Prince of Wales, later King Edward VII, had a private suite here, and paid several calls on Lillie Langtry when she was staying at the hotel in the years between 1877 and 1890. In the 1920s, the greatest crowds ever assembled on the beach at Saltburn, estimated at some 30,000 people, watched motor cars racing across the sands.

In 1959 Saltburn was the starting point for the morning 'Tees-Thames' restaurant car train to London, returning to Saltburn as the 1735 from King's Cross, the only through restaurant car train that British Rail operated each weekday to this resort on the North Yorkshire coast. Although popular with business people who enjoyed leisurely breakfasts and dinners en route, this convenient through train had a relatively short life, and was withdrawn at the end of 1962.

From Saltburn we take the train back to Marske and Redcar where sand dunes lead to the mouth of the Tees, on one of the most industrialized coastlines in Britain, extending northwards to the Tyne. At Middlesbrough we change trains, continuing up the coast to Seaton Carew, first developed by wealthy Quakers from Darlington, who in 1783 organized coach trips to the sands bordering Hartlepool Bay.

Hartlepool, named after the wild harts that roamed nearby forests, extends for several miles along the shore of Hartlepool Bay and its harbour contains an attractive historic quay portraying maritime life as it was at the time of Trafalgar. One of the most interesting exhibits is HMS Trincomalee, built in 1817, the oldest authentic British warship still afloat. Nearby is the restored paddle steamer 'Wingfield Castle'.

Between Hartlepool and Seaham, the coastline is spoilt by millions of tons of coal waste. Before the railway arrived, Lord Byron came to Seaham in 1815 to marry Anne Isabella Millbanke, the daughter of the Lord of the Manor. They were married in the drawing room of Seaham Hall (now a hospital), and then set off for their honeymoon at Croft-on-Tees, near Darlington.

Sunderland's seaside lies north of the River Wear at Seaburn, where the railway line veers away from the coast to join the east coast main line at Newcastle, whose station was opened by Queen Victoria on 29 August 1850, amid great celebrations to mark the occasion. The bills for the festivities, including a huge banquet, were sent to Buckingham Palace for payment. This so incensed the Queen that she vowed never to look upon Newcastle again, ordering her staff to close the view from her window whenever the Royal Train passed through the station.

Some years later, when her train from Portsmouth to Scotland was routed by the GWR via the industrial cities of Birmingham and Wolverhampton, she again ordered her servants to shut out the view, for she could not bear to see the grime and poverty in which so many of her loyal subjects had to live.

But we are here to celebrate. On 27 August 1936, the highest speed ever achieved by a steam train in scheduled service was recorded by A4 Class locomotive 'Silver Fox' from Newcastle to King's Cross. The train was the famous 'Silver Jubilee', and the circumstances, as recounted by O.S. Nock, were unusual. Just past Grantham, locomotive inspector Edward Thompson went through the tender to the footplate and stood behind driver Haygreen, saying: "Top a hundred" - with 154 fare-paying passengers on board, some in the restaurant car enjoying their meal.

Late Victorian scene at Saltburn, one of the first of many seaside towns created by the coming of the railway. It owed its development to Henry Pease, a Quaker ironmaster and director of the Stockton & Darlington Railway, who intended the resort to be a 'celestial city' for the recuperation of Teesside ironworkers. (NRM - Tripp22)

This order caught both the driver and fireman unprepared, since the official 'Silver Jubilee' handbook shows an average speed of 74.3 mph between Grantham and Peterborough. From 70 mph at Stoke summit, 100 miles from London, the train accelerated to 85 mph at Corby and reached a maximum of 113 mph at milepost 86, giving passengers the ride of their lives in setting the speed record for a steam train in revenue-earning service. Later the driver said : "If only the inspector had told me earlier what he wanted", as he was convinced that a greater speed could have been achieved with more advance notice.

A train on the Tyne & Wear metro from Newcastle Central station takes us to beaches easily accessible from stations at Tynemouth, Cullercoats, and Whitley Bay. The suburban area of Tynemouth is spread along the top of steep cliffs, with a series of beaches below, first at Prior's Haven, then King Edward's Bay and Long Sands, leading to Cullercoats, a small sandy cove between two stone breakwaters.

Although parts of this coast have been ravaged by industry, there are places where the shoreline is unspoilt, with beaches among the most under-rated in the country. Whitley Bay is the main seaside resort near to Tyneside towns, and attracts large crowds during summer weekends. It has a fine beach stretching for nearly two miles below steep slopes, with clean soft sands leading to a rock-studded shore where St Mary's Island and lighthouse mark the northern end of the bay.

The Tyne marks a boundary between Durham and Northumberland. After departure from Newcastle on the east coast main line, the next sighting of the sea is near Alnmouth, where the train speeds around a curve to reveal an attractive seaside town on the headland. Frequent excursion trains came to Alnmouth from Newcastle in the heydays of the 1920s and 1930s, but most trains today hurtle through Alnmouth, and only a brief glimpse of the sea is possible from the carriage window.

In the railway renaissance of the 1990s, the Aln Valley Railway project was launched at Alnwick Castle on 24 February 1997 to rebuild and operate the three-mile branch line from Alnmouth to Alnwick, linking coast to castle. With a grant of £500,000 from the European Regional Development Fund, this will probably be the last standard-gauge revival project in Britain before the new millennium.

Railway history in Alnwick dates back to 1809 when a horse-drawn coal 'train' ran between Shilbottle Colliery and the town. Passenger train services started in 1850, and prospects of royal visits to the castle, inhabited by successive

Dukes of Northumberland, resulted in a grand new station at Alnwick in 1887.

The estuary of the river Aln changed direction into the North Sea in 1806, stranding Alnmouth's Saxon church among sandhills on the southern shore. Only the ancient foundations remain, and in summer sunshine the sands provide visitors with a quiet place to enjoy the seascapes, or to watch pleasure boats on the estuary.

Leaving Alnmouth, the train heads inland again towards Berwick-upon-Tweed, passing close to the village of Beal, where the main street leads towards Holy Island, also named Lindisfarne, one of the cradles of Christianity in England. The causeway crosses two miles of sand and mud at low tide to reach the island.

At high tide this causeway is covered by the sea, and tidal currents are dangerous. The castle was built c.1550, and restored in 1900 as a private dwelling. The ruins of the 11th century priory nearby are open to the public. Just south of Beal the railway line comes closest to the castle, and on a clear day the distant view may be enjoyed for several miles.

Holy Island is seven miles northwest of the Farne Islands, thirty in number, on which the greatest number of breeding grey seals in Britain are to be found. The furthest island, Longstone, was where Grace Darling, the lighthouse keeper's daughter, heroically rescued the crew from the stricken 'Forfarshire' in 1838. The nearest mainland villages are Seahouses and Bamburgh, whose castle is one of the most impressive on this coast. In Bamburgh's churchyard is the shrine-like tomb of Grace Darling, commemorating her bravery.

The approach to Berwick-upon-Tweed from the south is far more interesting by train than by car, for the line hugs the coast for several miles, while the road goes inland. Two bridges and a viaduct now span the Tweed: an old 17th century bridge, and a 1925 bridge alongside, while further upstream is Robert Stephenson's famous Royal Border viaduct of 1850. This was opened by Queen Victoria on the same day she opened Newcastle station, where George Stephenson had been honoured a few days earlier for his many contributions in building Britain's railways.

Berwick has fine medieval walls, vital defences during the conflicts between England and Scotland from 1147 to 1482, when the town changed hands fourteen times. While the walls have been well preserved, there is not much left of the castle built by Edward I, which was almost completely demolished when the railway station was built.

This historic town has been plundered, captured, burnt, rebuilt, besieged and recaptured on several occasions. It has seen massacres and been starved into surrender by both sides; no other place on this coast has been subjected to so much violence and slaughter over the centuries.

The border between England and Scotland was first established along the River Tweed in 1157, and for some distance west of Berwick it follows the river inland. But three miles before the Tweed flows into Berwick, the boundary line heads north then east to reach the coast north of Marshall Meadows Bay. Thus Berwick has a border girdle of three miles beyond the town to leave no doubt that its citizens must pay their taxes to Northumbria County Council.

Scotland's East and North coasts

**From scenes like these old Scotia's grandeur springs
that makes her loved at home, revered abroad.**

Robert Burns (1759-1796)

Scotland has 30,000 miles of roads and only 1,400 miles of railway routes, so an occasional journey by road may be required to reach some of the interesting places along this coast, since Dunbar is the only station near the sea on the east coast main line between Berwick- upon-Tweed and Edinburgh, a distance of 58 miles. There is a five-mile branch line from Drem to North Berwick, but most express trains from the south do not stop at Drem or Dunbar. To reach these stations it is usually necessary to take a train from Edinburgh (Waverley).

Between Berwick-upon-Tweed and the Firth of Forth lies one of Britain's most precipitous coastlines. As the train speeds north across the border, there is a brief glimpse of the sea near Burnmouth before we head inland to avoid cliffs and headlands guarded by ancient castles facing stormy waters of the North Sea.

Four miles beyond Burnmouth is Coldingham Bay, leading to St Abb's, a small fishing village protected from northwest winds by St Abb's Head. The cliffs near here rise to almost 400ft and are among the highest on the east coast of Britain. Ahead is Fast Castle, a battered stone fortress dating from the 16th century, joined to the mainland by a narrow neck of land. Access to the ruins is by a footpath along the cliffs from St Abb's Head, or from Redheugh Beach to the west, up the slopes of Telegraph Hill. The castle was stormed by the English in 1547 and retaken by the Scots two years later. In Sir Walter Scott's 'The Bride of Lammermuir', Fast Castle is 'Wolf's Crag', the tower of Edgar of Ravenswood.

Near Cove Harbour the main line approaches the coast, heading for Dunbar, which developed as a holiday resort after the railway arrived in the 1850s, bringing the town within easy reach of Edinburgh, 28 miles away. In 1842, when the harbour was blasted from the rocky shore, most of Dunbar Castle was destroyed. A few ruins remain to remind us of the town's sieges, and that its name means 'fort on the point', where Cromwell's army battled Scottish covenanters in 1650. The great conservationist John Muir was born here in 1838, emigrating to America and founding the first national park there in 1890.

From Dunbar station there are pleasant walks to the sea front, and westwards to Belhaven Beach and Tyne Sands. Beyond these sands it is easier to reach interesting local coastal areas from North Berwick station.

Approaching North Berwick by train, a massive conical hill called the Law (613ft) dominates the scene, and in fine weather provides good views from its summit. When the branch line from Drem was built, North Berwick rapidly became a fashionable seaside resort and residential area for those who worked in Edinburgh and wished to live beside the sea.

The town's tree-lined Quality Street leads to a small, snug harbour flanked by beaches where the sands are bordered by outcrops of rock and low-tide pools. In the summer there are boat trips to Bass Rock, Tantallon Castle, and other points of interest along the coast, such as the small islands of Fidra, Lamb, and Eyebroughty, all bird sanctuaries.

Tantallon Castle, built on the edge of a sheer cliff and protected inland by a massive rampart and ditch, is three miles east of North Berwick. The castle was built c.1375 as a fortified home of the Douglas clan, frequently attacked during the turbulent years of clan wars, and besieged for the last time

in 1651 by the English under General Monk. The best view of Tantallon (which sounds as if it should be in Cornwall), is obtained from a small cove to the south of the castle.

Gin Head, close to Tantallon Castle, is the nearest point of land to Bass Rock, just over a mile out to sea and almost 350ft high. It was a religious retreat in the 7th century, then a fortress and prison, and now has a lighthouse to guide ships safely past this hazardous part of the coast.

From North Berwick we take the train to Edinburgh, heading towards the Firth of Forth, known long ago as the Scottish Sea. Centuries of industrial development and pollution along the south shore between Seton Sands and Edinburgh have left their mark, giving a grey tinge to beaches at Cockenzie, Prestonpans, and Musselburgh. It was at Prestonpans that Bonnie Prince Charlie won his greatest victory over the English in 1745.

The train sprints through the outskirts of Edinburgh and enters Waverley station below Princes Street, one of Britain's most famous and beautiful boulevards. Nearby are the National Gallery, Scott Memorial, Castle, St Giles' Cathedral, Parliament House, and several excellent museums. Henry James considered Scotland equal to Greece in its beauty, music, and historic monuments, with Edinburgh the Athens of the north. The skyline around Waverley station is of great historic and architectural interest, and well worth viewing by taking a stroll through the public gardens on both sides of Waverley while waiting for a train at Britain's largest railway station.

There is so much to see in Edinburgh that a week is hardly enough to enjoy its many handsome buildings, fine parks and gardens, places of historic interest, panoramic views from the

Passengers look distinctly scarce as a train for Drem prepares to leave North Berwick in July 1954. Lack of traffic plagued this branch from the outset, although there was a period when the town's good beaches and bracing air brought family holiday-makers flocking to the resort. As was so often the case in Scotland, golf was also a major attraction with two courses being opened shortly after the arrival of the railway. (T.J. Edgington)

hills, and to sample the fine shops and restaurants along Princes Street and the 'Royal Mile'. But we have a long way to go by rail around the coasts of Britain, so after a stroll through the gardens above the tracks, we board a train to Aberdeen.

From Edinburgh, the train speeds towards the famous Forth Bridge, whose approaches give fine views over the waters of the Firth of Forth, and across to the coastline of Fife. When the train reaches the massive cantilever spans, the scene is partially obstructed by all the steelwork, so it is best to be prepared for a fast entry on to the bridge itself in order to see as much as possible of the Firth from the viaduct leading to the main spans. When floodlit at night, the bridge is a grand sight from either shore.

It took seven years (1883-1890) to build the Forth Bridge, which completed a rail link between the Lothians and Fife that had been promoted for over half a century. Lessons learned in the tragic Tay railway bridge disaster influenced the design and construction of this gigantic cantilever structure, one of the most impressive rail bridges in the world. A tunnel under the Forth had been proposed in 1805, but for another 159 years the vehicle ferries continued to provide a vital link

CAPE WRATH

DUNNET HEAD

DUNCANSBY HEAD
+ *John o'Groats*

Scrabster
+
Thurso

SINCLAIR'S BAY

Georgemas •

• Wick

Altnabreac • Scotscalder •

Forsinard •

○ *Lybster*

Kinbrace •

Scaraben
(2054 ft) +

LOCH SHIN

Kildonan •

Helmsdale •

Rogart •

Brora •

+ *Dunrobin Castle*

Invershin • Lairg •

Golspie

Culrain • *Loch Fleet* +

○ *Dornoch*

Ardgay •

Tain •

Lochluichart •

Ben Wyvis
(3429 ft) + Invergordon •

Lossiemouth ○

Fraserburgh

Garve • *Ben Wyvis* Alness •

Findhorn

Banff ○ St Combs ○

Strathpeffer ○

Dingwall • BLACK ISLE

Nairn • +
Forres •

Elgin •

○ PETERHEAD

Muir of Ord •

Keith •

+ *Bullers of Buchan*

INVERNESS + *Culloden*

Huntly •

Slochd Summit +
(1315 ft)

Grantown-on-Spey

Insch •

Carrbridge •

Inverurie •

+ *Sands of Forvie*

Aviemore • ▲ STRATHSPEY STEAM RAILWAY

Dyce •

ABERDEEN ■

Balmoral
Braemar + ○ *Ballater*

Kingussie •

Newtonmore •

Stonehaven •

• Dalwhinnie

○ *Inverbervie*

+ *Druimuachdar Summit (1484 ft)*

• Blair Atholl

+ *Pass of Killiecrankie*

Montrose •

■ PITLOCHRY

Broughty Ferry •
Arbroath •
Carnoustie •

Dunkeld &
Birnam •

DUNDEE ■

Golf Street •
Barry Links •

TAY

Monifieth •

Leuchars •

PERTH ■

ST ANDREWS

Lochty ▲

Largo ○

Kirkcaldy
Kinghorn

Earls
Ferry ○

North Berwick •

BASS ROCK

Burntisland
Aberdour •

INCHCOLM

FORTH BRIDGE ▼

• *Tantallon Castle*
Dunbar •

Bo'ness ▲

Cove Harbour
+ *Fast Castle*

EDINBURGH

Prestonpans •

• Drem

+
ST ABB'S HEAD
+ *Coldingham Bay*

○ *Burnmouth*

SCOTLAND

■ BERWICK-UPON-
TWEED

N

LEGEND

■ RAILTRACK STATION

• FORMER STATION

○ FORMER STATION

▲ PRESERVED
STANDARD GAUGE

▽ NARROW GAUGE

+ PLACES NAMED IN TEXT

ENGLAND

0   10   20   30   40   50   60

MILES

The incomparable Forth Bridge, photographed in 1957 before its majesty was dented by the building of the parallel road bridge. A local for Stirling is heading across the massive cantilever spans as the ferry William Whitelaw *waits patiently at the ramp. (Colour-Rail/D.A. Kelso)*

across the Firth until the road bridge was completed in 1964.

The Fife peninsula which separates the Firths of Forth and Tay was once described as "a beggar's mantle fringed with gold," for there is a great concentration of population, industry and wealth along the two Firths. Several small islands dot the Firth, and of these Inchcolm is the most interesting, with its well-preserved abbey of St Colm, accessible to visitors by boat from Aberdour. In Shakespeare's 'Macbeth', Inchcolm is mentioned in as "an island close to heaven" while elsewhere it has been described as "the Iona of the east".

In Victorian times, Aberdour was a favourite retreat for Edinburgh businessmen who travelled from the city by train to their seashore villas, built facing south and protected from north winds by trees on the hills behind them. Aberdour station is noted for its fine floral displays, and the southern shores of Fife are Scotland's 'Riviera', where small sheltered bays face the sun for most of the day.

From 1850 to 1890, Burntisland was the northern terminus of the Firth of Forth rail ferry, the first in the world, an example of the abundant inventive genius that has flourished for centuries in Scotland. Along Pettycur Bay there is a fine crescent beach near Kinghorn, and at Kirkcaldy the train leaves the coast, heading north across Fife, stopping at Leuchars, the nearest station to St Andrews, one of Britain's most historic and mellow coastal resorts, whose university is the oldest in Scotland.

St Andrews proudly displays its glories and patrimony from medieval times, when it was the ecclesiastical capital of Scotland. The cathedral was founded in 1171 and completed seventy years later, but three centuries of neglect after the Reformation brought it to ruin. Much of the dressed stone was used to build secular structures in the town until 1826, when a preservation order was finally issued. Today, the lofty remains of the medieval cathedral and priory on a hill overlooking the harbour form one of the most impressive historic sites in Britain, recalling a catholic Scotland of long ago.

A place of pilgrimage for golfers from all over the world, St Andrews welcomed kings and bishops who played here long before the club was founded in 1754. There is an air of grandeur in the wide sweep of St Andrews Bay, where sea breezes have a uniquely Scottish tang. The shoreline to the east of the town is rocky, while at the other end of St Andrews Bay the West Sands extend for two miles to the mouth of the Eden estuary.

One of the many attractions of St Andrews is its remoteness from industrial landscapes laced by motorways. Six miles south of the resort is a short length of preserved railway track owned by the Lochty Private Railway, on which the A4 Class Pacific locomotive 'Union of South Africa' operated under private ownership. In recent years this paradigm of stream-lined locomotives has shown its abundant power in steam excursions on several main lines around Britain.

On 25 March 1967, during the final hurrah of main line steam in Scotland, the 'Union of South Africa' hauled an eighteen-coach train over Druimuachdar summit on the main line between Pitlochry and Aviemore, reaching speeds of up to 80 mph en route. It was estimated that the locomotive developed some 2,000 hp, demonstrating the power that could be generated by manual effort in heaving coal on to the firebed as the train climbed up and over the line summit.

From Leuchars, we travel north to the second Tay Bridge, built in 1887 to replace one that collapsed while a passenger train was crossing during a gale eight years earlier. Some of the remains of the piers of the first bridge may still be seen as the train crosses the spans to Dundee, Scotland's fourth largest city.

Today, in the dominant high-tech industrial age, more than 1,300 acres of public parks and gardens provide peaceful green oases overlooked by the Dundee Law, a volcanic hill 571ft high, from whose summit there are fine views of the Firth of Tay, and the coasts of Fife and Angus. Among all the modern construction, there are some interesting Victorian and Georgian buildings in Dundee, a city with considerable historic interest, and civic pride.

Spanned by rail and road bridges, the wide Firth of Tay provides Dundee with a natural deep-water harbour, one of the best on this part of the coast. The sea's influence reaches 23 miles up the Tay to Perth, the great Highland hub for railway journeys north to Inverness, east to Aberdeen, south to Edinburgh, and west to Glasgow.

The fastest, and certainly the most spectacular railway route north to Inverness is from Perth through the mountains to the sea, so we will take a quick return trip on this important main line before resuming our travels up the coast from Dundee to Aberdeen, then onwards through Elgin and Nairn to the Moray Firth, entering Inverness via the coastal route.

The station at Perth dates from 1850, when it served trains of the Highland, Caledonian, and North British Railways. On 7 August 1888, five days before the 'Glorious Twelfth', the early morning train from Perth to Inverness comprised a total of 37 carriages, including passenger coaches, sleeping cars, saloons, horseboxes, and vans from ten railway companies all over Britain. Three locomotives were required, and it is not surprising that after climbing to the line summit at Druimuachdar, the train was 72 minutes late at Kingussie, with Slochd summit still ahead. This was one of the longest passenger trains ever to run over these two mountain passes.

On 11 August 1912, the eve of the 'Glorious Twelfth', over 800 coaches of Britain's railway companies passed through Perth station with passengers, horses and hounds, en route to Highland estates for the traditional shooting parties, which were then at their peak. Such was the importance of Perth during those great years of highland railway travel that it is difficult to visualize the busy Victorian and Edwardian scenes in what is now a relatively quiet passenger station for most of the day.

Not far from Perth station are some pleasant walks along the west bank of the Tay, Scotland's longest river (117 miles). To the east stands Kinnoul's wooded hill (728ft), one of the best natural viewpoints from any urban area in Scotland, with sweeping views of Perth and the Tay, as well as a panorama of hills on the horizon.

Perth was one of Queen Victoria's favourite station stops on her many railway journeys to and from Balmoral. In her lifetime of rail travel, she refused to eat a meal cooked on the train, and by the time the royal party from the south reached Perth, everyone was very hungry. Large breakfasts were prepared at the Station Hotel for those travelling in the royal entourage, while the Queen usually took her meal in the privacy of the royal waiting room at the station.

Today, well-appointed station hotels at Perth and Inverness provide comfortable accommodation and an opportunity to enjoy some Victorian ambience as well as modern facilities, choice Scottish cuisine, and the warm welcome that awaits all guests at a highland hotel. At Inverness, when the time comes to leave for the south on the 'Highland Chieftain', there is always time to enjoy a full Scottish breakfast in the hotel dining room at 0700 and walk from the lobby to the train for departure at 0755.

We now leave Perth for our trip through the mountains to Inverness, heading up the Tay valley to Dunkeld & Birnam. William Shakespeare stayed at Dunkeld in 1601 on a journey to the north of Scotland with his players, and it was near Birnam Wood that he learned about King Macbeth, and later wove the story into one of his finest plays.

Pitlochry, with its admirable setting in the Tummel valley, is the tourist centre for this part of the Highlands. Ahead is the Pass of Killiecrankie where the River Garry cascades through a narrow gorge, famous for the 'Soldier's Leap' across a seventeen foot gap during a battle here in 1689. Through the train window, this dramatic spot may be seen briefly on the left side just before the train plunges into Killiecrankie tunnel.

After leaving Blair Atholl station, with its famous white castle on the right, a long climb commences to reach Britain's highest main line railway summit at Druimuachdar (1,484ft). This is a route to enjoy, regardless of the weather, which can change quickly in the mountain passes. With today's diesel trains, the climb from either direction is smooth and seemingly effortless, especially on board the 'Highland Chieftain', the only weekday InterCity 125 train from London (1200) to Inverness (2006).

Between Blair Atholl and Culloden Moor there are 27 miles of main line above 1,000ft. At the pass of Druimuachdar, marked by a summit board on the left, the train leaves Perthshire and enters Inverness-shire, descending through Dalwhinnie, Newtonmore, and Kingussie to Aviemore, where the Strathspey Railway operates the country's most northerly standard-gauge heritage line, part of the original main line from Perth to Inverness, before the present shorter route via Slochd summit (1,315ft) was built.

Trains on the Strathspey Railway run from Aviemore station along the Spey for five miles to Boat of Garten, on a section of the 35 mile line to Craigellachie which served several whisky distilleries for which the Spey region remains world-famous. From Aviemore the train climbs for ten miles through Carrbridge to Sloch summit, then it is downhill most of the way to Inverness, with fine views from the viaducts across the rivers Findhorn and Nairn before crossing Culloden viaduct on the approach to Inverness.

We shall return to this highland capital via Aberdeen, and in the meantime take a southbound train back to Perth so that we may complete the popular Highland railway circuit formed by stations at Inverness, Perth, Dundee and Aberdeen.

From Perth the train travels along the Firth of Tay to Dundee, Broughty Ferry, Monifieth and Carnoustie, whose championship golf course beside the North Sea is acknowledged by many famous players as the finest in Britain, and one of the greatest in the world. There are three railway stations in two miles on the line to Aberdeen, the first at Barry Links, followed by Golf Street and Carnoustie, so this part of the coast is well served, whether it be to play golf on one of the many courses, or to explore nearby sandy shores.

Arbroath may claim a role as capital of Scotland. On 6 April 1320 a gathering of noblemen led by Robert the Bruce made a declaration of independence which was sent from Arbroath Abbey to the Pope at Avignon. When the famous Stone of Scone used during coronation ceremonies was taken from Westminster Abbey in 1951, it was discovered later on the high altar at Arbroath Abbey. Founded in the 12th century, the abbey is one of the most impressive ruins in Scotland and known to sailors as 'the Arbroath O', for a light that used to burn in a large circular window in the south transept as a navigational aid.

The coast to the north of Arbroath is wild and rocky, with cliffs and caves best seen from the sea in calm weather, for the tides can be very hazardous along this shoreline. Lunan Bay, eight miles from Arbroath, has a fine sandy beach over two miles long flanked by rocky headlands, while above stand the ruins of Red Castle. In the 16th century the formidable Lady Innermeath held this castle against a force led by her husband, who trapped her in the tower which he then set ablaze. She was saved by the timely arrival of an army commanded by the Provost of Dundee. Scotland's turbulent history throughout the ages is enriched by countless heroic deeds of its nobility.

Montrose is almost surrounded by salt water, and at high tide its basin becomes a 2,600 acre seawater lake. The town has many fine buildings and pleasant gardens, dating from the period when it was a winter resort for the rural aristocracy of Angus. At one time several railway lines radiated from Montrose, including a branch line along the coast to Inverbervie, which was used for overnight stabling of the 'Northern Belle' in the 1930s.

Between 1950 and 1972, Scotland lost nearly 4,000 miles of railway track from a total of 7,300 miles, suffering a greater proportion of closures than either England or Wales. Most of the scrapped Scottish railway track was exported from Montrose in the 1960s to feed steel furnaces in Belgium and the Netherlands.

Stonehaven was built where two rivers, Carron Water and Cowie Water, meet between rocky headlands. The ancient town, known as Old Steenie, was the creation of George Keith, 5th Earl Marischal, who also built the harbour. The new town of Stonehaven was founded in 1795, and by 1895 the harbour provided shelter to over 120 fishing vessels, which are now outnumbered by sleek yachts and pleasure craft. Three miles south of the station is Dunnottar Castle, built on a crag towering 160ft above the sea.

Of all Scotland's castles by the sea, Dunnottar is one of the most spectacular and formidable. Its landward approach is through a narrow rocky gorge, and it is easy to see how defenders inside the castle walls defied an English army for 8 months in 1651-52. Cromwell's troops attempted to capture the Scottish crown, sceptre, and sword of state which were hidden in the castle, but they were foiled by a fisherman's wife who smuggled them out in a basket, which was then hidden in Kinneff Church, six miles south.

Three miles north of Stonehaven the train travels near the sea for several miles, turning inland at Newtonhill, then back to the sea near Cove Bay before heading into Aberdeen, the largest seaside resort in Scotland, and Britain's third largest fishing port. This is the great granite city whose prosperity still depends upon the sea, whether it be oil, shipbuilding, or fish,

The power of the kirk!   The station buildings at the important fishing port of Fraserburgh attempted to mirror the nearby edifice but simply could not compete.   Seen here in 1954, the terminus was part of the now decimated network of the Great North of Scotland Railway. (T.J. Edgington)

which together contribute to make Aberdeen the economic capital of northern Britain. The city's charter dates from 1179, and a papal bull was obtained in 1494 for the creation of a university at Aberdeen, the fourth oldest in Britain.

The long sandy beach which stretches between the Dee and Don rivers is two miles from the railway station. North of the Don estuary, the beaches extend for a further ten miles, making Aberdeen a popular seaside resort, and even at the height of summer the beaches are rarely crowded. In addition, there are 3,000 acres of parks in and around Aberdeen, as well as many other amenities and attractions in this richly endowed city. In the western suburbs are the Rubislaw quarries, which for two centuries supplied most of the granite to build Aberdeen, and to pave the streets of many towns in Britain, leaving a vast hole 450ft deep in the ground when the quarries were closed in 1970.

At one time there were ten stations in 6.3 miles between Aberdeen and Dyce on the line to Inverness, and ten stations between Aberdeen and Peterculter (7.5 miles) on the former line along which royal trains passed on their way to Ballater for Balmoral. The last royal train left Ballater in October 1965, travelling in 'Queen's weather' (rain) on its way south, and when the line was lifted, 'royal sleepers' were sold to the public as souvenirs.

Aberdeen is well-served by trains from London, with the 'Aberdonian' as lineal descendant of the east coast expresses of 1895 which raced the rival west coast expresses to Scotland. When the Forth Bridge was completed in 1890 it opened up a much shorter east coast route and made competition for the lucrative passenger traffic more intense as trains raced to reach Aberdeen first. There was a close finish on several occasions, when east and west coast trains converged early in the morning at Kinnaber Junction, three miles north of Montrose. Whichever train was offered first to the signalman at Kinnaber got the right of way on the single northbound track, and led the race for the final 38 miles to Aberdeen.

It should be mentioned that the man on duty in the signal box at Kinnaber was employed by the Caledonian Railway, whose trains came in from the west coast main line. Of the 42 trains that raced from London to Aberdeen between 29 July and 21 August 1895, the west coast trains won all but two races, even though they had to travel 539.7 miles versus 523.2 miles by the east coast trains.

The scene as trains raced through the night from London to Scotland was described in the September 1888 issue of the Pall Mall Gazette thus:

"A foreigner taken on to the midnight platform at Shap in the nights of August would have been surprised to see five expresses roaring through within two hours, one laden with

'Horses and Carriages only', another full of beds and lucky people whose rest the North Western Railway will not allow to be broken by the entry of a single passenger between Euston and Perth, all five steaming without a stop from Preston to Carlisle.... Down the adjacent Eden valley he might almost have heard the three Midland night expresses, two sweeping without a stop from Skipton to Carlisle.... Away on the east coast, five Great Northern trains would be doing similar deeds."

The 'Aberdonian' received its official title in 1927, and was one of only four trains in Britain to retain its title throughout WW2 . In 1972 the 'Aberdonian' name was transferred to the noon departure from King's Cross, arriving in Aberdeen at 2109. After HSTs were introduced on the east coast main line in 1978, the noon 'Aberdonian' received its HSTs in the summer of 1979, immediately cutting 102 minutes from the timetable, including stops at Darlington, Newcastle, Edinburgh, and Dundee. The 1998/99 winter timetable listed the 'Northern Lights' as the fastest train from King's Cross to Aberdeen on weekdays, departing from King's Cross at 1030 and arriving in Aberdeen at 1731.

North of Aberdeen is one of the longest unbroken lines of sand dunes in the Highlands. At the Sands of Forvie, the top of the highest dune reaches 180ft above sea level. This is now part of a National Nature Reserve where large numbers of sea birds feed and breed. The ruins of a church which was once the centre of village life at Forvie may be seen in the sands two miles north of Newburgh Bar.

The farmlands of Buchan, as this northeast corner of Aberdeenshire is known, end suddenly north of Forvie Ness in a series of high cliffs linked by ravines. In fierce storms, waves rage against the cliffs and into the caves, notably at the Bullers of Buchan where there is a ravine 200ft deep and 50ft across, into which the sea bursts through a natural arch. When Dr Johnson and Boswell visited this 'monstrous cauldron' in 1773, the weather was so calm that a local boatman was able to row them in with ease and safety. The nearest railway station to this part of the coast is Dyce, twenty miles to the south.

Peterhead, Scotland's most easterly town, no longer has railway service, nor does Fraserburgh to the north.The sole surviving railway line to the north and west of Aberdeen runs inland through castle and whisky country to Elgin, once the hub of a busy railway network, where one branch line went north to the sea at Lossiemouth, terminus for the longest sleeping-car journey in Britain, a distance of 609 miles from King's Cross.

Other lines from Elgin went south along the Spey, west to Inverness, and two lines to the east, one along the Moray Firth shore, and the other through Keith and Huntly to Aberdeen. Only part of Elgin's former station remains, while the ruins of the great cathedral dominate the town and are well worth a visit, for it is considered to have had the finest design of all Scottish cathedrals.

Twelve miles to the west is Forres station, three miles from Findhorn Bay, and the quiet fishing and holiday village of Findhorn, once a busy port on what is known as the 'Banff-shire Riviera'. It is here that the 'Findhorn Garden' community was created to farm the sandy soil, nourished with organic materials to yield rich harvests of fruit and vegetables.

Nairn has an attractive railway station, opened in 1855, one mile south of beaches on each side of the estuary. To the east, fifteen miles of forest from Nairn to Burghead form the most thickly- wooded coastline in the British Isles. Most of the trees were planted in the 1920s to reclaim once-fertile land that was covered by sand deposited by storms of previous centuries. With its fine location on the Moray Firth, Nairn is a popular holiday resort, and from its shore there are good views across the Moray Firth to Black Isle, and on clear days the summit ridge of Ben Wyvis (3,433ft) may be seen, twenty miles away.

The popularity of Nairn as a holiday resort was due largely to Dr Grigor, who practised medicine here in the 1850s. He recommended the cool, dry summer climate to his patients, and by 1888 Nairn was firmly established in the directory of 'Baths and Wells of Europe', which described the town as a "flourishing watering place with first-rate arrangements." Just west of Nairn station is Balblair, site of the Duke of Cumberland's camp before he marched his army twelve miles to Culloden Moor where he defeated the brave Scottish clansmen on 16 April 1746.

It was a decisive victory for the well-equipped forces of George II, who outnumbered the 5,000 Scots by almost two to one, in a battle that lasted only an hour and destroyed all hopes of an English crown for Bonnie Prince Charlie. The graves of some 1,200 clansmen who died at Culloden in the last major battle on British soil are marked by cairns. Trains on the main line from Inverness to Perth pass less than a mile from the field of battle as they climb up through Culloden Moor and over the Findhorn viaduct to Slochd summit.

The Highland capital of Inverness is at the centre of an area of outstanding natural beauty, rich in history and legend. John Ruskin (1819-1900) described Inverness as "a jewel clasping the folds of the mountains to the blue zone of the sea," and to him the Beauly Firth was "one of the world's loveliest estuaries." Prime Minister Lloyd George made British political history here in 1921 by convening the first Cabinet meeting ever held outside London. He was in the Highlands, and saw no reason why he should leave, when his colleagues could easily take the train north and enjoy some fine Scottish hospitality and scenery while attending to the nation's business.

The Station Hotel at Inverness is convenient for those planning early departures or late arrivals by train. It opened in 1854, four years before arrival of the first express from London, and was the flagship hotel of the Highland Railway

TAYSIDE AND DEESIDE

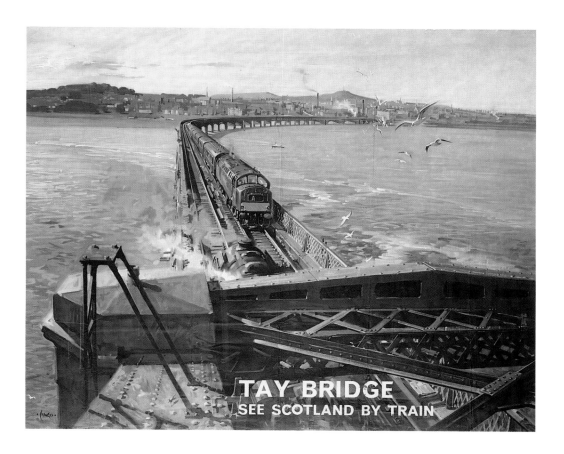

Terence Cuneo, 'the railway painter of the century', bravely climbed the high girders of the Tay Bridge in order to capture its impressive lines. The date was about 1957 when steam haulage was giving way to diesel. Dundee is in the background.

TAY BRIDGE
SEE SCOTLAND BY TRAIN

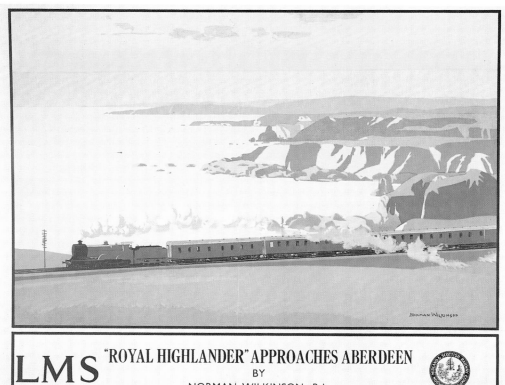

The 'Royal Highlander', a sleeping car express from London, runs along the coast as it approaches Aberdeen. The artist, Norman Wilkinson, was a noted marine painter who made a major contribution to the art of camouflage.
(NRM/Science & Society - 2)

LMS **"ROYAL HIGHLANDER" APPROACHES ABERDEEN**
BY
NORMAN WILKINSON, R.I.

Company, whose coat of arms may still be seen in the stained glass roundels of the Strathconon dining room. If you stay and dine here, you may well be served with silverware embossed with railway monograms, a nostalgic touch from the heydays of travel by train in the highlands from 1910 to 1939.

Inverness is the terminus from which trains depart for the Kyle of Lochalsh, Wick, Thurso, Aberdeen, Edinburgh, Glasgow, and the south. A week is needed to explore all rail routes radiating from this busy station, where hikers and climbers may be seen boarding a train to one of the lonely stations on the Kyle or Wick/Thurso lines in order to explore the far north, or to climb a 'Munro' (Scottish mountain whose summit is 3,000ft or higher) listed in the ScotRail Guide for the West and North Highland lines.

There was high drama in building Scotland's railways through the mountains to the coast, so before leaving Inverness let us pay homage to three remarkable men who dominated the highland railway scene in the nineteenth century, on whose routes we have already travelled, and along which we will be roaming by train for the next few days.

Joseph Mitchell was the great civil engineer of the Highland railway network and a cast plaque in Inverness station marks his achievements. Sir Alexander Matheson accumulated immense wealth abroad, and returned to devote his fortune to development of railways in his native land. Andrew Dougall was a fierce young man with a gift for organization, who came to Inverness from Perth to manage the railways that were financed under Matheson's fiscal leadership and built to Mitchell's visionary plans. The evidence of their collective efforts is on the tracks we take north, south, east and west out of Inverness station today.

Our first journey will be to Wick, 162 miles and over four hours by train from Inverness. On departure from Inverness, the train crosses the Ness on a bridge built in 1990 to replace the original stone structure destroyed by the river in full flood the previous winter. The train then slows to a crawl to cross the old Clachnaharry swing-bridge over the Caledonian canal which enables vessels from the west coast of Scotland to reach the Moray Firth and North Sea via Loch Lochy, the Great Glen, and Loch Ness, along a sixty-mile canal and loch waterway. We will see the other end of this canal at Banavie, on the line from Fort William to Mallaig.

The train now heads due west along the south shore of the Beauly Firth. On a clear day the views across the Firth to the north are superb, and are included among a personal selection of the finest sea views from the train in Britain (Appendix 4). To travel on this line in the Spring is to double the pleasure in viewing seascapes and landscapes before dense foliage obscures some of the scenery. At the far end of the Firth, the train turns nearly 180 degrees to cross the Beauly River and reach Muir of Ord station, the only railway station between Inverness and Dingwall.

Dingwall is the junction for the Kyle and Wick/Thurso lines. We will travel north to Wick first, then to Thurso before returning to Inverness or Dingwall for a train to the Kyle of Lochalsh. In contrast to the road and rail hub of Inverness, with its maze of busy streets and traffic, the town of Dingwall on the Cromarty Firth is a quiet and pleasant place for an overnight stay before boarding a train westwards to the coast.

The tranquillity at Dingwall station today is a far cry from the tumult of WW1, when thousands of military personnel en route to Invergordon and Scapa Flow were given refreshment here. It is recorded that 134,864 cups of tea were served by staff at Dingwall station during the four years of conflict. In both world wars the railway lines to Thurso and Wick were of great strategic importance in such famous sea battles such as Jutland in WW1, and the pursuit and sinking of the Bismarck in WW2.

From Dingwall the train to Wick and Thurso runs on the west side of Cromarty Firth to Alness, where in fine weather a huge monument may be seen high on a hill on the left side of the train. This triple arch is called 'The Gate of Negropatam', built by philanthropist Sir Hector Munro with local labour to relieve unemployment in the nineteenth century.

Three miles beyond Alness is Invergordon, at one time a large naval base, and scene of a Royal Navy mutiny in 1931 as a protest against pay cuts. Across Cromarty Firth is Black Isle, which is neither black nor an island. Its name derives from a climate so mild that snow rarely settles at ground level in winter, when nearby mountains are covered in white, and ploughed fields are usually black. From Invergordon, the train passes Nigg Bay, which at extreme low tide reveals over ten square miles of sands with several deep and dangerous channels.

Tain is the quiet and dignified centre of a rich farming area bounded by the firths of Cromarty and Dornoch. When the tide is out, a large sand and shingle beach stretches for over six miles from Ferry Point to the village of Inver on the south shore of the Dornoch Firth. One of the last great saints of the Celtic church, St Duthus, was born in Tain c.1000AD and died in Ireland in 1065. His remains and relics were finally brought back to Tain in 1253. From 1493 to 1514, King James IV made seven pilgimages to Tain, one of those rare places in Britain where time has not effaced marks of a medieval culture from the landscape we see today. In 1966 Tain marked its 900th anniversary as a royal burgh, and one of its roads is still known as the King's Causeway.

When builders of what became the Highland Railway to Wick and Thurso reached the Dornoch Firth, a crossing was proposed near Meikle Ferry, but money was not available to build a bridge across the wide firth. The Duke of Sutherland offered £42,500 to the railway company if it would take the line round to Lairg in order to open up the interior of his vast

estates. His proposal was accepted.

The route we take today is the Duke's choice, a forty-mile detour up the Firth and inland to reach the sea again at Golspie. From Tain we head west for several miles along the south shore of Dornoch Firth, where wide expanses of bright water are rimmed by hills and woodland scenery, with the mountains of Sutherland in the distance.

At Ardgay the train heads inland, crossing the River Carron near Bonar Bridge to reach Culrain station, where Carbisdale Castle looms above the railway line and the River Oykel. This castle, maintained and operated by the Scottish Youth Hostel Association, is at one of the most isolated and dramatic sites in Britain, yet it still has a network railway station to serve hostellers.

On leaving Culrain, the train crosses the River Oykel on a high iron viaduct to Invershin. When this viaduct was completed in 1863, the railway provided the only river crossing for several miles, and issued tickets for one half-penny to take passengers by train from Culrain to Invershin. This was said to be the lowest fare between any two stations in Britain at that time.

After leaving Invershin the train climbs up the Shin gorge and across Achany Glen to Lairg station, near the southeast end of Loch Shin, the longest inland loch (seventeen miles) in the northern Highlands. To reach Lairg, the railway navvies had to blast uphill through solid rock, a difficult and expensive section of line to build. Nevertheless, the Duke of Sutherland paid the bills for the railway to force its way on his chosen

Furthest North. The small terminus at Thurso, photographed in 1992. The next station westwards is Kyle of Lochalsh, over 200 miles distant. (John Hadrill)

route through Lairg to reach his castle by the sea at Dunrobin.

Lairg station is at a crossroads of the northern Highlands, with roads leading to all four points of the compass, notably to harbours at Ullapool, Lochinver, and Kinlochbervie in western Sutherland, as well as to the extreme northwest tip of Scotland around Cape Wrath. The most northerly 'Munro' is fifteen miles from Cape Wrath, and was only recently awarded the accolade, for maps had shown Foinaven's summit as 2,890ft, until more accurate measurement showed a height of 3,000.25ft, just enough to add it to the official list of Munros.

From Lairg, the train heads eastwards down Strath Fleet to the sea, which at high tide reaches up Loch Fleet to the railway embankment. On the opposite shore of the loch is Skelbo Castle, and while Loch Fleet may not compare in grandeur with other lochs on the west coast, nor with the great firths to the south, it has a rare natural beauty.

When the Highland Railway extended its line into Sutherland and Caithness in the 1870s, a causeway was built to carry a branch railway past Loch Fleet, south of Golspie, to reach the town of Dornoch. The railway has long gone, and the nearest station is now Golspie, seven miles by sea and eleven by road from Dornoch, but we will make a brief visit to Sutherland's county town, with its attractive beaches and royal golf course

SCOTTISH BYWAYS

Few railways have seen a more drastic reduction of their network than the Great North of Scotland, serving sparsely populated country north of Aberdeen and east of Inverness. The six-mile branch from Tillynaught to the small coastal port of Banff was closed to passengers in 1964, shortly after this photograph was taken of 2MT 78045 waiting to leave the terminus with its neat overall timber roof. (David Sutcliffe)

Gourdon, on the branch from Montrose to Inverbervie, was often used to provide a quiet overnight stop for the LNER 'Northern Belle' cruise train. In more recent times, the pick-up goods is heading south away from the harbour in July 1964.(M. Mensing/Colour-Rail SC599)

Largo, on the straggling line along the Fife coast from Thornton Junction to Leuchars Junction via St Andrews. B1 61343 is crossing the viaduct over the harbour with a through train from Crail to Edinburgh. (Colour-Rail SC639)

The Banff branch passed close to the golf course, served from 1913 by its own halt. Sea, sand and sunshine form a memorable picture as a 4MT 2-6-4T leaves with a seven-coach train in June 1957. (T.B. Owen/Colour-Rail SC240)

End of the line. Lybster, terminus of a branch from Wick and at 935 miles the furthest point it was possible to travel by rail from Penzance. The branch ceased to feature in 'Britain's longest rail journey' when it was closed in 1944. (NRM - LGRP7872)

dating from 1616, the third oldest in the world.

Dornoch's magnificent cathedral dates from 1239, but a fire in 1570 left only the tower standing, so the building we see today is a splendid restoration sponsored by the Duchess of Sutherland in the 1830s. It is the most northerly cathedral on mainland Britain, and a great ecclesiastical treasure-house, elegantly restored in all its glory.

A stone on the southern edge of the town marks the spot where Scotland's last witch was burned in 1722. Ten miles to the west is Skibo Castle, Andrew Carnegie's gift to himself after giving libraries to three thousand towns in Britain and North America. Near Dornoch's parish church, the tower of the medieval castle built for the Bishops of Caithness has served as a tollbooth, courthouse, and prison. It is now part of the Dornoch Castle Hotel.

The train reaches the sea again near Golspie, a town overlooked by a massive statue of the first Duke of Sutherland, standing two miles inland on the summit of Beinn a'Bhragaidh (1,293ft). A climb to the peak is rewarded not only by a closer look at the first duke, but also views in fine weather along the coastline and across Loch Fleet to the Dornoch Firth and beyond. The vast and mostly desolate county of Sutherland, which includes parts of Scotland's north, west, and east coasts, is Europe's most sparsely-populated countryside.

Golspie was a small fishing port in Victorian times and is now a tourist centre, with a beach that extends south for three miles to the entrance of Loch Fleet. The town has prospered as a place of business for the estates of successive Dukes of Sutherland, whose lands extend from the North Sea to the Atlantic.

The jewel in the ducal crown is Dunrobin Castle, two miles north of Golspie station, and set in wooded parkland overlooking the sea, with its own station for visitors to the castle in the summer season. Parts of the castle are more than 500 years old, but most of the structure dates from the 1920s, and from the train it has a magical appearance in its setting beside the sea, more like a palace in the French style than a Scots castle, the grandest residence on the northeast coast of Scotland.

When Queen Victoria visited Dunrobin Castle by train in

September 1872 as guest of the Duke of Sutherland, she was surprised to learn that he had driven the locomotive from Inverness to Bonar Bridge, where he joined the Queen in the royal saloon for the remainder of their journey to his private station.

Two locomotives and three coaches had been built to meet the private needs of this immensely rich duke, and he maintained the right to run his own train from Inverness northwards, having personally financed the line around the Dornoch Firth to Golspie and Helmsdale. Prior to national-ization of the railways in 1948, each successive Duke of Sutherland retained this right, and also the right to travel in the ducal carriage between Dunrobin and London.

The workers building his railway had great respect for the Duke of Sutherland. One 'navvy', striking his pick into the earth, and raising his ungainly form to admire His Grace who was driving a locomotive out of Dunrobin Station, said to his mate: "There, that's what I call a real duke! Why, there he is a-driving of his own engine on his own railroad, and a-burning of his own blessed coals!"

During the summer months, when the castle and grounds are open to the public, trains stop at Dunrobin station beside the castle gates, where for more than a century visitors have come to this great estate by the sea, with its stately castle and gardens. In June 1998 Lord Strathnaver opened a new museum at the station which was restored with help from the Small Station Society, a group formed to revive the beauty of Britain's lesser-known stations.

Three miles north of Dunrobin Castle is Strathsteven, where three young ravens were captured for the Duke of Sutherland in 1947, and sent by him to the Tower of London when the resident raven population had dwindled to one. According to legend, Britain will be invaded when the Tower's last raven dies.

Coal was mined at Brora as early as 1529, and in the 1870s the Duke of Sutherland developed several industries on his estates around Brora. First, he invested in the sinking of a new shaft for mining coal close to the seashore at Strathsteven, where he also established a brick and tile works. He then built a railway workshop in Brora to produce steam locomotives, although only one was completed before the premises were converted to other uses.

It is fitting that one of the most elegant and powerful steam locomotives ever built in Britain (1938) is named 'Duchess of Sutherland', preserved today for all to admire its handsome appearance and enormous latent power. In September 1998 it was announced that another locomotive of this class, the 'Duchess of Hamilton' would be rebuilt to its original stream-lined configuration in maroon and gold livery, 58 years after the last resplendent LMS streamliner disappeared under a dull coat of WW2 black. The project, sponsored by the National Railway Museum and VSOE is expected to take two years to complete.

The ScotRail West and North Highland Rail Guide titled 'Rathad Iarainn nan Eilean' (the Iron Road to the Isles) lists several interesting walks from Brora station, including a distillery where Sutherland's only single-malt whisky is made. Other stations on this line from which walks are described in the rail guide include Helmsdale, Invershin, Golspie and Invergordon.

Between Brora and Helmsdale the railway runs beside the sea for most of the ten-mile journey, giving close-up views of the sea and sands, with scattered shingle and rocks. In late afternoon sunshine, with hills hemmed by pebbled beaches, views from the train as it hugs the coast are outstanding.

Helmsdale nestles among steep hills where the fertile Strath of Kildonan meets the North Sea, from whose waters lobsters are taken into the harbour and put in a sea-water pound for grading and shipment. The railway can go no further north from here, for ahead is the formidable Ord of Caithness, over 400ft high, marking the county boundary between Sutherland and Caithness, which together form one of Europe's last wildernesses. Several place names on this coast relate to 12th century Viking settlements which for centuries had closer links with Scandinavia than with the rest of Scotland.

The hundred miles of rugged coastline in Caithness rank among the finest and most isolated in Britain. From Helmsdale, the train climbs westwards up the Strath of Kildonan, then north through mostly deserted moorland, with scattered hunting lodges served by stations at Kinbrace, Forsinard, Altnabreac and Scotscalder. In clear weather, Scaraben (2,054ft) can be seen to the right of the train, and there are also good views to the west as the train reaches the line summit of 708ft above sea level, midway between Forsinard and Altnabreac stations. Two miles east of Altnabreac, the long and gradual descent to Wick and Thurso begins, with a stop at Georgemass Junction to divide the train into separate sections for Wick or Thurso.

Only during heydays of the 'Glorious Twelfth', and in two world wars has this line seen heavy rail traffic, when trains from the south passed through this desolate part of Scotland either with shooting parties, or with military personnel en route to bases in the Orkneys and Shetlands. The greatest population here is of wild animals, and deer can often be seen from the train between Helmsdale and Scotscalder.

Railway travel in the extreme north of Scotland is not distin-guished by high speed, for the lines are almost entirely single track, with sharp curves and some steep gradients. To make the long journeys to Wick and Thurso more enjoyable in the 1930s, the LMS introduced restaurant cars on two of its titled trains, the 'Orcadian' and the 'John o'Groat'.

The 'Orcadian' ran all year from Inverness, and included a third-class overnight coach from Glasgow, whose

Inverness, a curious terminus with its forked platforms for the Wick/Kyle and Aberdeen/Perth lines. 5MT 45192 is ready to to take a train of 'blood and custard' stock west to Kyle of Lochalsh in July 1955. Note the tiny Station Frame signal-box.
(T.J. Edgington/Colour-Rail SC662)

Dornoch, only 29 miles from Inverness for a straight-flying seagull but 88 miles by rail, in part because the 'Far North' line detoured through Lairg to serve the vast estates of the Duke of Sutherland. The Dornoch branch was noted for its mixed trains, one of which is waiting to leave the terminus in July 1955 behind ex Highland Railway 0P 55053. (T.J. Edgington/Colour-Rail SC134)

D5330 prepares to leave the neat little station at Wick with the up mail. In LMS days this was the terminus for a third-class overnight coach from Glasgow, whose passengers endured a weary journey of fourteen hours for the 342 miles. (Colour-Rail DE1710)

Helmsdale, marking the point where the 'Far North' line turns inland and heads up the Strath of Kildonan to some of the most desolate moorland in Britain. 3P 54495 is shunting the yard in August 1960. (F.W. Shuttleworth/Colour-Rail SC840)

passengers endured a weary journey of fourteen hours for the 342 miles from Glasgow to Wick. They did, however, have plenty of time to enjoy meals in the restaurant car before it was detached at Georgemas Junction. The 'Orcadian' also included through coaches from Inverness to Thurso, justifying its title by connecting with the ferry from Scrabster harbour to the Orkneys.

The 'John o'Groat' ran in summer only and included restaurant car service all the way to Wick, the most northerly point reached by a restaurant car in Britain. Only 23 minutes of latitude prevent Thurso from claiming to be the most northerly railway station in the British Commonwealth. This distinction is held by the rail terminus at Churchill on the shore of Hudson Bay in Canada.

Robert Louis Stevenson described Wick as "the bleakest of God's towns". His father, a civil engineer, had built a new breakwater here, and this collapsed in a violent storm, so perhaps his son's judgment was influenced by the catastrophe, which brought criticism upon his father. The fickle weather can make or mar a visit here, and if the sun is shining on the town it is a pleasant place for a stroll down to the harbour, or for a walk around Wick Bay to South Head and the Castle of Old Wick, two miles south of the station.

In October 1998 the first preserved main line steam train for more than 35 years brought a full load of railway enthusiasts to Wick and Thurso. The train consisted of seven immaculately restored coaches in classic LMS maroon and gold livery which sparkled in the autumn sunshine as long white plumes of steam floated above the single-line track along some of Scotland's most impressive coastal scenery between Helmsdale and Golspie.

The road from Wick to John o'Groats passes close to Sinclair's Bay, which at low tide has a three mile sandy beach, the longest on the Caithness coast, and one of the oldest inhabited houses in Scotland (Ackergill Tower). John o'Groats cannot claim to be the most northerly point of land or to have the most northerly road in mainland Britain; these are located twelve miles to the west at Dunnet Head, two miles closer to the North Pole. But John o'Groats is such an attraction for travellers that few visitors stepping from the train at Thurso make the twelve-mile trek to the lighthouse at Dunnet Head,

300ft above waters of the Pentland Firth.

In 1990, when Peter de Savary became the first person to own properties at both Land's End and John o'Groats, there were plans to develop the site of Britain's most northerly hotel as a tourist mecca similar to Land's End. Fortunately, geography has placed John o'Groats at so great a distance from large centres of population compared to Land's End that this tip of Scotland remains relatively unscathed.

Dunnet Bay has two miles of sands and dunes, accessed from a road that follows the coast from Wick to Thurso. On a sunny day in Spring, the fertile countryside around Thurso, and displays of daffodils on the sea front, make us wonder whether we really are in the most northerly town on mainland Britain. There are times when Thurso, sheltered from strong westerlies by Holborn Head, can be as temperate as many coastal towns in the north of England, and a walk along the shore can, in favourable weather, be as enjoyable as one along the Yorkshire coast, 350 miles to the south.

Two miles northwest of Thurso is Scrabster Harbour, where ferries sail to the Orkneys and Shetlands, maintaining a vital lifeline to 25 inhabited islands out of a total of 170 islands and islets. Like inhabitants of the Isle of Wight and Cornwall, who do not consider themselves to be part of England, inhabitants of the Orkneys and Shetlands do not count themselves as part of Scotland until they leave the islands to go to the mainland. In both the Orkneys and Shetlands the largest islands are named Mainland, and at Kirkwall the great cathedral of St. Magnus stands proudly as the most northerly in Britain.

The coast west of Thurso and south from Cape Wrath forms a 500-mile barrier pierced by many large sea lochs fringed by menacing mountains which no railway has ever penetrated. Our next station westwards from Thurso is the Kyle of Lochalsh, 236 miles by train from Thurso, via Inverness. The wild and remote coastline between these stations is the least accessible in Britain by rail or road, with the greatest distance between any two adjacent coastal railway stations on the railway network.

We therefore return from Thurso to Inverness (or Dingwall) to take the train across Scotland on the spectacular Kyle Line to Skye, then southwards to visit some of the western isles that are easily accessible from railheads alongside Atlantic waters.

To the Western Isles

"I know where I'm going."

Title of 1945 film starring Wendy Hiller and Roger Livesey,
with evocative scenes of travel by train and boat to the Western Isles of Scotland.

Almost 800 islands and islets lie off the northern and western coasts of Scotland, from the Orkneys and Shetlands in the far north, to Ailsa Craig in the south. About 130 of these islands are inhabited, and several are served by ferries from railheads at Thurso, the Kyle of Lochalsh, Mallaig, Oban, Wemyss Bay, and Ardrossan.

The rail map of Scotland shows large gaps along its west coast, and as we start our travels to stations serving the western isles, we celebrate the survival of services to the Kyle of Lochalsh and Mallaig, both of which came under threat of closure in the 1970s. Fortunately, there are now increasing numbers of passengers travelling on what are regarded as the two most scenic railway routes to the sea in Britain.

Back in the Highland railway hub of Inverness after our journeys to Wick and Thurso, a walk beside the River Ness is always pleasing, with Inverness castle and museum on one side, and the cathedral on the other, while swift waters of the Ness flow beneath bridges that link east and west sides of Inverness, all within easy walking distance of the station.

Trains from Inverness to the Kyle of Lochalsh take 2.5 hours to cross Scotland from the North Sea to waters of the Atlantic Ocean, a journey along 82 miles of track that took 35 years to complete. Construction began in 1862, and the line was opened as far as Stromeferry on Loch Carron, ten miles short of the Kyle, on 10 August 1870.

Another 27 years were to pass before sufficient money could be found to complete the line from Loch Carron to the Kyle itself. On 2 November 1897, the first train to thread its way through rock cuttings on the final ten miles between Stromeferry and the Kyle of Lochalsh arrived at the new railway terminus, to be welcomed by a large crowd brought over by ferries from Skye to witness this historic event.

Four years of blasting through rock to a depth of 80ft in places, and construction of the rail terminus with berths for ferries, had cost the Highland Railway Company a total of £270,973 (about £25 million in 1999 values), of which the government contributed one-sixth. This is the most expensive ten miles of railway line to the sea ever built in Britain.

From Inverness to Dingwall we travel the same route as Wick/Thurso trains, described in the previous chapter. Just beyond Dingwall station, the Kyle line veers away from the Wick/Thurso line and heads west through the town, crossing the River Peffery and climbing to what was the junction for Strathpeffer Spa, described as "the sanatorium for the British Isles" after a visit to the spa by King Edward VII.

In the summers before WW1, a through coach for this popular Scottish spa was attached to the express from London to Inverness, and in 1911 the 'Strathpeffer Spa Express' left Aviemore every Tuesday, bypassing Inverness station and stopping only at Dingwall on its way to the spa, which was on the opposite side of the valley to the line we take to Kyle. But Strathpeffer, having first refused a railway, was one of the first to close after WW2, and the last train left the Spa station on 2 March 1946.

The Kyle train climbs up the north side of Strath Peffery to reach the first line summit (458ft) at Raven Rock, traditional meeting place of ravens on one day of the year, a variable date. The train then descends beside Loch Garve to Garve station, a passing place for some trains on the single track.

In 1890, six branch lines were proposed to link west coast

RAILS TO THE ISLES

The western end of the Kyle of Lochalsh line runs through stunning scenery alongside the tidal waters of Loch Carron. One of its more colourful moments occurred on 21 June 1960, when restored 'Jones Goods' 103 was used to work the early morning mixed train to Dingwall in connection with filming for the 'Railway Roundabout' television series. (Derek Cross/Colour-Rail P79)

The Isle of Skye forms an incomparable mountain backdrop to Kyle of Lochalsh station. Little has outwardly changed since the evening train to Inverness was photographed in May 1973, although in reality completion of the Skye Bridge in 1995 has brought huge changes to local life. (T.J. Edgington)

A Morris 8 GPO van and MacBraynes AEC lorry add a distinctive period touch in August 1959 as K2 61787 Loch Quoich arrives at Fort William. Today even the station has gone, to be replaced by a more utilitarian structure a little further up the line. (R.E. Toop/Colour-Rail SC326)

Morar, last station before Mallaig on the West Highland Extension Line, has a superb setting. The village is laid out almost as if on a model railway; among many features of interest are the petrol pumps of the tiny garage by the level crossing. In the background the Morar River runs down to the sea from Loch Morar, the deepest in Scotland. (A.A. Harper)

fishing ports with existing highland rail routes, and one of the proposed lines was from Garve to Ullapool, but it was never built. Two lines were completed: Fort William to Mallaig, and Stromeferry to the Kyle of Lochalsh. The other three unsuccessful proposals were for lines from Achnasheen to Aultbea; Lairg to Laxford; and Culrain to Lochinver.

From Garve, the train climbs to Corriemuillie Summit (429ft), descending to Lochluichart, whose original station was submerged in the construction of the Conon Valley hydroelectric dam in 1954, which raised the level of Loch Luichart by 25ft, flooding the old railway line for two miles. This was one of the first lochs in Scotland to be used for the supply of electricity to the Scottish power grid.

Further upstream, the train passes Loch a'Chulinn and Loch Achanalt to reach Achnasheen station, with its hotel, visited by Queen Victoria on one of her several Highland tours in September 1877. The landlord, Murdo McIver, was a devout Presbyterian, whose observance of the Sabbath was so scrupulous that when the Queen arrived by coach from Loch Maree one Sunday afternoon, he declined to provide fresh horses, and refused to post her mail. The Queen, upset and helpless, ate a plate of cold roast beef and retired early for the night.

Achnasheen ('field of storm') is the half-way station along this route. It used to be a passing place for trains, but they now meet at Strathcarron or Garve. Heading west from Achnasheen, the train climbs above Loch Gowan (to the right) and at Luib Summit (646ft) reaches the watershed of Scotland, where the River Carron flows west to the Atlantic Ocean, while the River Bran flows east to the North Sea.

Down through Glencarron Woods, with Carn Gorm (2,870ft) and Moruisg (3,026ft) on the left, and Carn Breac (2,223ft) on the right, the train stops on request at Achnashellach, one of three halts built as private stations at the insistence of landowners, who had at first opposed the railway, but who later wished to benefit from its proximity and convenient train services. The other two private railway stations were at Lochluichart (still open) and Glencarron (closed).

With the closure of Glencarron station in 1966, Achnashellach is now the nearest station for mountain climbers and hikers heading for the seven local 'Munros' listed in the ScotRail guide. The station nestles in a pleasant wooded glen, part of Achnashellach forest, with mountain peaks rising beyond the treetops. From here, the Carron valley widens as the train continues its descent to Strathcarron station at the head of Loch Carron, the great sea loch whose south shore carries the railway line to the Kyle of Lochalsh.

From Strathcarron, the train threads its way alongside the loch for sixteen miles, with fine views across the loch and over the Inner Sound to Skye. There are stations at Attadale, Stromeferry (the original terminus), Duncraig, Plockton, and

Duirinish, before reaching the terminus at Kyle. Plockton is an attractive village in its setting beside the loch shore, with a fine aspect of mountains, woodlands and islets across the water. It is a popular sailing centre, and from the train one can often see yachts and dinghies sailing or moored near the loch shore.

This section of the route always reveals fresh scenes as tide, wind and weather change along a fascinating coast-to-coast line that is visually rewarding for all of its 82 miles. Wild life abounds, and sea otters or perhaps grey seals can be seen from the train as it travels beside the waters of Loch Carron, while birds of prey soar above the forests. On the loch shores, herons and other waders search for food in tidal waters.

After leaving Plockton station, the train clings to the edge of the sea, with views across the Inner Sound to Skye, Raasay, Scalpay, and several smaller islands. Across Loch Carron's wide mouth, the hills and mountains rise above Applecross as the train rounds the shoreline, darting in and out of deep rock cuttings to reach Kyle of Lochalsh station.

A one mile channel separates Kyle station from Kyleakin on Skye. The crossing was made by Caledonian MacBrayne ferries until the controversial Skye Bridge was completed in 1995, closing down the ferry service. For almost a century, the ritual of arrival by train and a trip on the Skye ferry was enjoyed by countless visitors, who often made the crossing several times in one day to enjoy the sea views, as the ferry ride was free for those on foot.

When the line from Fort William to Mallaig was completed in 1901, passengers arriving at Kyle of Lochalsh station were also able to use Skye as a huge stepping-stone, taking (until 1995) the ferry across to Kyleakin, then island bus via Broadford to Armadale, and a ferry across the Sound of Sleat to Mallaig, terminus of the scenic West Highland Line from Glasgow and Fort William, thus completing what has become a classic railway circuit. Buses now provide the link between Kyle station and Skye.

Until WW2, the LMS operated two titled trains on the Kyle line to provide connections with ferries to and from Skye, and also with the steamship service between Kyle and Stornaway on the island of Lewis in the Outer Hebrides.

The first train in the morning from Kyle was the 'Lewisman', departing at 0505 with passengers from the overnight Hebridean ferry. At this early hour there was no restaurant car on the train, so passengers usually slept during the three-hour journey to Inverness, and had breakfast at the Station Hotel on arrival. Meanwhile, the 'Lewisman' was prepared for its return to Kyle at 1015, this time with a restaurant car, reaching Kyle at 1340.

The other titled train between Inverness and Kyle was the 'Hebridean', whose restaurant car provided a full Scottish breakfast on departure at 0725 from Inverness. This was especially appreciated by those who had sat up all night in the

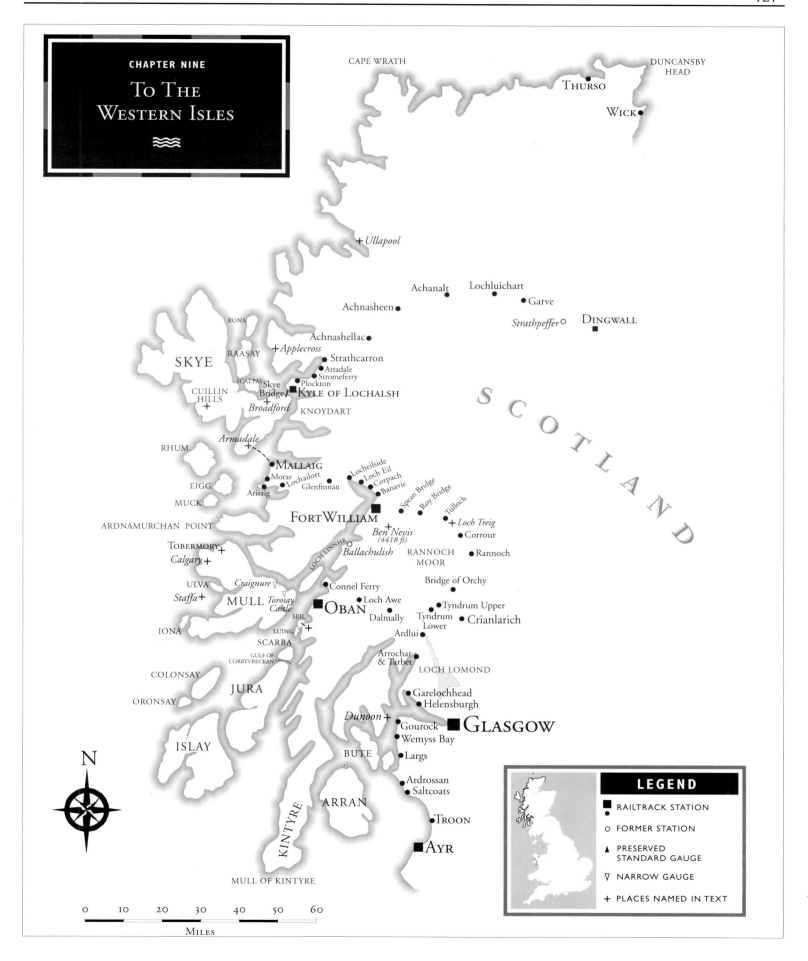

CHAPTER NINE

TO THE
WESTERN ISLES

≈≈≈

CAPE WRATH

DUNCANSBY
HEAD

● THURSO

● WICK

+ *Ullapool*

Achanalt ●   Lochluichart ●
                                        ● Garve
Achnasheen ●
                              Strathpeffer ○   ■ DINGWALL

RONA

Achnashellac ●

+ *Applecross*   ● Strathcarron
                          ● Attadale
RAASAY   Stromeferry
                          ● Plockton
SKYE   SCALPAY
                    Skye   ■
            Bridge ● ⌐ KYLE OF LOCHALSH
CUILLIN
HILLS   +
        + *Broadford*   KNOYDART

Armadale
+
RHUM   ● MALLAIG   Locheilside ●
        ● Morar   Loch Eil ●
        ● *Lochailort*   Corpach ●
EIGG   *Arisaig* ● Glenfinnan ● Banavie ●

MUCK   Spean Bridge ●
                                            ● Roy Bridge
ARDNAMURCHAN POINT   Tulloch ●
                        FORT WILLIAM ■   + *Loch Treig*
TOBERMORY +
Calgary +   Ben Nevis +   ● Corrour
                        (4418 ft)
                  Ballachulish ○   RANNOCH
ULVA   *Craignure* ▽ LOCH LINNHE MOOR   ● Rannoch
Staffa +   Bridge of Orchy ●
        MULL *Torosay*   ● Tyndrum Upper
            Castle   ● Connel Ferry Tyndrum ●
                SEIL   ● Loch Awe   Lower ● Crianlarich
IONA   LUING + OBAN ■ Dalmally ●
        SCARBA   Ardlui ●
GULF OF
CORRYVRECKAN   Arrochar ●
                              & Tarbet
COLONSAY   LOCH LOMOND
        JURA
ORONSAY   ● Garelochhead
                        Dunoon +   ● Helensburgh
                              ● Gourock ■ GLASGOW
                              ● Wemyss Bay
ISLAY   ● Largs
                BUTE
                              ● Ardrossan
ARRAN   ● Saltcoats
KINTYRE
                              ● Troon
                              ■ AYR

N

MULL OF KINTYRE

0   10   20   30   40   50   60
MILES

LEGEND

■ RAILTRACK STATION

● •

○ FORMER STATION

▲ PRESERVED
STANDARD GAUGE

▽ NARROW GAUGE

+ PLACES NAMED IN TEXT

SCOTLAND

Ballachulish, from 1903 to 1966 the terminus of a branch from Connel Ferry which offered relatively easy access to Glencoe. The slate quarries, creating surroundings reminiscent of Blaenau Ffestiniog, are clearly visible in this view of the late afternoon train to Oban awaiting departure in August 1964. (J.S. Gilks)

The push-pull service from Craigendoran enters Garelochhead in exquisite spring sunshine in May 1959. The motive power is C15 67460. (D H Beecroft/Colour-Rail SC385)

spartan third-class coach attached to the overnight sleeping car train from Glasgow to Inverness. The 'Hebridean' reached Kyle at 1031, and with a quick turnaround, departed for Inverness at 1045.

For many years, one restaurant car was shared between the 'Lewisman' and the 'Hebridean', with transfer usually taking place at Achnasheen. Passengers on the westbound 'Lewisman' who had not finished their lunch when the train reached Achnasheen had the choice of either missing the rest of their meal in order to get to Kyle, or staying in the restaurant car as it was switched to the eastbound 'Hebridean' bound for Inverness.

Some passengers who enjoyed the excellent Scottish food, good company and service on this train had planned to stay on board the restaurant car anyway for the scenic ride to Achnasheen and back to Inverness. Such were the pleasures of rail travel in the Highlands in the 1930s.

After WW2, the title 'Lewisman' did not reappear, but the 'Hebridean' survived until the 1990s as the 1040 to Kyle, with observation car, live commentary, and buffet service. A supplement was payable for travel in the observation car, bookable in advance at Inverness, well worth the surcharge for a round trip of 164 miles across Scotland and back

During the century of ferry service between Kyle and Skye, there must have been many who would sing or hum the 'Skye Boat Song' on the way over, even though it was written for Bonnie Prince Charlie's longer voyage across The Minch from the Outer Hebrides to Skye. One wonders if those crossing the bridge to Skye will sing the song with such sentiment.

On a clear day the 30-minute sea crossing from Armadale on Skye to Mallaig provides fine views of Rhum, Eigg , Muck, and Ardnamurchan Point, the most westerly point in mainland Britain. To the northeast, hills and mountains of the western highlands present an impressive backdrop across the water on the approach to Mallaig, terminus of the last major railway line to be built in Britain.

On this part of our journey along Scotland's west coast, we have reached Mallaig from the Kyle of Lochalsh via Skye and ferry from Armadale. For travellers from the south there are trains from Glasgow (Queen St) to Fort William and onwards to Mallaig, as well as an overnight 'Caledonian Sleeper' from London (Euston) to Fort William, with a change of train to reach Mallaig.

In celebration of rail journeys to the west coast of Scotland, we recall Britain's last dinner, bed and breakfast train, which ran until the late 1970s from London (King's Cross) to Fort William, with through coaches to Mallaig. This train offered two restaurant cars en route: one from London to York (for dinner), and one from Glasgow to Fort William (for breakfast). Several third-class coaches were also attached to the train, making a total of sixteen coaches for the long overnight haul to Scotland. The journey from King's Cross to Fort William took 14.25 hours.

The demise of this train in an age of ebbing elegance has deprived us of Britain's finest year-round long distance sleeping car service. On departure from King's Cross, dinner was served, to be enjoyed at leisure for two hours before settling into a comfortable berth all the way to Fort William. Alternatively, one could still get a good eight hours sleep after dinner, and a full breakfast after leaving Glasgow, with the added pleasure of seeing the most scenic part of the route to Fort William and Mallaig during and after breakfast in the dining car.

Over eleven years passed, from 23 October 1889 to 1 April 1901, before all 164 miles of the West Highland line from Glasgow (Queen St) to Mallaig were completed along shores of sea lochs, over the hills, high above fresh water lochs, and over desolate moorland. This difficult route required the building of 663 bridges, 13 tunnels and 43 viaducts.

Notable civil engineering achievements in creating this line included construction of the great Horseshoe Curve and viaducts on mountain flanks between Tyndrum Upper and Bridge of Orchy, the crossing of Rannoch Moor, the forcing of a track through the rocky Monessie gorge between Tulloch and Roy Bridge, and the spanning of Glen Finnan with a huge concrete viaduct, the first of its kind in the world.

Today's 'Caledonian Sleeper' from London (Euston) to Fort William meets daylight before leaving Glasgow's suburbs, so we will highlight the route from Garelochhead, where the train starts its first climb into the Highlands. The 132 miles of line from Gare Loch to Mallaig are the most consistently scenic in Britain, and the opening of the Glasgow to Fort William section on 11 August 1894 was an occasion for ceremonies all along the route. Never before in Britain had over one hundred miles of railway to the sea been opened in one day, nor was there a rail line of equal length in Britain with so few communities along the way.

From near sea level beside the Clyde, the train climbs to 560ft above Garelochhead and Loch Long, before descending to Arrochar and Tarbet station, crossing the narrow strip of land that separates Loch Long (a sea loch) from Loch Lomond, the largest area of fresh water in Britain, 23 miles long and six miles wide at its southern end. There are brief views of Loch Lomond through the trees until the northern end of the loch is reached at Ardlui, at the start of a long climb up Glen Falloch, crossing the high viaduct over the gorge at Dubh Eas (black water) where the train is almost as high above the water as on the famous Forth Bridge.

The 'West Highland Way', a 95-mile footpath from Milngavie (near Glasgow) to Fort William, crosses the railway line in Glen Falloch and continues through the glen to Crian-larich and onwards to Bridge of Orchy station, where it heads across Rannoch Moor to Fort William. This footpath was the first long-distance path to be established in Scotland and can be accessed from several stations along the line.

By now the train has climbed to over 1,000ft as it approaches the rail junction of Crianlarich, with Ben More (3,843ft) and Stobinian (3,821ft) to the east, and Beinn Oss (3,374ft) guarding the route west. The train usually divides here, one section heading west to Oban, while the Fort William coaches prepare to leave for the long climb to Rannoch Moor.

From Crianlarich, the train to Fort William climbs up the west flank of Strathfillan to Tyndrum Upper station, where there are fine views of the valley below. Two miles beyond Tyndrum, as the train clings to the mountain sides, it approaches the famous Horseshoe Curve between Beinn Dorain (3,524ft) with its elegantly curved profile, and Beinn Odhar (2,948ft), giving impressive views from the two viaducts that carry the line towards Bridge of Orchy.

After a brief stop at Bridge of Orchy station, the train follows the River Orchy to its source at Loch Tulla, climbing high above the loch until, on the left, the ruins of Achallader Castle may be seen partly hidden among farm buildings as we pass through the remnants of Crannach Wood, part of the great Caledonian forest which once covered most of northern Scotland.

Continuing its climb, the train starts its long haul across the 400 square miles of Rannoch Moor, a bleak area of peat bogs, heather, streams and lochs surrounded by mountains. Near the eastern edge of the moor is a large painted sign beside the track: 'Soldiers Trenches - 1745' marking the area of the moor where troops camped during the Jacobite rebellion. At the centre of the moor is Rannoch station, near Loch Laidon. When the great roadbuilder Thomas Telford surveyed a road across Rannoch Moor, he selected an almost identical route to that taken later by the railway, but concluded that a road was not feasible, so he abandoned the project.

The trackbed on which we ride today was built by floating the line on a bed of branches carrying thousands of tons of ash, earth, rocks, and crushed stone until a stable base for the track was established across black roots, pickled for ages in the bog, all that remained of a vast forest. This is the great tableland of Scotland, with Rannoch station situated on the most desolate high plateau for rail travel in Europe.

When crossing Rannoch Moor by train in fine weather one can appreciate the immense landscape all around this high level moorland rimmed by mountain peaks, as solitary as any place in Britain, with only the occasional remains of ancient stone shelters to remind us of transient life here during past centuries.

Financial problems in building the railway across Rannoch Moor brought construction to a halt in 1893. The workers could not be paid until J.H.Renton, one of the West Highland directors, contributed the necessary funds from his personal bank account to complete the line. He drove in the ceremonial 'last spike' and is commemorated by a sculpted memorial that stands on the platform at the north end of Rannoch station.

There is just one road that pierces into the heart of Rannoch Moor, the B846 between Rannoch station and Tummel Bridge, where it joins the B8019 to Killiecrankie, then the A9 to Pitlochry. Only the railway has succeeded in crossing Rannoch Moor, and this is a journey to relish all the way from Bridge of Orchy to Tulloch, below Loch Treig.

After leaving Rannoch station there is a fine view on the left along Loch Laidon to Black Mount. The only snow shed in Britain is at Cruach cutting near Corrour, and Loch Ossian is to the right, the highest loch (1,269ft) of any significance in Scotland. Corrour station is one of the most isolated stations on the railway network, with a wind generator at the east end of the platform to provide electrical power. Just beyond Corrour station, the line summit of 1,347ft is reached, and from here it is downhill most of the way to Fort William, a distance of 28 miles.

The ScotRail guide lists ten 'Munros' accessible from Corrour station, the greatest number of mountain peaks over 3,000 ft close to a rail station in Britain. At the edge of Rannoch Moor the train makes a steep descent of 415 vertical feet beside Loch Treig to reach Tulloch station, with its Swiss-style buildings, restored and re-opened in June 1998 as a hostel for walkers and climbers.

After Tulloch station the train continues through the Braes o' Lochaber and Monessie Gorge to Roy Bridge station, close to Keppoch House, the ancient home of Clan McDonell. In the 17th century, a fierce battle in Glen Roy between the McDonells and the MacIntoshes was the last time that highlanders used bows and arrows in combat.

Beyond Roy Bridge we cross the Spean to reach Spean Bridge station near to a monument commemorating Commandos who trained here in WW2. Continuing our descent, we approach the lower northern flanks of Ben Nevis, with Leanachan Forest on the left and Inverlochy Castle on the right, before entering the railway terminus on the east shore of Loch Linnhe.

In travelling from Rannoch Moor to Fort William the train has passed three sides of the Ben Nevis range, first approaching from the east above Loch Trieg, then along the Braes o' Lochaber to the north and finally rounding its lower western flanks above Fort William. It is a massive mountain, with a circumference of 24 miles at its base.

Fort William is the largest town on the west coast of the Highlands north of the Clyde. Its name commemorates a fort dating from 1654 which was rebuilt during the reign of William III (1689-1702). Ironically, the fort which stood for 240 years was not demolished by battle or siege, but by the coming of the West Highland Railway, when the fort was removed to make

way for locomotive sheds and tracks in the goods yard.

Completion of the West Highland line from Glasgow to Fort William in 1894 brought many visitors to the region and made the town a business centre for the West Highlands, just as Inverness, at the other end of the Caledonian Canal, is the business centre of the East Highlands. Fort William was the first town in Britain to have its streets lit by locally-generated hydroelectric power.

The railway terminus at Fort William welcomed the last passenger train operated by British Rail, the night sleeper that left London (Euston) on 31 March 1997 as a British Rail service, and arrived in Scotland the next day as a privatized National Express train. Today's Caledonian Sleeper services to Fort William are operated by ScotRail and run nightly except Saturdays.

Loch Linnhe is the largest sea loch along 400 miles of Scotland's west coast from Cape Wrath to Fort William. It is 34 miles long and four miles across at its widest point near Ballachulish. A branch line once ran south from Ballachulish Ferry station along the loch shore to Appin, then across the Strath of Appin to Loch Creran, Benderloch, Connel and Oban.

This is yet another of Britain's former branch lines whose closure prevents us from exploring this part of the coast by train. It was the only railway route north of Glasgow that was

Glory days. The evening train for Glasgow leaves Fort William in the North British era behind Glen Oichy *and the now preserved* Glen Douglas. *Today the largest town on the west coast of Scotland north of the Clyde, Fort William owes much of its current importance to the completion of the West Highland Railway in 1894. (NRM - 1112/82)*

built for some twenty miles up the west coast of Scotland. The train hugged the shoreline of Loch Linnhe as far as Ballachulish Ferry station, then continued along the south side of Loch Leven, almost reaching into Glencoe.

The coastline around Fort William marks the southern end of the Great Glen, a sixty-mile gash which cuts across Scotland from Oban to Inverness. The rivers Lochy, Oich and Ness link their respective lochs along this glen, which provided an ancient waterway and portage, later converted into the Caledonian Canal. Loch Ness contains the largest volume of water in any inland Scottish loch, reaching a maximum depth of 980ft.

From Fort William, the train to Mallaig heads west around the fringes of the town, passing Inverlochy Castle, then crossing the River Lochy to reach Banavie. Just beyond the station is a swing bridge over the Caledonian Canal, one of

Telford's engineering masterpieces, with a set of eight locks he named 'Neptune's Staircase', raising vessels 64ft for the start of their journey across Scotland to Inverness.

As we travel west from Banavie and look back along Loch Eil towards Fort William, the summit of Ben Nevis (4,406ft) appears more impressive and worthy of its title as Britain's highest mountain. Four miles northwest of Fort William, near Corpach, Loch Linnhe meets Loch Eil, where the line to Mallaig keeps close to the shore before crossing the five-mile barrier of land that separates Loch Eil from Loch Shiel.

At the far end of Loch Eil, the train starts its climb up to Glenfinnan, whose viaduct is one of the most-photographed railway structures in Britain. The contractor for this master-piece of concrete construction was Robert McAlpine, who built several concrete viaducts on the line to Mallaig, all of which have endured the test of time. Glenfinnan viaduct is 1,250ft of elegantly curved concrete, supported by 21 arches, an impressive testimony to Victorian vision, engineering skill, and refusal to be intimidated by the awesome terrain. Further along the line, Borrodale railway bridge was the longest (128ft) single span concrete bridge in the world when completed in 1901.

Glenfinnan viaduct forms a backdrop to the most famous memorial along the line, Bonnie Prince Charlie's monument at the head of Loch Shiel, where he landed on 19 August 1745 to start his ill-fated crusade that ended at Culloden. Exactly 250 years later a great crowd assembled near the railway viaduct to commemorate this historic event.

While the tall monument beside Loch Shiel marks the place where the Prince landed, the spot where his standard was raised is on higher ground, marked by a rock on which was chiselled an inscription to record for posterity this heroic gathering of the clans. The rock remained buried for decades under long grass until uncovered by a shepherd.

On leaving Glenfinnan station, with its museum and gift shop, there are good views down Loch Shiel as the train continues to climb through rock cuttings, oak woods, and over several streams until the shores of Loch Eilt appear. Ahead is Lochailort station, the site of one of the largest construction camps when this line was built nearly a century ago. Two thousand workers were based here to force a route through to Mallaig across the headlands of South Morar, excavating rock cuttings and blasting tunnels on the approach to Arisaig, the most westerly railway station in Britain.

While being rowed across Loch Ailort, Sir Harold Boulton was inspired to write the 'Skye Boat Song' when he heard the melody from his boatman. The words of the song were formed in Sir Harold's mind during an overnight railway journey across the highlands, and written down the next morning.

Between Lochailort and Mallaig are some of the most spectacular sea views to be seen from a train, if islands are included as criteria. Let us list some of them: Eigg with its massive Sgurr (1,289ft) presiding over the sea, aloof and mighty as a battleship; Rhum; Muck; and in the distance, the tip of Skye. To the southwest is Ardnamurchan Point, jutting twenty miles further into the Atlantic than Land's End in Cornwall.

A narrow neck of land separates the sea from Loch Morar, Britain's deepest lake (1,017ft), whose waters cascaded over one of Scotland's finest waterfalls, the Falls of Morar, before they were tamed to feed a hydroelectric station. Loch Morar still has its tourist attraction, for it is the domain of Morag, a legendary monster who appears only to foretell the death of a MacDonald of Clanranald. The coastline around Morar, where one sandy bay leads to another, is perhaps seen best on a day in May or June, when the Hebrides have, on occasion, recorded the highest daily sunshine figures for the British Isles.

As the train weaves its way along the coast we reach the famous sands of Morar, with beaches formed of quartz grains, washed by crystal clear waters of the Atlantic, giving a sparkling appearance under clear skies. From Morar station to Mallaig it is seven minutes by train and a world away from London. Here, along the tracks of the West Highland Railway, are wonderful and ever-changing colours of mountain, sky and sea, all difficult to capture in a photo from inside a moving train, or even standing with tripod beside the tracks, as Eric Treacy, the great railway photographer, modestly explained:

"I suppose every photographer has his vision of his ideal picture. So far I haven't got it, and I don't suppose I ever shall. Whatever it is, I shall search for it all my life...."

Mallaig has an interesting origin. In the early 1800s, Lord Lovat devised a plan for his extensive estates at North Morar, settling sixteen crofters on this rock-bound peninsula at the mouth of Loch Nevis. Each settler was given four acres of land on which to eke out a living, until the railway arrived to transform a poor crofting settlement into one of the busiest fishing ports on the west coast, and a favourite tourist destination.

When the Mallaig extension opened in 1901 it provided the fastest transportation ever seen on this remote and isolated part of the coast. The 'Iron Road to the Isles' was far more comfortable, reliable and faster than any cart on rough tracks, and it enabled large catches of fish to be sent by train to distant markets. Mallaig harbour was the departure point for the 'Stornaway Mail', a daily steamship service that connected with the overnight train from King's Cross, making it possible to travel from London to the Outer Hebrides in less than 24 hours.

Some ScotRail trains to Mallaig connect with Caledonian MacBrayne ferries to Skye (Armadale), Eigg, Canna, Rhum and Muck. A circular trip to these islands is one of the finest excursions by ferry from mainland Britain. During the summer season, 'Jacobite' steam trains between Fort William

and Mallaig are so popular that a British cabinet minister was reportedly unable to obtain seats for himself and his family to travel on the 'Jacobite' one day in August 1996.

In 1998 the 'Jacobite' service celebrated its fifteenth year as the only steam train operating a scheduled service on Britain's railway network, and during that time ten steam locomotives have worked the West Highland Line, providing some fine action scenes for photographers. This most westerly outpost of steam has proven to be one of railway preservation's great success stories. The luxury land cruise train 'Royal Scotsman' has also been steam-hauled over the Mallaig line.

Such is the appeal of a journey by steam train to Mallaig that over eighty days of 'Jacobite' specials were scheduled for 1998, and turntables have been acquired for installation at each end of the line so that locomotives will always face the direction of travel, for improved visibility by footplate crews and to increase the aesthetic appeal to railway photographers.

Steam train excursions to the Kyle of Lochalsh with the 'Jacobite' train were run on a trial basis for two days in October 1997 at the end of the Mallaig season, marking the centenary of the first train from Inverness to the Lochalsh pier in 1897. This may lead to the return of scheduled steam services on the Kyle Line in the summer, similar to those of the 'Jacobite' to Mallaig. Much will depend on continued public support, for we are now in the age of "use them or lose them" for some preserved standard and narrow-gauge lines, as well as for steam

Mallaig, created by the railway out of a hamlet to provide at one and the same time a packet station giving new access to the islands, a fishing port and a tourist centre. It also marked the end of one of the epic train journeys of Britain, the section from Fort William being used today by the immensely popular 'Jacobite' steam specials. (NRM - 432/89)

locomotive journeys on the Railtrack network. Happily, the lure of steam locomotive excursions appears to be as strong as ever.

Oban is our next destination, so we will return to Fort William, stay overnight, and leave on the early morning train to Crianlarich, changing there for Oban, taking a seat on the right side in all three trains to enjoy the best views of sea and mountains. For the journey from Mallaig to Fort William, and onwards to Crianlarich, here are some highlights to watch for: the sands of Morar; Loch Eilt; Glenfinnan, Loch Shiel and monument; Loch Eil, with Ben Nevis in the distance; the Monessie Falls; the climb beside Loch Trieg to reach Rannoch Moor; the crossing of Rannoch Moor to the Bridge of Orchy, followed by the Horseshoe Curve with viaducts on each side of the valley; and the descent from Tyndrum Upper station along Strathfillan to Crianlarich.

We should not leave Rannoch Moor without mention of the 'West Highland baby'. Many years ago, as the train from Fort William to Glasgow started its ascent beside Loch Trieg to the

Oban, gateway to the isles, was praised by Queen Victoria as 'one of the finest spots we have seen'. A Glasgow train is departing in 1913, a year before the Caledonian Railway inaugurated its famous Pullman service to the port complete with an elegant observation car Maid of Morvern.
(NRM - LGRP 7952)

moor, the guard told a doctor: "We're going to have another passenger". There was nowhere on this desolate moor to seek help, so the mother-to-be was taken to a first-class compartment, next to that occupied by the Marquess and Marchioness of Bute, who helped in collecting towels and boiling water from the dining car, in the true spirit of 'noblesse oblige'.

At Crianlarich, a Scots-Canadian nurse on her way back to Canada boarded the train and assisted at the birth, which occurred near Craigendoran. The baby was named after the nurse and doctor, although some versions of this episode had the engine driver, fireman, or guard providing the first names.

The West Highland Railway established Crianlarich as the half-way station between Glasgow and Fort William, where passengers could have a meal before the long haul over Rannoch Moor. This tradition continues today in the spacious refreshment room at the station. The Callandar and Oban Railway came here too, from the east through Glen Dochart, and we shall take the only surviving part of this line for 42 miles along the route of the 'Lord of the Isles' to Oban.

From Crianlarich we travel along Strath Fillan, where the line to Fort William and Mallaig may be seen climbing to Tyndrum Upper station on the north side, while we take the other side of the valley to Tyndrum Lower station. The train descends through Glen Lochy and Dalmally to the head of Loch Awe where there is a good view of Kilchurn Castle, stronghold of the Campbell clan since 1450.

Loch Awe is longer than Loch Lomond, and there are boat trips in the summer from the pier near the station. A huge Victorian mansion in the Scottish baronial style stands above the station in a magnificent setting among woods on the hillside facing the loch. The panorama opens up as we continue along the western arm of Loch Awe to the Falls of Cruichan railway station.

Inside Ben Cruichan is a huge hydroelectric generating station, where water turbines and electrical generators operate in a cavern large enough to house the Tower of London, buried 3,000ft below the summit. This is one of the hidden wonders of the Highlands, and guided tours are offered inside the 'hollow mountain' where water plunges down from a large reservoir high on Ben Cruichan (3,689ft), whose name is the war cry of the Campbell clan.

At the western end of Loch Awe the train enters the narrow rock-walled Pass of Brander, with the flanks of Ben Cruichan on one side and steep screes on the other, forming the dark gorge of the well-named River Awe, a dramatic setting for Sir Walter Scott's 'Highland Widow'. The high peaks around here may be "dignified by cloud and mist", or perhaps lit by a sun "shining among mists and resting clouds"- to quote Dorothy Wordsworth, who came to Loch Awe in 1803 with her brother William. He was attracted to loch castles (especially Kilchurn) - "ruined, at rest, and all silent in their age."

Emerging from the Pass of Brander, we turn west towards Taynuilt station near Loch Etive, where the line meanders through woods and rock cuttings to Connel Ferry, from whose bridge the 'Falls of Lora' may be seen when tidal waters flow over a ledge of rock at the narrow entrance to Loch Etive, a fjord-like sea loch at the southern end of Loch Linnhe. This spectacle, best viewed at mid-ebb Spring tides, is Europe's only seawater falls.

If train time and ebb tide do not coincide, there are compensating views from the train as we look across the loch to the hills at Benderloch, near to the former branch line to Ballachulish. From 1903 to 1966 trains crossed the great steel cantilever bridge now used by road vehicles travelling between Connel and Ballachulish.

From Connel Ferry the train climbs to over 300ft in the hills above Oban, with brief views to seaward on our descent to one of the busiest ports on Scotland's west coast. For more than a century Oban has been the rail terminus for passengers taking one of the Caledonian MacBrayne ferries to Mull, Colonsay, Tiree, Coll, Lismore, and islands of the Outer Hebrides. The harbour is sheltered from Atlantic storms by the island of Kerrera, and a stroll along Oban's attractive esplanade lined with hotels and guest houses usually rewards the visitor with interesting sightings of ships arriving from or departing for the Western Isles.

When the railway arrived in 1880, tourists from all over Britain came to this pleasant resort gateway to the isles, for at that time Oban ('little bay' in Gaelic) was the only port on the west coast of Scotland with railway service. The town now ranks high among the major holiday resorts of Scotland, and much of its revenue comes from tourism, trade, and travel to the islands.

Queen Victoria came here by sea and gave the royal seal of approval, calling Oban "one of the finest spots we have seen." A century earlier, James Boswell and his famous companion Samuel Johnson travelled the hard way overland and were more restrained, yet relieved, to find in Oban a "tolerable inn'" where they stayed in 1773. Calling for a glass of whisky, Johnson exclaimed: "Come, let me know what it is that makes a Scotchman happy!"

Oban's conspicuous Victorian folly, McCaig's Tower, was built on a hill above the town, and is visible from the station platform. It was planned as a replica of the Colosseum in Rome, to contain a museum, art gallery, and family memorial in the grand spirit of Scottish romanticism and philanthropy, with the intention of relieving local unemployment, but the tower was never completed.

McCaig's Tower celebrated its centenary in 1997, and from the viewing platform the mountains of Morvern provide a spectacular backdrop for the islands of Kerrera, Lismore, Mull, and Maiden, especially at sunset. Two other prominent landmarks in Oban are the pink granite cathedral, and the

remains of Dunollie Castle which has stood guard over the narrow entrance to the sheltered bay for almost 600 years.

The seascapes and landscapes near Oban that inspired Mendelssohn, Johnson and Boswell still create the same magic for visitors today. This is an area of contrasts, from busy harbours at Oban and Tobermory, to the golden beaches of Coll and Tiree; from the spectacular mountain scenery of Lorn and Mull to quiet sea lochs dotted with yachts of many colours and nationalities; to nearby Iona, cradle of early Christianity in Scotland. Nowhere is the past so present as in the west highlands and islands of Argyll.

In 1914, the Caledonian Railway operated a Pullman service from Glasgow to Oban with an observation car named 'Maid of Morvern'. This was the first railway observation car to run in Britain, and was followed by similar observation coaches on the scenic Kyle and Mallaig lines. While coaches on today's trains from Glasgow (Queen St) to Oban are more functional than the elegant carriages of the 1920s and 1930s, the grand title 'Lord of the Isles' has been retained for the morning Glasgow-Oban service, connecting with Caledonian MacBrayne ferries, one of which is also named 'Lord of the Isles'.

Mull is one of the most attractive of the western islands, and its proximity to Oban makes it a very popular tourist destination. It has the only railway on a Scottish island, a narrow-gauge line between Craignure Pier and Torosay Castle, operated in season by the Mull & West Highland Steam Railway, which opened in June 1984, along a 1.25 mile route of 10.25 inch gauge. At the sheltered bay at Craignure the views on a clear day across the Sound of Mull to the Isle of Lismore, to Duart Castle, and to Ben Nevis are outstanding. From the summit of Ben More (3,170ft) there is a grand panorama, with Tobermory fourteen miles to the north.

The coastline of Mull is more than 250 miles in length, making it third in circumference of Scotland's western islands. It is deeply carved by sea lochs, and has many sandy bays, coves, cliffs, caves, and waterfalls. The sea to the west is studded with islands, including Iona, a place of pilgrimage where 62 kings are said to be buried, and which in 1997 marked the 1400th anniversary of St Columba's death.

Six miles north of Iona lies Staffa, a small uninhabited island with one of the most dramatic natural wonders in the British Isles. Staffa's black basalt columns rise high above the caves, the most famous of which is Fingal's Cave, discovered by a party of scientists sailing to Iceland in 1772, and celebrated by Mendelssohn in his famous overture.

Tobermory, with its bright multi-coloured buildings on the waterfront, is a popular haven for yachts and cabin cruisers from many parts of Britain and Europe. The harbour is an ideal base from which to explore the western isles, and lochs along the west coast of Scotland. A galleon of the ill-fated Spanish Armada sought shelter and sank in Tobermory Bay in 1588,

and while some relics have been recovered, the search continues for more treasures buried in the bay. On the west coast of Mull, is Calgary - 'bay of clear waters'- which has conferred its name, through a Scots-born Commissioner of the 'Mounties', to the great Canadian city of Calgary.

There is so much to see and explore among the islands off Scotland's west coast, using railheads at the Kyle of Lochalsh, Mallaig, Oban, Wemyss Bay, and Ardrossan that we must leave it to the guidebooks to provide information on the many destinations served by Caledonian MacBrayne ferries. But before leaving Oban, 'Gateway to the Isles' and 'Capital of Lorn', there are four islands to the south that we will visit, two by ferry, and two on foot.

The first is Colonsay, destination for Wendy Hiller and Roger Livesey in the delightful 1945 film 'I Know Where I'm Going', in which an overnight train journey north to Scotland was followed by a terrifying sea journey by small boat to Colonsay through the very real Gulf of Corryvreckan, between Scarba and Jura, whose ferocious whirlpool nearly drowned them.

One of three southern islands of the Inner Hebrides (Jura and Islay are the other two), Colonsay is set like a stepping-stone in the sea between Scotland and Ireland. It is served by ferry from Oban, and has delightful sandy beaches on its southern and western sides. The coast south of Kiloran Bay is impressive, with waves surging over rocks at the base of high cliffs, accessible only on foot.

Concourse at Largs, built by the Glasgow & South Western Railway and rebuilt by the LMS. The town, one of Scotland's top tourism centres, has a wide shingle beach and a regular ferry service to Millport on the island of Great Cumbrae. (T.J. Edgington)

The small island of Oronsay is close to Colonsay and may be reached on foot with great care at low tide across the Strand, a 1.5 mile sandy channel between the two islands. Spring tides allow between three and four hours access; local advice should be sought and tide tables consulted before attempting the crossing on foot.

Legend has it that Saint Columba made his first landfall on Oronsay after leaving his native Ireland. Standing on Ben Oronsay, he could see the hills of Ireland, and fearful of homesickness and weakening of resolve, he sailed north to Iona and founded a community that was to become the centre for the spread of Christianity in northern Britain.

The third island we shall visit is Jura, served in the summer season by ferry from Oban to Port Askaig on Islay, then another ferry across the narrow Sound of Islay. This sparsely-populated island is best explored on foot. The Corryvreckan whirlpool may be seen from Jura's northern tip, and is usually at its most ferocious in September when tides are often given added impetus by strong Atlantic westerlies.

George Orwell chose to live on Jura in 1948 in order to write his novel '1984'. For the few visitors he invited to his isolated retreat at Barnhill, the journey from London took two days and required six modes of transportation: by train up the west coast main line to Glasgow; then another train to Gourock; by ferry to Tarbert on Kintyre; bus across Kintyre to Kilberry; boat for twelve miles across the Sound to Craig-house on Jura; taxi to the end of the road; and finally a hike for the rest of the way to Barnhill.

Journeys such as this are no longer so strenuous or rare, as more people set out to explore the wilder and remoter western isles, served by ferries that link 23 islands to the mainland and to each other via 52 ports and terminals. The popular 'Island Rover' tickets and 'Island Hopscotch Tours' offered by Caledonian MacBrayne enable some interesting multi-island itineraries to be planned, starting from railway stations on Scotland's west coast.

Midway as the gull flies between the rail terminus at Oban and the northern tip of Jura is the island of Seil, linked to the mainland by its unique 'Bridge over the Atlantic'. This handsome single span stone bridge was built by Thomas Telford in 1792 and provides road access to the island and to the ferry across to Luing. After the defeat of the Jacobite army at Culloden and the flight of Bonnie Prince Charlie from Scotland, the wearing of a tartan kilt was banned, so islanders going to the mainland would change from their traditional kilts at the inn beside the bridge. This inn is still called Tigh an Truish, 'the house of the trousers'.

To return to Oban from Seil, the most practical route is by road, a distance of about ten miles, of which four miles are beside Loch Feochan, a sea loch meeting the Firth of Lorn southeast of Kerrera, Oban's sentinel island. The next railway station on Scotland's west coast is Gourock, a distance of 129 miles by rail from Oban, via Crianlarich to Glasgow (Queen St), then from Glasgow (Central) to Gourock.

There are frequent ferry services from Gourock to Dunoon, a popular coastal resort on the Cowal peninsula, offering remoteness from industrial Clydeside, yet good access to Glasgow. The sub-tropical palms found in gardens here are evidence of the sheltered coastline's mild climate, unequalled anywhere else in the world at the same latitude.

Wemyss Bay, the next station on our journey down the coast, is the departure point for Bute, another interesting island off Scotland's west coast. Rothesay is the island's principal town and ferry harbour, boasting one of Scotland's best-preserved medieval castles. There are several small bays of red sand backed by fields and rolling farmland on Bute's west coast, while on the southeast side is Kilchattan, with fine views across the Firth of Clyde to Great Cumbrae and Little Cumbrae islands.

Bute provides a pleasant alternative route from Glasgow to the western isles, starting with a train from Central station to Wemyss Bay, then ferry to Rothesay, followed by a combination of road and ferry to Rhubodach, Colintrave, Portavadie, Tarbert, Kennacraig, Islay and Colonsay to Oban. This is one of several rail/sea/road routes to the islands, and although the example given is longer than the journey by train from Glasgow to Oban, it provides an excellent opportunity to see more of Scotland's west coast and the sea highway that links islands to mainland stations.

Largs, sheltered by the island of Great Cumbrae, is one of Scotland's top tourism towns, with blue waters of the Firth of Clyde lapping its shores, and the green hills of Clyde Muirshiel Regional Park at its outskirts, offering pleasant walks and fine views of the islands, notably Cumbrae, Arran, and Bute. Its sea front faces a wide shingle beach, scene of one of the most famous battles of medieval Scotland, in which a Viking army was defeated on 2 October 1263, enabling the Scots to secure command of the Clyde, and opening the way for re-possession of the Hebrides.

There is a regular ferry service from Largs to Millport on Great Cumbrae, which has the smallest cathedral in Europe, built in 1876 and known as 'the cathedral of the Isles', with a nave measuring 40ft by 20ft and a spire 123ft high.

Ardrossan faces Arran, an island with some of the most dramatic landscapes around the Firth of Clyde. No British island of its size can match the variety of its scenery and complexity of its geology. From the summit of Goat Fell (2,866ft) there are fine views across to the mainland and other islands, as well as sightings of ships and pleasure craft in the Firth of Clyde and to the west in Kilbrannan Sound, where Kintyre's 43-mile peninsula, the longest in Scotland, stretches across the horizon. The Mull of Kintyre is closer to Ireland than any other part of Britain.

Arran's Brodick Castle has a violent history that goes back to the early 14th Century. In the course of just over one hundred years it was burned down and rebuilt three times. Today the castle and its 65-acre woodland garden are carefully tended by the National Trust for Scotland. Arran has been called "Scotland in miniature", where islanders continue to make their living from the soil and the sea, just as they have done for generations, their lives governed by tides and ferries to and from their island.

At Ardrossan, and its neighbour Saltcoats, we have drawn a boundary line to close this chapter, for Arran is the most southerly of the islands served by rail and ferry on Scotland's west coast. The next seaside resort on our railway circumnavigation of mainland Britain will be Troon, reached by train from Glasgow, or from London (Euston) via Carlisle, Dumfries, Kirkconnel, and Kilmarnock, a shorter and more scenic route than via Glasgow.

West coast main line routes to the Sea

**Of Albion's glorious Isle the wonders I write
The sundry varying sights, the pleasures infinite.**

Michael Drayton 1612

The 401 mile west coast main line from London to Glasgow approaches the sea at only one place along its entire length, and that is at Hest Bank, three miles north of Lancaster, and 233 miles from London. To reach resorts covered in this chapter, we go first to Glasgow Central station, named in the 1998 Railtrack awards as Britain's most passenger-friendly large station.

Before leaving Glasgow for the coast, a few days to explore this great city on the Clyde are recommended, for this is one of Europe's most cosmopolitan cities, diverse in its architecture, with a wide range of attractions for the visitor. Glasgow was named Europe's City of Culture in 1990, and City of Architecture for the year 2000. To Sir John Betjeman it was the finest Victorian city in the world, and a walk along the 'Merchant City Trail' which passes close to Queen Street station on George Square provides a good sampling of Glasgow's Victorian heritage, which includes, after London, the largest and most diverse collection of art galleries and museums in Britain.

On departure from Glasgow Central, Troon will be our first seaside destination. When the Glasgow-Ayr railway opened in 1840, Troon developed rapidly as a port and seaside town, spreading towards Prestwick and Ayr to form the most popular resort area on the west coast of Scotland. This is the heart of Scotland's golf coast, with more courses here than on any comparable length of coastline in Britain.

Prestwick, the oldest incorporated borough in Scotland, extends southwards to Ayr, well known to Robert Burns for its "honest men and bonnie lassies." It is the closest town to his birthplace at Alloway, now a hallowed shrine and museum.

From all over the world, visitors come to pay homage to "the bard sublime", as Wordsworth called him.

In summer months, Ayr is thronged with visitors. Yet there is a feeling of spaciousness and contentment along the seashore, with sailboats and pleasure craft moving across Ayr Bay, while residents and visitors enjoy a pleasant walk on the sands or through the parks and gardens near the elegant terraces and town houses of this attractive resort.

The Clyde coast extends southwards as far as Stranraer, and becomes more rocky, with sea cliffs rising to 200ft at the Heads of Ayr. The most spectacular feature of this coastline is Culzean Castle, built by Robert Adam in 1777 on cliffs overlooking Culzean Bay, with 560 acres of woods and gardens. These grounds, together with the castle, formed Scotland's first country park in 1969, all maintained by the National Trust for Scotland, "certainly the most magnificent country park in Britain" according to one guidebook. Culzean has also won a Tourism 'Oscar' as the best long-established attraction in Scotland. The closest railway station to the castle is Maybole, four miles away.

Three miles south of Culzean are the remains of Turnberry Castle, childhood home of Robert the Bruce. Turnberry owes its early development as a resort to the opening in 1906 of a branch line and hotel by the Glasgow & South Western Railway, to rival the Caledonian Railway's luxury hotel and golf course at Gleneagles on the main line between Stirling and Perth. To cater for visitors from the south, sleeping cars for Turnberry were attached to London-Glasgow overnight trains until the outbreak of WW2. All passenger services on the six-mile branch line from Maybole were withdrawn in March 1942.

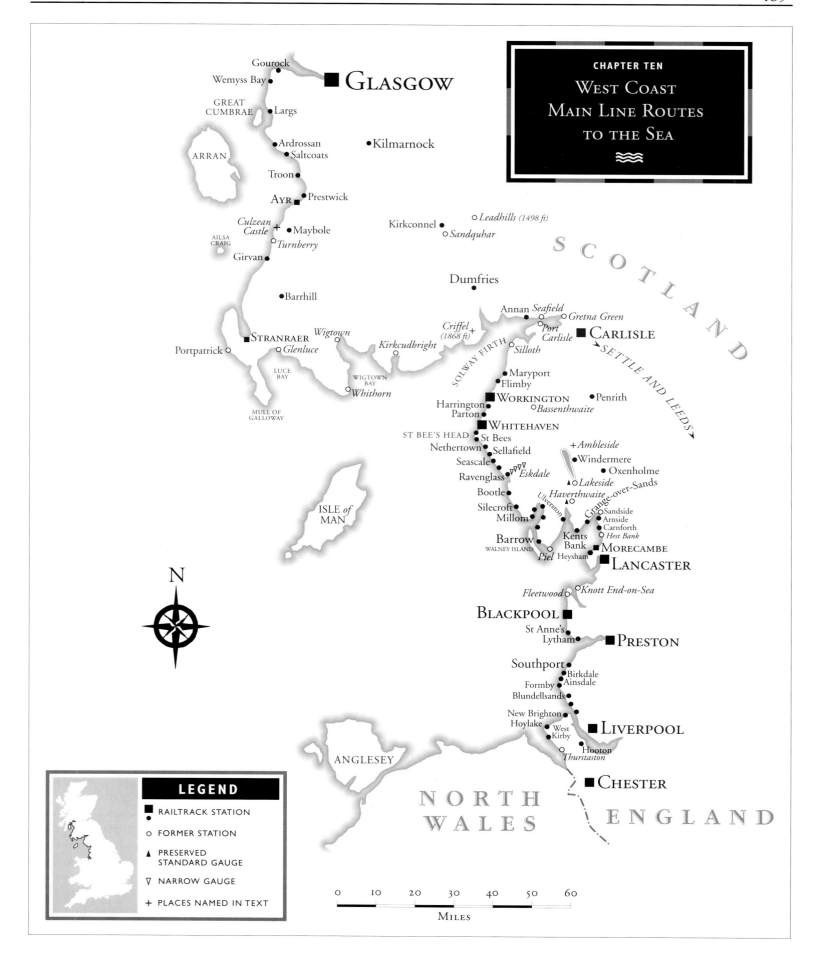

Gourock
Wemyss Bay
GREAT
CUMBRAE
Largs
ARRAN
Ardrossan
Saltcoats
Troon
AYR Prestwick
Culzean
Castle + Maybole
AILSA
CRAIG Turnberry
Girvan
Barrhill

GLASGOW

Kilmarnock

Kirkconnel Leadhills (1498 ft)
Sandquhar

Dumfries

SCOTLAND

Annan Seafield
Seafield Gretna Green
Criffel Port
(1868 ft) + Carlisle
SOLWAY FIRTH Silloth

CARLISLE

SETTLE AND LEEDS

Wigtown
STRANRAER
Glenluce
Portpatrick
LUCE
BAY
WIGTOWN
BAY
MULL OF
GALLOWAY
Kirkcudbright
Whithorn

Maryport
Flimby
WORKINGTON Penrith
Harrington Bassenthwaite
Parton
WHITEHAVEN
ST BEE'S HEAD St Bees
Nethertown Sellafield
Seascale
Ravenglass Eskdale
Bootle
Silecroft Ulverston
Millom
Barrow
WALNEY ISLAND
Piel Heysham
Kents
Bank

+ Ambleside
Windermere
Oxenholme
Lakeside
Haverthwaite
Grange-over-Sands
Sandside
Arnside
Carnforth
Hest Bank
MORECAMBE
LANCASTER

ISLE of
MAN

N

Fleetwood Knott End-on-Sea

BLACKPOOL

St Anne's
Lytham PRESTON

Southport
Birkdale
Ainsdale
Formby
Blundellsands

New Brighton
Hoylake West
Kirby LIVERPOOL
Hooton
Thurstaston

ANGLESEY

CHESTER

NORTH
WALES ENGLAND

0   10   20   30   40   50   60

MILES

A rail-tour departs from Silloth in June 1964, three months before closure led to scenes of unprecedented hostility including a mass sit-down on the line. The two preserved Scottish locomotives are symbolic, as Silloth was a unique case of an English resort being developed by a railway company based in Scotland. The North British directorate even forbade the playing of cricket, on the grounds that the hard balls could injure waiting passengers, and instructed local sportsmen to play bowls instead! (Derek Cross)

Two centuries ago, Girvan thrived on fishing and its textile industry. When the railway line reached here, many people came to see Girvan's great tourist attraction, the huge granite pile of Ailsa Craig, ten miles offshore. This volcanic island, with its lighthouse and castle soars 1,109ft above the sea.

From Girvan station, the train climbs inland through rock cuttings and glens to Barrhill, the only station between Girvan and Stranraer (52 miles). On this lonely moorland, a line summit of 690ft is reached at Chirmorie near the Ayrshire-Wigtown-shire boundary, before a long descent to the sea at Stranraer.

It would be difficult to find a more isolated route for two former titled trains of Britain than that between Girvan and Stranraer. The steam-hauled 'Irishman' and 'Fast Belfast' struggled up the single track from Girvan, with long gradients of 1 in 54 and 1 in 67 that led to the shortest sea crossing (39 miles) to Ireland. This justified the latter title, until the train was withdrawn after WW2, while the 'Irishman', known to railwaymen as 'The Paddy', survived until 1967. Diesel trains now operate between Glasgow and Stranraer, connecting with ferries to Larne.

Situated at the head of Loch Ryan, Stranraer is protected from rough waters of the Irish Sea by a 1.6 mile breakwater, one of the longest in Britain, reaching out into deeper waters of the loch at low tide. Most visitors to Stranraer are in transit between Scotland and Ireland, and the port has only limited appeal as a seaside town, but it provides a good base for exploring the Galloway coast, which curves around successive bays, headlands, and river estuaries between Luce Sands and Kirkcudbright.

Portpatrick, on the opposite side of the peninsula from Stranraer, was once a ferry port and railway terminus. Severe gales on this exposed coast closed the port for days on end, and all ferry services to Ireland were transferred to the sheltered harbour at Stranraer, resulting in closure of the branch line across the peninsula. However, Portpatrick remained a favourite place for Irish couples to get married, with its quick and profitable business in easy weddings, noted in contemporary journals as "landed on Saturday, called on Sunday, married on Monday."

On this stretch of coastline there are no railway stations between Stranraer and Annan, a distance of some eighty miles. After crossing the border, the first station on the coast is Maryport, in Cumbria. The shortest rail route from Stranraer to Maryport is via Troon, Kilmarnock, Dumfries, Annan, and Carlisle, a journey of 172 miles.

On our way south from Kilmarnock and Kirkconnel, we follow Nithsdale to Sanquhar, where a former branch line to Elvanfoot climbed to the highest railway summit (1,498ft) ever built on Britain's rail network, at the boundary between Ayrshire and Lanarkshire near Leadhills, linking the two west coast lines from Carlisle to Glasgow.

It is unfortunate that this scenic southwest coast of Scotland between the Mull of Galloway and Annan has lost all its branch lines, notably those to Glenluce, Wigtown, Kirkcudbright, Whithorn, and Creetown. The closest station to these towns is now either Stranraer or Dumfries, with Kirkcudbright the largest coastal town, 25 miles by road from Dumfries station.

Kirkcudbright's waterfront is dominated by the gaunt ruins of McLellan's Castle, while along the western shore of the Dee estuary there are rocky coves and small sandy beaches. Tidal sands and saltings merge at the head of the bay, with the town standing on the eastern side, from whose shores the first boatload of settlers from Scotland to Nova Scotia sailed sadly yet hopefully away in 1622.

Twelve miles southeast of Dumfries the train approaches the Solway Firth, where wooded hills end in muddy river estuaries. The upper reaches of the Solway Firth are bleak, desolate and dangerous, with incoming tides moving swiftly across the sands and mud flats. In Sir Walter Scott's novel 'Redgauntlet', a Solway Firth fisherman warned the hero that "The tide advances with such rapidity upon these fatal sands that well-mounted horsemen lay aside hopes of safety, if they see its white surge advancing."

Seafield, on the Solway Firth, was at the northern end of what was Europe's longest railway viaduct when built over the sea in the 1860s, one of the great engineering achievements of that busy decade of railway construction. This viaduct joined the coasts of England and Scotland by means of 193 piers across the Firth, a distance of two miles. In 1881 it was severely damaged by winter storms and was closed for repairs until 1884.

All traffic between Annan and the Cumberland shore ceased in 1921, and the railway viaduct was dismantled in 1934. Only part of the embankment at Seafield survives, ending abruptly at Solway Sands, to remind us of the Victorian railway builders who dared to construct a line across hazardous waters of the Firth more than two decades before the Tay and Forth Bridges were completed.

Trains cross the border between Scotland and England near Gretna Green to reach Carlisle, great northern hub of the west coast main line, yet it is further east in longitude than Edinburgh on the east coast main line. Like York, Carlisle's Citadel station is an outstanding example of Victorian railway architecture, scene of some exciting train journeys, notably the races to Edinburgh in 1888, to Aberdeen in 1895, and the LMS record-breaking non-stop 401 mile run from London to Glasgow in November 1938. Citadel station celebrated its 150th anniversary in 1997.

Six rail routes radiate from Carlisle, and five of these go to or near the sea: north to Glasgow or Edinburgh via Carstairs; northwest to Dumfries, Kilmarnock and Glasgow; east to Newcastle-upon-Tyne, passing near Hadrian's Wall between Brampton and Haltwhistle; west to the coast of Cumbria; and south via Hest Bank beside Morecambe Bay on the west coast main line. The sixth route is the most scenic of them all, from Carlisle to Leeds, more popularly known as the 'Settle-Carlisle', providing a direct rail route between Carlisle and south Yorkshire.

This is the longest (112 miles), and certainly the most impressive of all trans-Pennine routes. It has the highest main line station in Britain, at Dent (1,150ft), four miles from the village, and 600ft above it. Such is the isolation up here that a person could spend the best part of a day at Dent station without seeing another soul, surrounded by splendid solitude.

Ribblehead viaduct is on a sixteen-mile section of line over 1,000ft above sea level, and the entire line is a civil engineering masterpiece with 325 bridges, 21 viaducts, and 14 tunnels. The late Eric Treacy, Bishop of Wakefield, named the Settle-Carlisle line as one of the three great wonders of northern England; the other two he identified as York Minster and Hadrian's Wall, the latter acknowledged to be the most important surviving memorial to the overseas military power of the Roman Empire.

There was once another railway to the sea from Carlisle, which ran beside Hadrian's Wall from Burgh-by-Sands to Drumburgh on its way to Silloth, a handsome town with acres of greensward and a sea front extending for miles, still waiting for the Solway holiday boom which never really happened. It was popular with residents of Carlisle, especially for its fine views across the Solway Firth to Scotland's most southerly hills, notably Criffell (1,868ft), eleven miles away.

The straggling railway route round the Cumbrian coast is never far from the sea, one of the more attractive stretches between St Bees and Sellafield being depicted in this early engraving. This section of the line was built by the Whitehaven & Furness Junction company, which gained notoriety as the country's least profitable railway. Its mainly mixed trains reputedly made long stops at several of the smaller stations so that the staff and crew could indulge in the traditional Cumbrian sport of cock-fighting.

Until 1921, some trains on this branch line swung north and crossed the railway viaduct over the Solway Firth to Scotland. The train from Carlisle to the Cumbrian coast travels inland for 28 miles before reaching the sea at Maryport. This was the route recommended by railway builder George Stephenson for the west coast main line between Lancaster and Carlisle, in order to avoid long climbs over, or tunnels through, the eastern fells of the Lake District.

But, in the tradition of the Romans who occupied this part of the coast, Stephenson's rival Joseph Locke chose a shorter and straighter line from Lancaster to Carlisle through the Lune gorge and over Shap, even though this meant steeper gradients. Locke predicted correctly that the power of future

locomotives would enable adequate speeds to be maintained for the long haul up Shap, and he would surely be impressed to travel today in comfort at 90 mph past the summit marker along the west coast main line he built through Grayrigg, Low Gill, and Tebay on the 22 mile climb to Shap summit, starting at Milnthorpe, just south of Oxenholme.

The 114 mile Cumbrian coast railway line south from Carlisle to Carnforth via Barrow is 26 miles longer than Locke's main line via Penrith, Shap, and the Lune Valley, but by taking this coastal route it gives us an opportunity to enjoy some fine sea views south of Maryport. From Flimby to Workington, and from Harrington to Whitehaven the train clings to cliff edges buttressed by stone walls to support the weight of track ballast and trains on steep slopes.

Whitehaven was attacked in 1778 during the American War of Independence by John Paul Jones in his privateer 'Ranger'. He was Scots-born and knew the port well, having served his apprenticeship here, and was awarded a gold medal by the U.S. Congress for his daring attack on Britain.

This part of the Cumbrian coast is exposed to the full fury of Atlantic gales, and there are several places near the railway line where wind-generator 'farms' are producing electrical power, not far from Sellafield's Calder Hall, the world's first nuclear power station to generate electricity on a commercial scale in 1956.

St Bees railway station is two miles from the red sandstone cliffs of St Bees Head (462ft) which form the only large mass of cliffs on the northwest coast of England. Seventeen miles of almost deserted beaches stretch south from the headland to Seascale and Ravenglass, where the rivers Irt, Mite, and Esk flow into the sea. Wooded slopes rise up behind this quiet fishing village which has three rivers, two railways, and one road through it.

The Ravenglass & Eskdale Railway was built in 1875, and has an interesting pedigree. The line was first built to a 3ft gauge on the speculation of mining a vein of iron ore first discovered in this area by the Romans. The mines failed in 1882, but the railway continued running until 1912. Three years later it was converted to 15 inch gauge, the smallest public railway in the world, then taken over in 1925, sold in 1948, auctioned in 1958, changing hands again in 1960.

As the Lake District's only narrow-gauge steam railway, the R&ER ('Ratty') line runs for seven miles from Ravenglass to Dalegarth, the terminus at Eskdale. With its fine locomotives and scenic route between mountains and sea, it attracts many visitors each year. In October 1998, three R&ER locomotives travelled behind the former 'Iron Curtain' to operate on Dresden's 4.5 mile Parkeisenbahn. Two of the locomotives were steam: 'River Mite' and 'Northern Rock'; the third was a Lister diesel.

Two new steam locomotives were built in the 1990s at the company's workshops in Ravenglass and exported to Japan, a notable transfer of transportation technology, and a proud achievement for this great little railway. A journey along Eskdale in one of the R&ER steam trains, and a tour of the Ravenglass terminus will confirm that in the railway world 'small is beautiful' and longevity the norm, with the 'River Esk' celebrating its 75th year of service in December 1998.

There is a standard-gauge preserved steam railway not far away, which formerly linked Lake Windermere with Morecambe Bay and the Cumbrian coast. To reach the Lakeside & Haverthwaite Railway from Dalegarth station, we take the road eastwards over Hard Knott Pass, Wrynose Pass, through Little Langdale and Skelwith Bridge to Ambleside Pier, where pleasure boats depart for Bowness and Lakeside, terminus of the L&HR.

This railway was built in 1869, and the section now open is the only rail line in the Lake District that actually goes to a lake, England's largest. For nearly a century, trains on this line took passengers from Lakeside station down to the Barrow-in-Furness line which followed the northern shoreline of Morecambe Bay.

Passenger traffic reached a peak during the inter-war years, when special excursion trains from London, Leeds, Blackpool and Morecambe arrived at Lakeside station, where cruise boats were waiting to sail the length of Windermere to Bowness and Ambleside. But summer crowds and holiday traditions were not enough to justify keeping this branch line open all year, and passenger services were withdrawn in 1965.

Dedicated preservationists in this area, as elsewhere, accepted the challenge to restore steam train services on at least part of the line, and eventually succeeded. Early in 1971, British Rail isolated the tracks from the railway network, and after two years hard work by railway enthusiasts, the section between Haverthwaite and Lakeside (3 miles) was opened on 2 May 1973. The L&HR successfully combines a scenic railway journey with a variety of lake cruises around Windermere.

We now return to Ravenglass to continue our journey south along the coast to Barrow and around the shore of Morecambe Bay. Even at the height of summer it is easy to find miles of quiet beaches in south Cumbria, where only the cries of gulls and sounds of the sea may be heard. While this section of the coastline is relatively unknown to most holiday-makers, just a few miles inland is England's greatest natural tourist attraction, the Lake District.

The train continues southwards near a shoreline dominated by Black Combe (1,970ft), past Silecroft to Millom, close to the attractive Duddon sands, then around the estuary to Barrow-in-Furness, once a very busy station and now relatively quiet except when a train is due. Further along the coast is Ulverston, a port that became so choked by silt over the centuries that in 1796 the shortest, deepest and straightest canal in England was dug to re-open the port to the sea.

Ulverston station, with its clock tower and elegant canopies, is one of many fine Victorian buildings erected by the Furness Railway. The town has several modest claims to fame: as the birthplace of the Quaker movement; pole vaulting; Stan Laurel of Hollywood's Laurel and Hardy; and a world champion town crier. Hoad Hill (435ft), a mile north of Ulverston is topped by a replica of the Eddystone lighthouse, visible for miles around.

From Ulverston, the train crosses the Leven estuary at Cartmel sands on the northern fringe of Morecambe Bay. The station at Kents Bank overlooks the bay, as does Grange-over-Sands, noted for its ornamental gardens and retirement residences on what was known to Victorians as Cumbria's 'Riviera'.

When the railway arrived here in 1857, a sea wall was built to hold back high tides that occasionally covered what is now the main street. The shoreline at low tide is a mass of muddy silt, difficult and dangerous to venture across, for it is like walking through glue as the tide ebbs and flows.

Long before the railway came, Grange-over-Sands was a haven for many people crossing the hazardous sands of Morecambe Bay. The meandering route across the sands

Basic seaside terminus. Piel, until 1882 the port for Isle of Man and Belfast boats which sailed from a deep-water pier. When these were diverted to the new Barrow docks, Piel remained a popular venue with Barrovians until closure of the branch in 1936.

from Hest Bank to Kents Bank, near Grange, was a risky alternative to the long and tiresome overland journey by foot, horse, or cart around estuaries that flow into the bay. Many travellers paid a high price, losing their lives to the fast incoming tide, as they struggled to cross difficult sections of quicksand and mud intersected by channels of rivers flowing into the sea.

We cross the Kent estuary smoothly by train to reach Arnside, where a small tidal bore sweeps over the beach two hours before high water. The tidal bore was much more impressive before the railway viaduct was built over mud that was found to be 90ft deep in places. This viaduct provides fine views of the coast around Arnside, where a surprised Victorian gentleman on his first visit reported that the shore was covered one hour with ships, and then later with horses, carriages and pedestrians.

The Cumbrian coast line meets the west coast main line just

south of Carnforth station, where the classic railway film 'Brief Encounter' was made in 1945. Three miles south of Carnforth is Hest Bank, where guides usually set out with walkers to cross the sands only if the conditions of tide and weather are suitable. Most trains speed by Hest Bank, allowing only a brief view of the sea at high tide. To reach Morecambe, we change trains at Lancaster.

In 1848 the first train arrived at Morecambe, and it was not long before huge crowds from Lancashire and Yorkshire came by train for their holidays here, where the town's motto was: "Beauty surrounds, Health abounds." It was said that if Morecambe provided a smile on the face of workaday Lancashire, then Blackpool was its belly laugh. In competition for holiday business, each resort excluded the other from their respective maps of places to visit, even though more distant places were clearly shown.

Morecambe was the first place in Britain to have electric railway service between main line and sea front (1908), and the first to have electric illuminations along its promenade. It was also the last town in mainland Britain to operate horse trams along the sea front. At the peak of its summer season in the 1920s, over 100,000 visitors were lodged among a population of less than 20,000, and twenty churches and

'LA'AL RATTY'

The Ravenglass & Eskdale Railway, built as a 3ft gauge line in 1875 and converted to 15in gauge from 1915, has long had the nickname "La'al Ratty" ("la'al" is dialect for "little"). Worked by a preservation society since 1960, it now boasts a most impressive terminus at Ravenglass. (John Hadrill)

A spick and span River Esk poses for a group of interested admirers. The locomotive celebrated its 75th anniversary in 1998. (John Hadrill)

Heysham Harbour, once the terminus of the 'Ulster Express' boat train from London Euston. This view dates from May 1968 when steam was about to give way to diesel. The train on the right is a pigeon special to Ludlow. (Derek Cross)

chapels were built to cater for their needs. In 1924, over half a million people arrived by train between 26 June and 2 October.

The greatest and most enduring attraction at Morecambe is its bay, covering an area estimated at 174 square miles, the largest bite out of the northwest coast of England. The panorama from the sea front never fails to fascinate. On a clear day, the scene at low tide is one vast desert of sand and silty grey mud which is submerged rapidly as the tide comes in. Fine views across the bay to the mountains of the Lake District inspired one early guide book to describe Morecambe Bay as "our English Bay of Naples", a far cry from the fishing village entered in the Domesday Book as Poulton-le-Sands.

In the 1990s, Morecambe's impressive railway station on the sea front was converted into an arts and entertainment centre named 'The Platform', which also includes the town's travel centre. A smaller station has been built nearby, while a supermarket and various other commercial buildings now occupy the area where platforms long enough to take trains of twelve coaches led into the old station. The famous LMS art deco Midland Hotel which opened in 1933 opposite the station has fortunately survived, and is now named 'The Midland Grand Hotel'.

From the age of steam to the advent of nuclear power, "cheap and cheerful Morecambe" has been adopted as the resort of choice by many visitors from Lancashire and Yorkshire, who prefer its fine mountain backdrop to the flatness that surrounds the Fylde coastline. Those favouring Blackpool in turn deride Morecambe's northern landscape as "all wind, water, and walking".

Heysham is a mixture of residential areas, docks and industry, with a deep water channel leading to the open sea. The harbour was built by the Midland Railway in 1904 to provide services to the Isle of Man and Belfast in competition with other railway companies on Britain's west coast. The name 'Ulster Express' was conferred on the Euston-Heysham boat train in 1927, and for some years the first-class section included an open saloon coach with leather-upholstered armchairs originally built for the 'Royal Scot' service.

During WW2, the boat train ran incognito, returning with its title and dining cars in October 1945, until withdrawn from service in April 1975. It was the last steam-hauled named train on British Railways. The Heysham branch line from Lancaster remains open, taking passengers to Heysham docks for ferry services to the Isle of Man.

From Heysham to Blackpool our rail route is via Morecambe, Lancaster and Preston, to reach the greatest cluster of seaside resorts created or developed by Britain's railways, at Fleetwood, Cleveleys, Blackpool, Lytham, St Annes, and Southport. This part of the Lancashire coast between Fleetwood and Southport includes over twenty miles of developed shoreline north of the Ribble, and is the premier holiday playground of industrial northwest England.

In 1840 the first train from London arrived at Fleetwood, where ships took passengers north to Ardrossan, to complete their journey by train to Glasgow. Queen Victoria travelled this route in 1847, though in the reverse direction, when returning from Scotland to Windsor. The west coast main line from London to Glasgow was completed in 1848, and Fleetwood then lost its importance as a passenger port, gaining status as a holiday resort under the guiding hand of Sir Peter Hesketh-Fleetwood, owner of large estates around Poulton-le-Fylde.

Fleetwood has lost its passenger trains, but can still be reached easily by frequent trams that run along the promenade, or close to it, from Blackpool. Around the Fylde coast from Fleetwood, the beaches at Cleveleys link with

those of Blackpool, famous for its tower, three piers, extensive sands and golden mile of entertainments, attracting more than eight million visitors each year.

The season here extends far beyond the traditional summer holidays, with conferences, trade shows and many other events in the autumn and winter. Seven miles of sea front are dominated by the 518ft high tower, completed in 1894 at the peak of Victorian engineering exuberance, the tallest structure in Britain at the dawn of the twentieth century, and still the most spectacular man-made landmark on this coast.

No other place in Britain is so overwhelmingly dedicated to providing fun and entertainment for the masses as this big, brash, seaside resort. When the first visitors arrived in the 18th century, Blackpool was just a small seaside village, yet as early as 1789 the habit of sea bathing became popular here, following publication of a booklet outlining the etiquette to be followed by those daring enough to try the novelty of immersion in waters of the Irish Sea.

The railway reached Blackpool in 1846, enabling industrial Lancashire's huge population to take holidays by the sea for the first time. All over the northwest, factories and businesses would close down for a week or more in the summer to allow workers and their families to travel by train to Blackpool or neighbouring resorts along the coast, with beneficial results such as those described in a contemporary journal:

"Crowds of poor people from the manufacturing towns who

Morecambe Promenade's spacious concourse in its heyday, complete with hanging baskets and other botanical effects. It has now been demolished, commercial buildings occupying land where long platforms led into the station. Until 1963 the town had a second terminus at Euston Road, noted for its facade of vivid yellow bricks.

have a high opinion of the efficacy of bathing, maintain that in the month of August there is physic in the sea, physic of the most comprehensive description, combining all the virtues of all the drugs in the doctor's shop, and of course, a cure for all varieties of disease."

In 1895, before corridor trains came into general use, a group of first-class season ticket holders who lived in Blackpool and worked in Manchester persuaded the Lancashire &Yorkshire Railway to attach several first-class saloons to the morning and evening business trains for their exclusive use, complete with attendant and refreshments. Thus was born the 'Blackpool Club Train'. It was so popular that a third-class reserved saloon was added, and this service lasted for 44 years until the austerity of WW2 took away its comfortable saloons and attentive staff. The train continued to run without club coaches during the war, but did not regain its former prestige or fast timings when peace returned.

After the grouping of Britain's railways in 1923, a vice-

Morecambe Promenade once welcomed holiday-makers by the thousand from the mill towns of both Lancashire and the West Riding. It also had a pioneer electric service to Lancaster and Heysham which began as early as 1908. One of the three-car trains is seen at the terminus in 1964, two years before services were withdrawn
.(R. Herbert/Colour-Rail DE525)

A railway photographer's dream! A strong off-shore wind carries the smoke well clear of the train but the water is calm enough to give some impressive reflections in the bright sunshine. A steam-hauled enthusiasts' special is crossing Newbiggin viaduct, near Ravenglass, in May 1975 behind B1 1306 Mayflower *and A3 4472* Flying Scotsman. *(Colour-Rail P23)*

The things they do at Blackpool! Taste goes by the board as 'Compound' 41101 is repainted in garish yellow and red to head a Daily Mirror 'Andy Capp Special' to the Fylde Coast resort in 1959. (P.J. Fitton/Colour-Rail BRM1280)

No other resort in Britain has seen such huge crowds arriving by train during this past century as has Blackpool. Today traffic is greatly diminished, but colourful decorations still provide a touch of cheer for visitors at Blackpool North station, completely rebuilt in 1974 to meet modern requirements. (John Hadrill)

president of the LMS, who had a house near Blackpool, decided that a new fast train from London was needed to improve service to this popular resort. The 'Blackpool & Fylde Coast Express' was therefore introduced, departing from Blackpool at 0825 and arriving in London at 1250. For its return journey to the sea the train left Euston at 1710, stopping at resorts on the Fylde coast and arriving in Blackpool at 2157.

The train was manned alternately by Blackpool and London crews, but whereas the Blackpool men had four hours' turnaround time in the afternoon to enjoy the sights of London, their colleagues driving the express from London arrived in Blackpool too late at night to sample the many attractions of this lively resort. As many steam locomotive crews knew only too well, restlessness was a condition of railway life, and early wake-up calls for the next trip after a late night shift came all too quickly.

No other resort in Britain has welcomed such huge crowds arriving by train during this past century as has Blackpool. On one Saturday in August 1935, a total of 467 trains arrived at, or departed from, the resort's stations, while in 1938 over six million passengers came in 22,000 trains to this great metropolis of pleasure beside the sea.

The most famous illuminations in Britain bring visitors from all over the country for a brilliant extravaganza in September and October, when illuminated trams glide along an incandescent wonderland by night. The British Tourist Authority named Blackpool's Pleasure Beach as Britain's top free attraction in 1996, with 7.5 million visitors, and there is no seaside town in Britain that is better served by train. The 1998 winter timetable listed 76 trains each weekday from Preston to Blackpool, with its four railway stations: North, South, Pleasure Beach, and Squire's Gate.

Yet, almost lost among the strident and crowded entertainments, there is another unobtrusive and tranquil Blackpool, a resort of spacious parks, bowling greens, rose gardens, tennis courts, and art galleries, for those who prefer recreation away from the madding crowds. Seven miles of promenade and beaches are long enough to allow crowds to disperse the further one walks, or rides, from the resort's noisy epicentre near the tower and piers. From Blackpool South station, trains follow the coast down to stations at St Annes and Lytham, where the four miles of lawns, gardens and parkland along the sea front are in pleasant contrast to its boisterous neighbour.

Lytham's famous windmill stands beside the lifeboat museum on the sea front at Lytham Green, a short walk from the station. The promenade that joins Lytham to St Annes attracts visitors and residents alike for a leisurely stroll along to the pier at St. Annes, especially on a summer's evening with the sun setting over the water, and distant views across the Ribble estuary to Southport.

Established as health resorts at the same time as Blackpool,

both Lytham and St Annes retain a traditional seaside town atmosphere, with Victorian buildings, entertainments, sporting activities, and acres of greensward beside the sea, stretching round the coast from Lytham's white windmill to St Annes' elegantly restored pier dating from 1885, one of the most exotic of British piers, with its chinese-style kiosks and elegant ironwork.

In October 1998, Lytham's unique 'Pebble Mosaic' was completed in Clifton Square, a short walk from the station and sea front. This is one of the finest contemporary mosaics in Britain, over 26ft in diameter, whose subtle colours look best after rain has put a shine on them.

To reach Southport, six miles across the Ribble estuary from Lytham we change trains at Preston and Wigan, a journey of nearly fifty miles. Most of Southport's main promenade is on land reclaimed from the sea to create an attractive sea front, with extensive gardens, a marine lake and funfair. The station is about a mile from the beach.

In the 18th century, an enterprising innkeeper named William Sutton built the first sea-bathing house here on sands that reach almost as far as the eye can see in both directions. The tide goes out a long way from the dunes of soft sand and sea grass which extend southwards to Birkdale, Ainsdale, and Formby, all served by trains on the Southport-Liverpool line which was completed in 1850 and electrified in 1904.

The first train from Wigan arrived at Southport in 1848, and by 1851 its population was twice that of Blackpool. From 1882 to 1952 the Cheshire Lines Railway ran trains through sandhills along the coast between Liverpool and Southport, a journey that ended at the elegant Lord Street station, now a bus station. After closure of this line, a road was built on top of the old trackbed leading to Ainsdale-on-Sea.

With its fine location and many attractions, Southport has remained a favourite holiday and residential resort. Lively summer crowds on the promenade and along fashionable Lord Street are in contrast to the tranquillity one can find in parks, gardens, and miles of pleasant walks along the sands where it is usually safe to wade in shallow waters as the tide ebbs and flows.

All trains from Southport to Liverpool now travel inland through Birkdale and Ainsdale to Formby, an old fishing village by the sea. Grassy dunes and pine woods lead down to a broad sandy beach that sweeps north for eight miles to Southport. The National Trust controls 400 acres of dunes and shoreline, bought by public subscription in 1967 as part of 'Enterprise Neptune' to preserve the nearest unspoilt coastline to Liverpool and its northern suburbs.

Liverpool gained in prominence as a major port in the 18th century, and the city's fortunes, like those of Bristol, were founded on maritime trade all over the world, notably in sugar, tobacco, cotton, and countless other raw and manufactured

Blackpool Central, still a hive of activity in July 1963. Just over a year later it was closed, services terminating at the less convenient South station. It is a far cry from the days before the war, as instanced in 1938 when 22,000 trains brought over six million passengers to this big and brash resort dedicated to providing fun and entertainment for the masses. (F. Dean)

goods. In 1840, Samuel Cunard began the world's first steamship service across the Atlantic Ocean from Liverpool, and while the city now concerns itself with many more industries than shipping, it still retains distinctive waterfront landmarks from the great era of sea trade and travel.

From 1893 to 1956, electric trains on the Liverpool Overhead Railway travelled beside the city's extensive docks, giving passengers convenient access and spectacular close-up views of all the ships berthed along the waterfront. While other uses have been found for many of the famous docks, their names endure to remind us of the Cunard steamships and the great white fleet of 'Empress' ships of Canadian Pacific that berthed here during the heydays of sea travel which coincided with the lifetime of the overhead railway.

In order to see the famous Liverpool skyline, we will take a ferry over to New Brighton instead of a train under the Mersey. New Brighton was named and developed by James Atherton of Everton, who had ambitions to make it the Brighton of the north. But the railway, an essential catalyst, was a long time in coming, not reaching the town until 1888, fifty-eight years after Liverpool's first train.

The Wirral peninsula, bounded by the Mersey and Dee estuaries, is reached by trains from Liverpool and Chester. At its tip, the Wirral is seven miles across, with its east side facing industrial Merseyside, while its west side is another world on the peaceful estuary of the Dee, with green fields, quiet beaches, and views across to the coastline of North Wales.

Few areas of comparable size in Britain can match the variety and contrasts of the Wirral, with its saltings and ever-shifting sandbanks; three small islands on which seals bask; boating on the Shropshire Union Canal as it meanders into Cheshire; the Mersey, where ships pass along one of Europe's busiest waterways; and the Wirral Way, a restoration marvel along the former railway line from West Kirby to Hooton. This is one of

WEST COAST POSTERS

ENGLAND'S LATEST   SEASIDE HOTEL

MIDLAND HOTEL MORECAMBE

AN *LMS* HOTEL

ARTHUR TOWLE CONTROLLER LMS HOTEL SERVICES

The Midland Hotel at Morecambe, built to Oliver Hill's exciting modern design in 1933. It was too much for Arthur Towle, the LMS Hotel Services Controller, who thought it would frighten off traditional visitors!

GREAT CENTRAL RAILWAY.

BLACKPOOL

FOR GORGEOUS SIGHTS

FOR PARTICULARS OF **TRAIN SERVICE, FARES AND OTHER INFORMATION** APPLY AT ANY GREAT CENTRAL STATION

The 'gorgeous sights' are presumably these three Blackpool belles rather than the distant Tower. This early poster was issued by the Great Central Railway, which had ambitious but unfulfilled plans to reach the famous West Coast resort. (NRM/Science & Society - 3)

Left: *Grange over Sands, a small resort on the shores of Morecambe Bay, was originally developed by the Furness Railway. Both the town and its railway station have changed little down the years.*

Southport Chapel Street in the early 1900s, the car arguably more interesting than the ponderous Italianate facade. The wording above the entrance indicates that this resort was popular in the woollen districts of the West Riding as well as the cotton towns of Lancashire.

several places in Britain where a 'rails-to-trails' conversion has brought a new attraction for visitors to the area.

The twelve-mile Wirral Way is a showpiece of transformation from former branch railway line to country park, where the old trackbed is now a pathway connecting with a further fifteen miles of footpaths and bridleways in the Wirral. The old Thurstaston station is now a visitor centre, with platforms still intact, surrounded by grassy areas and trees within a few hundred yards of the sea.

When the railway was built here in 1886, Thomas Ismay of Cunard fame insisted that the line detour around his property near Thurstaston, forcing it nearer to the shoreline, which makes the walk along the Wirral Way all the more enjoyable today. The only station building to survive completely is at Hadlow Road, and it has been restored to look as it did in the heydays of the 1950s. Three miles east of Hadlow Road the pathway ends at Hooton, where we take a train to Chester, our gateway into Wales.

Chester is an important railway crossroads on the main line from London to Holyhead, and has direct rail services to the Wirral, Liverpool, Crewe, Manchester, Shrewsbury, and beyond. The city is strategically located between the estuaries of the Mersey and the Dee, with the border between England and Wales at its western outskirts.

In the centre of this ancient walled city established by the Romans is the great red sandstone cathedral, near to the unique shopping galleries known as 'The Rows'. Chester is an ideal base for exploring nearby coastal resorts, and if time is limited, a walk along the walls and 'Rows' is recommended in order to enjoy the character of this fine and friendly city before boarding the train into Wales.

The three coasts of Wales

**All places that the eye of heaven visits
Are to a wise man ports and happy havens.**

William Shakespeare

The train from Chester into North Wales crosses the border shortly after leaving the station, and passes the low-lying Dee flats towards the estuary and open sea, travelling towards Flint whose castle was founded in 1281. The town grew inland from the castle gate, but when Victorian railway engineers drove their line up the coast they placed it between town and castle, the latter now a ruin but still visible from the train.

Until the 18th century, Flint was a prosperous port, but its access to the sea became too shallow and dangerous due to constantly changing channels of the Dee estuary, a marine wilderness of saltings, sandbanks and mudflats. After leaving Flint, the train speeds past Mostyn docks, then rounds the Point of Air to approach a resort area known as 'the golden coast of North Wales'.

Prestatyn was first settled by the Romans, and in medieval times was the fiefdom of princes of Powys, the most powerful of Welsh kingdoms. When the railway arrived in 1840, Prestatyn started its steady growth as a seaside resort, expanding rapidly when the LMS joined forces with Thomas Cook in the 1930s to build a holiday camp here.

Rhyl and Prestatyn, two of the liveliest resorts on the coast of North Wales, are set on an eight-mile stretch of sandy beach, with caravans and holiday chalets spread on both sides of the railway line. Rhyl's funfair dominates the western end of a wide promenade near the mouth of the River Clwyd.

At Abergele and Pensarn, the coastal features change. To the east are long sandy beaches, low dunes, and miles of holiday homes, while to the west are cliffs and rugged headlands, with the rail tracks curving close to the shoreline.

Since entering Wales we have been following the route of the famous 'Irish Mail', the world's oldest named train, which started service between London (Euston) and Holyhead in July 1848. Until 1939, a unique railway ritual was followed at every departure of the 'Irish Mail' from Euston, with the handing of a chronometer to the guard in order to provide precise Greenwich time to officials in Dublin. Each evening, an Admiralty messenger would hasten to Euston with the precious chronometer, which would be returned to London with the next 'Irish Mail' for checking and re-adjustment.

This was one of several railway traditions dating from the reign of Queen Victoria, which like the stationmaster's top hat, have all but disappeared. The 150th anniversary of the first 'Irish Mail' was celebrated by Virgin Trains on 31 July 1998, with special events along the route, including naming HST power car 43101 'The Irish Mail' at Euston. The train was boarded by an 'Admiralty messenger' in period costume, complete with chronometer, for the journey to Holyhead.

Colwyn was a cluster of fishermen's cottages and three farms when the first train arrived in 1858. The railway company added the word 'Bay' to the signs on the station platforms and in its timetables in order to attract more visitors. This is another example of railway enterprise in developing seaside towns around the coast, and business for the railway companies. Colwyn Bay is now a flourishing resort with a long promenade facing the gentle curve of the bay towards Rhos-on-Sea, Penrhyn Bay and Llandudno.

At Llandudno Junction the main line to Holyhead meets two branch lines, one north to Deganwy and Llandudno; the other south to Blaenau Ffestiniog. We shall travel on each one, after

WELSH HIGHLIGHTS

The Britannia Tubular Bridge, as it looked before the disastrous fire of 1970 forced a complete rebuilding. A steel-arched structure using the original masonry towers was opened in 1972 and a road deck above the rails added eight years later.
(B.J. Swain/Colour-Rail BRM476)

Conwy, where the huge castle at the best-preserved medieval fortress town in Britain, completely dominates the railway. The town was founded in 1283 on a rocky promontory, providing a natural defence against attack and a quarry for building stone. (John Hadrill)

Business is brisk at Bangor as 5MT 45130 arrives with a down express in 1956. Two miles from the Britannia bridge, the station once handled traffic to Pwllheli and Porthmadog via Caernarfon as well as main-line services to Holyhead.
(J.H. Moss/Colour-Rail BRM816)

Dovey Junction, in the middle of nowhere, where trains from Aberystwyth to Paddington would pick up through coaches from Pwllheli and Barmouth. The up Cambrian Coast Express passes some fine signals as it leaves the Junction in 1964; this popular service ran for the last time three years later. (J.B. Snell/Colour-Rail BRW830)

Once just a cluster of fishermen's cottages, Colwyn Bay was one of many resorts to develop along the North Wales coast following completion of the Chester & Holyhead Railway. The station was rebuilt in the 1980s, retaining its famous glass screen as well as a privately-developed restaurant, museum and shops, complete with a static display of a tank engine and coach. (NRM - E3115)

first visiting Conwy castle and walled town, generally considered to be the best-preserved medieval fortress town on Britain's coastline, easily reached on foot from Llandudno Junction station.

Conwy was founded in 1283, and in the space of only five years most of the important features of the town, such as castle, town walls, quayside, and street pattern were completed. The rocky promontory on which Conwy stands was a natural defence against attack, and also a quarry for all the stone needed to build the fortress. A climb to the top of the castle walls is rewarded by a fine panorama of the town, estuary, and valley to the south.

In contrast to the huge castle, the quayside boasts the smallest house in Britain, a 19th century cottage with a frontage of six feet and height of just over ten feet. Fishing boats line the harbour wall, and at the mouth of the Conwy estuary is Morfa Beach with its broad expanse of sand at low tide. Across the water is Deganwy station and Great Orme's Head overlooking Llandudno.

The largest resort in North Wales, Llandudno is set on a wide bay flanked by Great Orme's Head (679ft) and Little Orme's Head (454ft). The promenade is one of the finest in Britain, with Victorian and Edwardian hotels lining the sea front which still retains most of its original 19th century dignity and charm. The pier, dating from 1876, harmonizes with the natural splendour of its setting amid all the modern-day amusements.

The first settlement at Llandudno was around the church of St Tudno on the top of Great Orme, but this lofty windswept site was too small for expansion, so the town developed along Orme's Bay and later across the narrow peninsula to West Shore overlooking Conwy sands. Most of the shops and restaurants are located on or near Mostyn Street close to the sea, and today this compactness is a great attraction for visitors, just as it was for their Victorian predecessors more than a century ago.

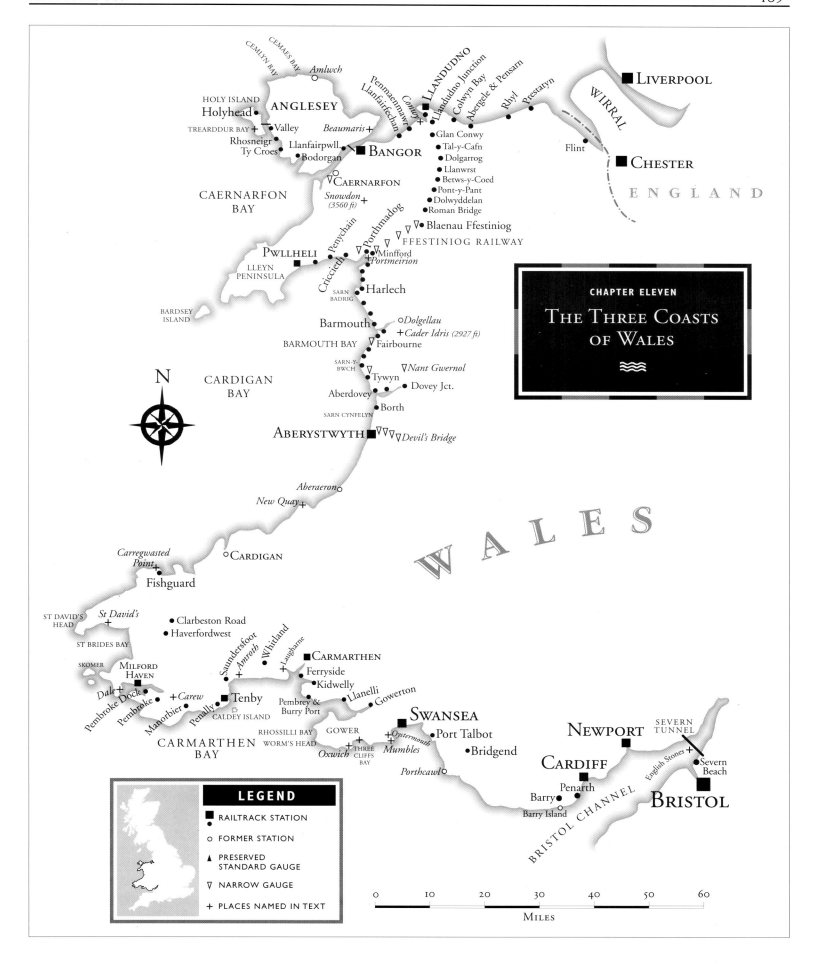

CEMAES BAY
CEMLYN BAY

Amlwch ○

HOLY ISLAND   ANGLESEY
Holyhead ■

TREARDDUR BAY + Valley   Beaumaris +
Rhosneigr
Ty Croes   Llanfairpwll.
          ● Bodorgan   ■ BANGOR

CAERNARFON   ▽ CAERNARFON
BAY

Snowdon +
(3560 ft)

Penmaenmawr
Llanfairfechan
Conwy
+
LLANDUDNO ■
Llandudno Junction
Colwyn Bay
Abergele & Pensarn
Rhyl
Prestatyn

● Glan Conwy
● Tal-y-Cafn
● Dolgarrog
● Llanwrst
● Betws-y-Coed
● Pont-y-Pant
● Dolwyddelan
● Roman Bridge

WIRRAL   ■ LIVERPOOL

Flint ●   ■ CHESTER

E N G L A N D

▽ ▽ ● Blaenau Ffestiniog
▽ FFESTINIOG RAILWAY

Porthmadog
Penychain   ▽▽ ▽ Minfford
Criccieth   + Portmeirion

PWLLHELI ■

LLEYN
PENINSULA

BARDSEY
ISLAND

SARN
BADRIG   Harlech

Barmouth   ○ Dolgellau
          + Cader Idris (2927 ft)
BARMOUTH BAY   ▽ Fairbourne

N   CARDIGAN
BAY

SARN-Y-
BWCH   ▽   ▽ Nant Gwernol
          Tywyn
Aberdovey   ● Dovey Jct.
          ● Borth
SARN CYNFELYN

ABERYSTWYTH ■ ▽▽ ▽ Devil's Bridge

Aberaeron ○
New Quay +

W A L E S

Carregwasted
Point +
Fishguard   ○ CARDIGAN

ST DAVID'S   St David's
HEAD   +   ● Clarbeston Road
          ● Haverfordwest
ST BRIDES BAY

SKOMER   Whitland
          MILFORD   Saundersfoot   Laugharne
          HAVEN   Amroth   ■ CARMARTHEN
Dale +   +
Pembroke Dock ■   ● Ferryside
+ Carew   ● Kidwelly
Pembroke ●   Tenby   Llanelli
          Penally   ● Gowerton
Manorbier   CALDEY ISLAND   Pembrey &
                    Burry Port

CARMARTHEN   RHOSSILLI BAY   GOWER   ■ SWANSEA
BAY   WORM'S HEAD   + Oystermouth   ● Port Talbot
          Oxwich +   THREE   Mumbles
          CLIFFS   ● Bridgend
          BAY
          Porthcawl ○

SEVERN
TUNNEL

■ NEWPORT

■ CARDIFF   English Stones
          + Severn
          ● Beach
Penarth
Barry ●   ■ BRISTOL
Barry Island ○

BRISTOL CHANNEL

LEGEND
■ RAILTRACK STATION
○ FORMER STATION
▲ PRESERVED
   STANDARD GAUGE
▽ NARROW GAUGE
+ PLACES NAMED IN TEXT

0   10   20   30   40   50   60
MILES

In recent years the slogan "Great Little Trains of Wales" has been used for the Principality's surviving narrow gauge railways. One of the favourite lines remains the Vale of Rheidol Railway, dating from 1902 when some passengers on the first train were so frightened by the experience that nothing would induce them to return except on foot!
(T.B. Owen/Colour-Rail BRW1296)

Steam on the sands. The Fairbourne Miniature Railway as it looked in 1960 before being rebuilt as a 12.25in gauge line. Barmouth is visible across the estuary. (David Joy collection)

Llandudno, served by its own branch running alongside the Conwy estuary from Llandudno Junction, has grown into the largest resort in Wales, although it has kept much of its early dignity and charm. A diesel-unit is about to leave on a service to Blaenau Ffestiniog in 1989 (above), a year before the terminus lost its overall roof. At this time the ticket barriers still retained their LMS motif (below). (T.J. Edgington - 2)

For over 25 years, until the outbreak of WW2, the 'Llandudno Club Train' made the longest journey of the 'club trains' that departed from Manchester to the seaside. The coaches assigned to this service included two luxurious twelve-wheeled saloons built originally for first-class passengers travelling in boat-trains between London and Liverpool.

On a difficult route from industrial Lancashire through Cheshire into Wales the 'Llandudno Club Train had some fast timings, serving resorts at Rhyl, Abergele and Colwyn Bay before leaving the main line at Llandudno Junction for the scenic run beside the Conwy estuary. But, like the 'Blackpool Club Train', it lost its fine saloons and attendants in September 1939, running incognito throughout WW2.

We leave Llandudno, changing at Llandudno Junction to board the Holyhead train, which crosses over to Conwy inside Robert Stephenson's tubular railway bridge (1848), then through Conwy to 'the big stone headland' which gives Penmaenmawr its name. The quarries here provide large quantities of stone for use all over Britain. There are fine views of Great Orme's Head, Conwy Bay, and Puffin Island from the new promenade built at Penmaenmawr in 1989.

The next station by the sea is Llanfairfechan, still dominated by Penmaenmawr mountain until the coastal plain is reached, as we head towards Bangor and the Menai Strait. The railway line follows the coast past Llanfairfechan to the Lavan Sands, a wide expanse of shingle and sand which used as a means to cross to the Anglesey shore before Thomas Telford built his graceful Menai Suspension Bridge, the longest in the world when completed in 1826.

Bangor is a busy commercial centre, university town, and gateway to Anglesey. Its cathedral is built on the remains of a monastery dating from AD 546, establishing Bangor among the oldest religious sites in Britain. From Bangor station it is just over two miles to the Britannia railway bridge (1849), another fine example of the engineering skill and enterprise that put Britain in the forefront of railway bridge construction. The bridge now carries a road as well as the main line to Holyhead.

The first station after crossing the Menai Strait has by far the longest name of any in Britain, requiring such space in timetables and on maps that it is usually shortened from 58 letters to 12 or less, simply Llanfairpwll, or sometimes Llanfair PG. It is the nearest station to Beaumaris which has the only one of Edward I's medieval castles built on an island. Although never completed, it is regarded as a good example of a concentrically designed fortress.

Where wooden warships once anchored to deliver supplies to the castle, yachts now moor in Beaumaris Bay, the principal sailing centre in the Menai Strait. Sheltered from prevailing westerlies, the east coast of Anglesey is an unspoilt holiday playground with sandy bays, rocky coves and clifftop walks. Puffin Island is a mile offshore.

The railway line to Holyhead crosses Anglesey on the west side of the island, approaching Malltraeth Sands and the Cefni Estuary two miles before Bodorgan station. Along this coast the sea has gouged the rocks to form indented sandy bays, reached from stations at Bodorgan, Ty Croes, Rhosneigr, and Valley, all within two miles of the coast.

Across the narrow strait between Holyhead Bay and Cymyran Bay is Holy Island, with Holyhead on its northern shore. The harbour is protected by Britain's longest breakwater (1.87 miles), completed in 1873 using stone quarried at Holyhead Mountain (719ft), using the broad-gauge Holyhead Breakwater Railway to bring more than seven million tons of stone from the mountain to the sea. Brunel, whose last broadgauge railway line was built in 1877, would surely have approved of the use of his seven-foot gauge for this line, which survived at Holyhead until 1913, when the trackbed was converted into a roadway

The rocky headlands of northwest Anglesey have been transformed by countless storms into a series of sandy bays. Most of the eight miles of cliffs and secluded coves between Church Bay and Cemlyn Bay are so remote that they can only be reached on foot. In the days of sail, this part of the coast had a history of tragic shipwrecks, and local legend claims that one of the many shipwreck victims was Saint Patrick. There is a church dedicated to the saint near Cemaes Bay.

Ferries and mailboats have operated between Holyhead and Dublin since the reign of Queen Elizabeth I. After its inauguration in 1848, the 'Irish Mail' was the fastest train out of Euston, with its passage reported to the LNWR company secretary each day. It was considered to be so important over all other arrivals that the Holyhead stationmaster always wore a buttonhole to greet the train, the first in the world to make use of water troughs between the rails for high speed refills along its 264 mile route.

Although most train passengers hurry through the station to board the ferry, Holy Island has much to attract tourists with time to explore the island, where no place is more than two miles from the sea. Holyhead Mountain (720ft) is Anglesey's best viewpoint, with a summit panorama that includes Snowdonia, the Lake District, the Isle of Man, Ulster's Mountains of Mourne, and Eire's Wicklow Mountains.

At the narrowest part of Holy Island is Trearddur Bay, a popular sailing and aquadiving centre, with clear waters and sandy beaches leading to secluded coves. Low tide at Rhoscolyn reveals a beautiful horseshoe of sand sheltered by rocky headlands, while to the east is another sandy beach at Silver Bay, accessible only on foot.

From Holyhead we return to Llandudno Junction to take the shortest route by train to Pwllheli, the next Railtrack station on the northwest coast of Wales. But before leaving the Menai Strait, we will travel eight miles by road from Bangor to Caernarfon, where the Welsh Highland Railway has started to rebuild a narrow gauge line between Caernarfon and Porthmadog to link the Menai Strait with Tremadoc Bay.

When work is completed on this narrow gauge railway project, trains will travel on a 25-mile line through Snowdonia to Porthmadog. The proposed route south from Caernarfon is via Dinas, Betws Garmon, Beddgelert, Nantmor, and Portreuddyn. In October 1997, the first steam train into Caernarfon since 1972 arrived from Dinas, puffing up close to the famous castle walls, and giving the town its second great tourist attraction, both within a stone's throw of each other.

Back at Llandudno Junction, we take a train south along the Conwy valley to Blaenau Ffestiniog, heading up the estuary and Vale of Conwy, to reach Tal-y-Cafn station, a mile from the famous Bodnant Gardens, high on the east side of the valley. As the train threads its way up the valley, wooded hills and mountains gradually close in on pastures along both sides of the river. Most of the stations along this line are small halts, and the only towns along the entire route between Llandudno and Blaenau Ffestiniog are at Llanrwst and Betws-y-Coed.

After stops at Dolgarrog and Llanrwst, we arrive Betws-y-Coed, a popular touring centre with nature trails, waterfalls, mountain lakes, wooded valleys, impressive bridges, and large forests. The Conwy Valley Railway Museum is in the former goods yard of the station and has a narrow- gauge steam railway, one of several that we see during our train journeys in Wales.

South of Betws, the train climbs through woods and rock cuttings to cross an impressive viaduct known as Cethin's Bridge, near Pont-y-Pant station. This is one of several places in Britain with a station on the Railtrack network, but hardly a village or even a house nearby.

Just after leaving Dolwyddelan station, the massive square shape of Dolwyddelan Castle may be seen on the right. This castle was the birthplace of Llewelyn the Great, Prince of Wales, whose fortresses in Snowdonia included castles on

the coast at Conwy, Harlech, and Criccieth, all close to their respective railway stations. After leaving Roman Bridge Station on the upper reaches of the River Lledr, the train continues its climb before plunging into a two-mile tunnel to emerge among man-made mountains of discarded slate that have accumulated during the past two centuries of production at the largest slate mines in the world.

There is no greater change in scenery between two ends of a railway tunnel in Britain than here, as we enter Blaenau Ffestiniog, terminus of the Conwy Valley Line, originally built to carry slate products to the sea for export to markets around the world. From a nearby platform at the station, trains of the famous Ffestiniog Railway depart for Porthmadog on a scenic thirteen-mile journey from the mountains to the sea, with the greatest vertical descent (700ft) of any narrow gauge railway in Britain.

Two years after this panorama of Penmaenmawr was photographed for posterity in 1883, the small town was described as a 'delightful and retired watering-place' with 'charming walks' as its main attraction. The scene has now been transformed by the building of the North Wales Coast Road, although the unstaffed station buildings have largely survived. (NRM - Cr.C48)

The line opened in 1836, with horses to haul empty wagons uphill to Blaenau, where slate was loaded and carried down to Porthmadog, mainly by gravity. Double-ended 'Fairlie' steam locomotives were introduced in 1869, operating on a gauge of only 1.96ft, and this rare type of locomotive is still in service today, an impressive sight when hauling a fully-loaded train up to Blaenau from sea level, with steam as white as snow

One of the Ffestiniog Railway's impressive double Fairlie locomotives poses for its admirers. Opened as early as 1836 to convey slate from Blaenau Ffestiniog to the port, this 1ft 11$^1/_2$ in gauge railway became a world leader when it adopted steam traction in the 1860s. After a long period of decline it is now one of Britain's premier preserved railways, offering a magnificent journey from the mountains to the sea. (John Hadrill)

drifting along the mountainside.

In 1955, part of the old line near Tanygrisiau was submerged beneath a hydroelectric reservoir, and had to be rebuilt in 1978 at a higher elevation. During construction of the new line, a spiral track was built on the mountainside, as well as a 310-yard tunnel, both unique for a British narrow-gauge railway.

The Ffestiniog Railway has several interesting passenger coaches, including those acquired and renovated from the Lynton & Barnstaple Railway, and the Welsh Highland Railway. Some of the seats in First Class coaches originally came from standard gauge Pullman Cars that once ran on British Rail, and most trains include licensed buffet cars and observation coaches.

The railway scene is certainly enhanced by the great little trains of Wales, and there is no better way to see parts of Wales than by steam trains that run on its narrow gauge railways, five of which go to the sea and connect with Britain's rail network. No other equivalent length of coastline in Britain has so many preserved narrow gauge railways as the west coast of Wales.

On departure from Blaenau Ffestiniog, the train heads to Tanygrisiau station, then travels above Tanygrisiau Reservoir to enter Moelwyn Tunnel and the spiral curves to Dduallt station (540ft above sea level). We then pass through Garnedd Tunnel to reach the restored Victorian-style station at Tan-y-Bwlch in the heart of Snowdonia National Park. The train continues its descent through rock cuttings and wooded slopes to Plas Halt, Penrhyn, and Minfford stations.

Minfford has two railway stations, one on the Ffestiniog line, the other on the Cambrian coast line between Pwllheli and Aberdovey. One mile south of Minfford is Portmeirion, a fascinating coastal village and architectural gem, containing the most remarkable collection of fine buildings assembled by one man in one place.

Sir Clough Williams-Ellis bought land here in 1925 when it was barren except for an old beach house and a decayed stable, just five miles from his ancestral home. His vision, fulfilled during the next 40 years, was to create a seaside village that enhanced its natural surroundings. From his travels as an architect, he was inspired in his choice of designs by Portofino in Italy, as well as other European locations. He selected buildings about to be demolished, which he acquired for restoration at Portmeirion.

The conspicuous campanile overlooking Tremadoc Bay contains stones from a 12th century castle and is visible like a lighthouse from far away. While others looked back to the past, Sir Clough's dedication to the future was in the form of this romantic village that slowly arose on a wooded Welsh hillside beside the sea.

Two miles away, the more pragmatic vision of William Madocks resulted in the building of a huge railway embankment across the estuary of the River Glaslyn, reclaiming several thousand acres of land and creating the harbour of Porthmadog. From Minfford the train travels across this embankment, known as 'The Cob', to the Ffestiniog Railway terminus beside the harbour.

At the other end of the town is the terminus of the Welsh Highland Railway, where trains run in season along a short southern section of the proposed line to Caernarfon. Across the road from the WHR station is Porthmadog station on the Cambrian coast line to Pwllheli, the furthest west we can travel by train on the Lleyn peninsula. Porthmadog has the distinction of three railway stations on three routes to the sea whose trains are run by three different railway companies.

On our journey from Porthmadog to Pwllheli, the rail line detours around Moel-y-gest (861ft) to reach Criccieth, and its ruined castle on the shore of Cardigan Bay. This was the scene of some fierce battles in the struggle for Welsh independence between 1282 and 1407. Criccieth is a small resort town which is ideal for visitors to wander along its shores and admire the panorama of Cardigan Bay. The castle ruins stand on a grassy headland close to the station.

Penychain station serves Butlin's 'Starcoast World', and the train runs alongside the holiday camp, with its huge roller-coaster silhouetted against the sky as we approach the station. This line formerly linked Cambrian coast stations with Caernarfon via Afon Wen junction, a mile east of Penychain station.

Pwllheli, traditional 'capital' of the Lleyn Peninsula, is journey's end for the Cambrian coast line, and a good centre for exploring the 'Land's End of North Wales', where it is said the spirit finds peace. It is twenty miles by road from Pwllheli station to the tip of this scenic peninsula, with narrow lanes meandering down to sandy bays sheltered by cliffs at the western tip of Lleyn near Myndd Mawr (524ft).

Bardsey Island stands two miles from the mainland across hazardous waters of Bardsey Sound, linking Caernarfon Bay with Cardigan Bay. Three visits by pilgrims to this 'Isle of 20,000 saints' were considered equal to a pilgrimage to Rome. The island is topped by a high hill (548ft) to the south of the abbey ruins, and the coastline to the north and east has been designated an area of outstanding natural beauty. According to legend, Bardsey was the final resting place of Merlin, the Arthurian wizard who was born near Carmarthen.

From Pwllheli we take the train back to Porthmadog, continuing along the Cambrian coast to Harlech, another of the impressive fortresses that ring Snowdonia. As we look up from the station beside the castle, it is hard to believe that when this fortress was built in 1283, ships could sail right up to the mound on which it stands. A short climb from the station platform leads us up to the castle ramparts, revealing distant Snowdonia. The fine panorama on a clear day is one of the chief rewards of surmounting Harlech's towers, before descending to catch the next train south along the coast of Cardigan Bay.

Castles dominate the three coasts of Wales that have seen fierce battles for sovereignty since medieval times. It is not surprising that the Great Western Railway, with services to more seaside resorts in Wales than any other company, named its largest class of steam locomotives 'Castles', and that 53 out of a total of 150 locomotives built between 1923 and 1950 were named for Welsh castles. Nor is it surprising that there is such a great concentration of castles in Wales, many of which were originally built by Welsh princes as a defence from attack by their neighbours, then later enlarged by royal successors.

Legendary lands lost beneath the sea are part of the folklore of the Cambrian coast between Harlech and Aberystwyth. Three great causeways (sarns) of stone run into Cardigan Bay, and the first is known as Sarn Badrig (St Patrick's Causeway) near Mochras Point, four miles south of Harlech. At extreme low tide, parts of this causeway, extending for fourteen miles under the waters of Cardigan Bay, are revealed. This has prompted visions of lost castles and churches in a land that is rich in myths. The two other sarns are also partially visible at low tide, one offshore from Tonfanau Camp north of Tywyn, and another opposite Wallog, north of Aberystwyth.

The sandy shores of Barmouth Bay extend southwards from Morfa Dyffryn for some nine miles, with the railway line running close to the sea at Llanaber on the approach to Barmouth. This section of the shoreline offers some fine sea views from the train, and there are also three narrow-gauge railways between Barmouth and Aberystwyth which we will visit as we travel along this part of the coast.

Barmouth, on the north shore of the Mawddach estuary, is a delightful holiday resort built around the harbour and hillsides leading down to the estuary and wide sea front. A wide sandy beach extends below the station and promenade to the river

A two-coach passenger service comes off Barmouth viaduct, which has long held a special place in the hearts of Welsh people. When the viaduct was closed in 1980, as a result of a wood-boring mollusc attacking the piers, there was such local agitation that BR was forced to take remedial action. Full re-opening to InterCity traffic in 1986 brought cheering crowds, with the locomotive on the special train being named Bont Y Bermo *(Barmouth Bridge). (J.S. Gilks)*

mouth, where fishing boats mingle with pleasure craft and ferry boats crossing the Mawddach to Penrhyn Point near Fairbourne.

Before arrival of the railway in 1866, Barmouth was a small fishing village isolated from inland towns by lack of a road along the Mawddach estuary. Terraced cottages lined the hillside, part of which was the first land in Wales to be owned by the National Trust in 1895. After more than a century of providing happy holidays, Barmouth fortunately remains on the railway network, attracting visitors to its beautiful sands and healthy seaside climate.

From Barmouth station there are pleasant walks along the north shore of the Mawddach estuary to Dolgellau, where use of the Welsh language is still very strong. John Ruskin (1819-1900), who chose to live in the Lake District, once said: "There is, in Britain, only one more beautiful walk than the walk from Barmouth to Dolgellau, and that is the walk back from Dolgellau to Barmouth."

Views between Barmouth and Dolgellau are dominated by the peak of Cader Idris (2,927ft), whose legend declares that if you spend a night on its summit you will awake as a poet, a mad person, or not at all. The Romans mined gold near Cader Idris, and in the 19th century Dolgellau was the centre of a short-lived gold rush. At the Gwyfynydd Gold Centre, visitors may still pan for gold and keep what they find, a tempting attraction for tourists with plenty of time to spare. In 1947, locally mined gold was used to make a wedding ring for Queen Elizabeth II.

Dolgellau, formerly served by the railway from Barmouth to Bala and beyond, is surrounded by mountains, which remind us that there are fourteen mountains over 3,000ft in Wales, compared to four in England and seven in Ireland. Even though Scotland has more than 280 'Munros', the Welsh peaks are generally more accessible from stations on Britain's rail network than those in Scotland, and equally challenging.

Southbound trains from Barmouth cross the estuary on an impressive one mile bridge to reach Fairbourne, where the smallest and shortest of the narrow-gauge railways in Wales runs to the end of the sandspit opposite Barmouth, with ferries crossing the water to complete a pleasant round trip by train and ferry. The 12.25-inch gauge track is two miles long, set close to the sea along its entire route. One of the steam locomotives is a replica of a 'Southern' type that was used on the old Lynton & Barnstaple Railway in Devon.

At extreme low tide, the sands along parts of this coast are a wondrous sight, notably near estuaries at Portmeirion, Barmouth, and Aberdovey, where vast areas of golden sand extend as far as the eye can see, revealing patterns that change with each receding tide. South of Fairbourne, the coastline changes in character as the sandy coastal strip is replaced by steep cliffs, forcing the railway to the edge of the coast before the train descends to Tonfanau, crossing the mouth of the River Dysynni to reach Tywyn, seaside terminus of the Talyllyn Railway.

This narrow-gauge railway was opened in 1866 to carry slate down to the sea from quarries above Abergynolyn, seven miles inland. In 1951, the derelict line was the first in the world to be taken over by a preservation group financed by public subscription and run by volunteers. The restored line extends to Nant Gwernol, whose station is situated in a natural ravine, an ideal starting point for walks to mountain waterfalls and former slate mining sites. Passengers travelling on this line are served by the Talyllyn's own titled train, 'The Quarryman'.

Tywyn's sea front faces three miles of sands extending south as far as Aberdovey Bar. There is a footpath through the dunes between beach and railway line from Tywyn to Aberdovey, an attractive village of neat colourful shops and houses facing the Dovey estuary. Like Barmouth, it is situated on the north side of a wide estuary, the last of the great submerged valleys which make indentations into the coast of Cardigan Bay from Pwllheli to Aberystwyth.

Travelling along the north shore of this estuary, five miles long and nearly two miles across at its widest point, the train reaches Dovey Junction, where we change trains in order to continue our journey down the coast to Aberystwyth.

This is the route of the former 'Cambrian Coast Express' from Paddington to Aberystwyth, with through coaches to Barmouth and Pwllheli. Introduced in 1927, it was a very popular train in the summer, with a restaurant car as far as Shrewsbury, and taking just under six hours to reach Aberystwyth from London. Withdrawn during WW2, and re-instated in 1951, it was the last titled train to survive on the main line between London and Shrewsbury.

From Dovey Junction station, the train to Aberystwyth makes its first stop at Borth, whose village is two miles long but only a hundred yards wide, hemmed in by the sea, the railway, and a peat bog. The beach is mostly shingle, and leads north to a spit of sand dunes facing Aberdovey. South of Borth the train heads inland to follow the vale of Rheidol into Aberystwyth.

The narrow gauge Vale of Rheidol Railway also comes into Aberystwyth station, and there is a third railway in Aberystwyth if we include the electric railway that climbs 430ft up Constitution Hill, a focal point for local leisure activities. When built in 1896 it was Britain's longest cliff railway, and from the summit there are fine views, especially from the camera obscura which overlooks this attractive resort, the largest on the Cambrian coast.

At the other end of the sea front, with its broad promenade and beaches, is a grassy hillock topped by the remains of another of Edward I's castles, best seen from the top of Constitution Hill, especially at sunset when the golden glow reflected from buildings along the sea front is followed by a floodlit panorama.

Known by Victorians as the 'Biarritz of Wales', Aberystwyth is home to the University College of Wales, National Library of Wales, Ceredigion Museum, and above all a place where Welsh myth and legend, history and tradition are kept alive and accessible after centuries of conflict with invaders.

A short walk from the sea front brings us to the terminus of the Vale of Rheidol Railway, whose steam trains were operated by British Rail for over twenty years after withdrawal of all their other steam locomotives from the rail network. The Vale of Rheidol Railway was eventually sold by BR in 1988, and it remains a popular tourist attraction, taking passengers on a scenic twelve-mile journey as the train climbs up to Devil's Bridge.

This railway has an interesting pedigree dating from December 1902, when some passengers on the first train were so frightened by the steepness of the gradients that nothing would induce them to return, except on foot. In the prosperous years before WW1, the railway was so popular that it was obliged to borrow a locomotive from the Ffestiniog Railway for several months in 1912 in order to provide additional services.

Such was the success of the Vale of Rheidol Railway that it was taken over in 1913 by Cambrian Railways, who were merged into the GWR in 1923. On 31 August 1939 the line was closed completely, and did not re-open until July 1945. British Railways took over the line in 1948, but revenue declined, and with the prospect of permanent closure looming, the railway was transferred from the Western Region to the London Midland Region of BR in 1968. With help from the Welsh Tourist Board, BR succeeded in raising the passenger count from a post-war low of 15,000, to 179,000 in 1975, a remarkable achievement.

The Rheidol trains depart from a platform that was

formerly used by BR trains to Lampeter and Carmarthen. On departure from Aberystwyth, the narrow-gauge track initially runs parallel to the main line which then veers north, while the Rheidol trains head eastwards to follow the river up into the mountains.

Beyond Aberffrwd, the gradient is 1 in 50 for the last four miles to Devil's Bridge, climbing almost 500 feet as the train twists and turns along the steep south side of Rheidol Gorge, with the river cascading far below. From here it is a short walk to Mynach Falls, Jacob's Ladder, and the three-tiered bridges of various vintages that span the chasm over the Devil's Punchbowl. The bridge attributed to the Devil is the lowest and oldest of the three.

There is no railway south along the Cambrian coast between Aberystwyth and Fishguard, a distance of 65 miles by road, or 270 miles by changing trains several times en route. On this part of the coast, Aberaeron was once served by a branch railway from Lampeter, while New Quay had to rely on the Aberaeron line for its nearest railway connection.

Aberaeron is an architectural delight, with its grand civic buildings and chestnut trees in front of Regency houses on the quayside. All this was the creation of one man, a local parson named Alban Gwynne, who inherited a large fortune and used it to develop Aberaeron into the surprising and delightful place it is today.

Dylan Thomas lived in New Quay in the 1940s, deriving inspiration for 'Under Milk Wood' and 'Quite Early One Morning' from his walks through the steep narrow streets of this quaint fishing town set on the hillside. The harbour, built in 1835, is one of the most sheltered in Cardigan Bay, and coastal trade flourished until the 1920s, when rail services on the nearby Aberaeron line proved to be faster and more convenient than shipment by boat. Meanwhile, New Quay was attracting a growing number of visitors, and the harbour is now one of the most popular sailing centres in Cardiganshire.

To reach Fishguard by train, we return to Aberystwyth to board the Shrewsbury train, travelling via Dovey Junction, Machynlleth, Caersws, Newtown, and Welshpool, crossing the border into England near Middletown, twelve miles west of Shrewsbury.

When this 81-mile line was built between Aberystwyth and Shrewsbury in the 1860s, the valleys of the Severn, Garno, Iaen, Twymyn, and Dovey rivers provided the best route with minimum cost to the builders. A railway across central Wales with no tunnels or major viaducts stands as a great tribute to the skill and enterprise of its Victorian engineers, whose only really challenging construction work involved forcing the line through mountainous country near Talerddig, midway between Dovey Junction and Newtown.

At the railway crossroads of Shrewsbury we take a train south to Craven Arms, branching off to cross the border again near Knighton, then to Llandrindod and Llandovery, continuing south to meet the main line west from Swansea to Llanelli, Carmarthen and Fishguard. This is a long journey from Aberystwyth and requires several changes of train, but it does provide splendid scenic views during two railway crossings of mid-Wales. The Tourist Board's travel brochure describes this part of Wales as: "A different country - a different world", and so it is.

Fishguard is a ferry port for travel to and from Ireland (Rosslaire). When the railway arrived here in 1906 after immense expenditure by the GWR in blasting through the rocky hillside on which the town stands in order to establish its station and sidings at sea level, a new breakwater and deep water harbour were built to attract Atlantic liners. But they rarely came, and Fishguard had to content itself with the GWR's 'Irish Mail via Fishguard' service. Until 1939 this titled express left Paddington each night at 1955, reaching Fishguard Harbour station at 0140 after a steep descent of 1 in 50 for two miles from town to dockside.

In August 1909, the GWR arranged with Cunard for the famous liner 'Mauretania' to call at Fishguard, which they claimed would save nearly 24 hours on the journey from New York to London, compared to the longer sea route via Liverpool. The GWR also had plans to lure the 'Titanic' and 'Olympic' here in 1911, without success. However the advantages of Southampton, with frequent fast trains to London, and closer links with Cherbourg and mainland Europe, were irresistible to Cunard, so the rival Southern Railway triumphed over the GWR in this instance.

Three miles northwest of Fishguard, at Carregwastad Point, is one of the least known of Britain's historic sites, which celebrated its 200th anniversary in 1997. A small stone on the headland above a remote and rocky bay marks the spot of the last foreign military invasion of Britain. On 22 February 1797, a large force of French troops led by an American general landed here under orders to attack Bristol and stir up republican sentiment among the population.

As with the Spanish Armada, storms at sea played havoc on this occasion with the French ships, and they were driven off-course into this remote corner of Cardigan Bay where the invaders landed, unexpected and unopposed. After looting the area, and several skirmishes with local troops, the invasion force surrendered on Goodwick Sands.

Cardigan, twenty miles northeast of Fishguard, has lost its railway service, but still retains its importance as a market town and tourist centre, with its sheltered location on the banks of the Teifi. It was a prosperous port when Cardiff and Swansea were small villages, but silting of the estuary and competition from the railways diminished its maritime importance.

The 170-mile Pembrokeshire Coast National Park is Britain's only park of such length entirely beside the sea. It is one of

Europe's longest stretches of protected coastline and its northern boundary ends here. It has been estimated that to walk the entire coastal path requires a combined ascent and descent of 32,000ft beside the sea, which offers as compensation more than thirty beaches along the way on which to rest and enjoy a walk in the waves.

Sixteen miles west of Fishguard Harbour station stands St David's Head and the northern shore of St Brides Bay. In order to visit this part of the coast, we take the road from Fishguard to St David's, then around St Brides Bay to St Ann's Head.

St David's (population about 2,000) is Britain's smallest city, and its cathedral is the largest ecclesiastical building in Wales, nestling in the peaceful Welsh countryside one mile from the sea. St David was the only native-born national patron saint in the realm, and after a pilgrimage to Rome he lived in this remote corner of Wales, having obtained from the Pope a special dispensation that two pilgrimages to St David's equalled one to Rome.

From St David's Head in the north to Martin's Haven in the south, the Pembrokeshire coastline thrusts westwards into the Atlantic. Rocky coves alternate with sandy beaches around St Brides Bay, with Skomer Island a mile offshore. The

Neyland, developed by Isambard Kingdom Brunel as a port for southern Ireland. His broad-gauge tracks reached here in 1856, but its heyday ended fifty years later when steamer services were diverted to Fishguard as part of the Great Western's dream to capture trans-Atlantic traffic. The Neyland branch lingered on, handling originating traffic in fish and rabbits, until closure in 1964. (NRM - FB521)

headland at St Ann's provides a fine view of Milford Haven Sound, and leads to three small beaches along the coast towards Dale, sheltered from all but easterly winds, and said to be the sunniest place in Wales.

To avoid the huge oil refinery and small estuaries between Dale and Milford Haven, we will head north from Dale to the nearest railway station at Haverfordwest, and take the train into Milford Haven.

Henry Tudor landed at Milford Haven in 1485 to first claim and then win the throne of England. Shakespeare paid Milford Haven a great compliment in writing: "and, by the way, tell me how Wales was made so happy as t'inherit such a haven." Nelson considered Milford Haven the best natural harbour he had seen, apart from Trincomalee (in what was then Ceylon), and few estuaries can match the tranquil beauty of Milford's upper reaches, especially along the Daugleddau estuary near Llangwm.

Much of the land upon which Milford Haven is built was owned by Sir William Hamilton, husband of Emma, Nelson's mistress. The harbours at Milford, Neyland, and Pembroke are the busiest on this coast, with huge supertankers unloading at the refinery, and other vessels heading for docks, berths and moorings around the shores of Milford Haven.

From Milford Haven station we take a bus to Pembroke Dock station to board a train heading east along the Pembrokeshire coast. We are once again in a countryside where castles abound, all close to the sea or river estuaries, and three have stations nearby at Pembroke, Manorbier, and Tenby. Another remarkable castle, Carew, is three miles north of Lamphey, the first station after Pembroke.

Manorbier station is a mile from the castle, which has a wonderful setting overlooking the sea, with cliffs on both sides of the beach, well worth a two-mile walk from the station. The peaceful village nearby retains a serenity from bygone days that one can find today in many Welsh villages.

This part of the coast has pathways on top of cliffs from Manorbier Bay westwards to Swanlake Bay, Freshwater East, Barafundle Bay, and Stackpole Head. To the east, cliffs extend as far as Lydstep Haven, where there are good views across the sea to Caldey Island, a religious centre since the 5th century. The island is easily reached by boats from Tenby harbour.

Penally station is near Giltar Point at the southern end of a wide beach, leading into Tenby, two miles away. The best approach to Tenby from Penally is along this beach which ends at St Catherine's Island, with its Victorian fort built in 1860. On the esplanade high above the sands are several elegant hotels and guest houses, some with private gardens on the edge of the cliffs, with views of Caldey Island. At ebb tide, St Catherine's Island is joined to Castle Hill by a sandy stretch of the south beach.

Tenby is one of Britain's most interesting and attractive resorts. With its narrow streets partially enclosed by 14th century walls, this ancient town beside the sea has a charm that few places in Britain can match. Its parish church of St Mary is the largest medieval church in Wales, and among its memorials is one to Robert Recorde, born here in 1510, who during a short life of 48 years was an eminent mathematician, astrologer, and Court Physician to King Edward VI and Queen Mary I (Bloody Mary). Recorde's most enduring achievement is his invention of the sign of equality (=), adopted throughout the world.

Many of the handsome houses we see in Tenby today date from the 19th century, mingling with medieval buildings such as the Tudor Merchant's House (c.1500), and St Mary's church in the centre of the town. Sir William Paxton, who designed the

famous Crystal Palace for the Great Exhibition of 1851 in London's Hyde Park, built the public bath house in Tenby at his own expense.

On the wall of Laston House beside the harbour is a Greek inscription from Euripedes whose translation reads "The sea washes away all mankind's ills." Thomas Huxley honeymooned here with his sickly wife Henrietta, who was cured of her ills and later bore him eight children. The naturalist Philip Gosse wrote a book about his holiday here in 1856, and then felt guilty of "opening up Eden to vandals."

The first train arrived in Tenby from Pembroke on 30 July 1863. Trains from London reached Tenby in 1866, via Cardiff, Swansea, Carmarthen, and Whitland. As one stands today on the long platforms of this well-preserved station, it is easy to picture the ten-coach GWR expresses from Paddington to Tenby (262 miles) arriving on summer Saturdays with hundreds of visitors heading for hotels, guest houses and beaches of Dinbych-y-Pysgod, ('little fort of the fishes').

In 1953, the Western Region of British Rail introduced the 'Pembroke Coast Express' to Tenby and Pembroke. It was the fastest scheduled steam train service from London into Wales, covering 133.4 miles from Paddington to Newport in 128 minutes. However, it was withdrawn in BR's cutbacks of the 1960s, and the best that BR could do in the 1990s was one through train on summer Saturdays from Paddington, with several stops en route to Tenby.

A short walk from the station to the esplanade high above Tenby's North Beach reveals a grand sea vista, with the coastline extending around Carmarthen Bay to the Gower Peninsula, while to the south a limestone headland shelters the harbour. In sunshine the tall and colourful Georgian houses have an almost Italian air, and summer visitors often return in the winter to enjoy the mild climate here, as they stroll on the two beaches, or walk along the Pembrokeshire Coastal Path.

In the June 1898 issue of the 'Railway Magazine', a writer commented: "Tenby has never catered for the rowdy picnickers with their accompaniments of ginger beer and sandwiches. Its clientele has always been of the respectable debonaire class who, satisfied with their treatment and the very moderate tariff, return year after year."

Beatrix Potter came here in April 1900, and painted some watercolours. Augustus John (1878- 1961) was born in Tenby, and with the perceptive eye of a painter he said of his native town: "You may travel the world over, but you will find nothing more beautiful; it is so restful, so colourful, and so unspoilt."

Saundersfoot station is over a mile from the sea front, with harbour, quays and beaches all very popular in the summer. To the northeast is Wiseman's Bridge, leading to Amroth, and Marros Sands. The beaches on this part of Carmarthen Bay were considered similar to those of Normandy, and were used in 1943 for rehearsals of the D-Day landings. Winston

Churchill, Eisenhower and Montgomery met at Wiseman's Bridge to witness the landings. Amroth marks the eastern end of the 170-mile Pembrokeshire Coast Path from Cardigan.

East of Amroth, rugged cliffs give way to long sandy beaches, high dunes, and lonely saltings of the Carmarthenshire coast. After leaving Saundersfoot, the train heads inland through Lampeter Vale towards Carmarthen, joining the line from Fishguard and Milford Haven at Whitland. This is the nearest station to Pendine and Laugharne sands, which together form one of the longest stretches of firm flat sand in Britain, used for several attempts on the world land speed record.

Laugharne (pronounced Larne), with its impressive castle ruins, nestles in a deep green valley beside the saltings and mudflats of the Taf estuary. Dylan Thomas spent his last years here, describing the town as " timeless, beautiful, tough, and barmy (both spellings)."

Four estuaries meet in Carmarthen Bay: the Taf, Tywi, Gwendraeth and the Loughor, and all have castles to guard them. We cross the Tywi on the approach to Carmarthen, the most westerly Roman military base in Britain, legendary birthplace of the wizard Merlin. In its railway heydays Carmarthen was an important railway junction, with main lines running west to Fishguard, Pembroke and Milford

A tramcar on the Swansea & Mumbles Railway runs past beached yachts on the shores of Swansea Bay. This six-mile line was the first railway to provide a public passenger service when it was opened in 1807 for haulage 'by men, horses or otherwise'. It came close to fulfilling the wishes of its creators by employing horse, steam, petrol, diesel and electric traction before closing in 1960 after a life of 155 years. (Colour-Rail/A.A. Jarvis)

Haven, and north across Wales to resorts at Cardigan, Aberystwyth, and Aberaeron.

In 1950, Carmarthen was given its own titled train, the 'Red Dragon', from London via Cardiff and Swansea, until it was withdrawn in timetable changes of the 1960s. This train left Paddington at 1755, but with time-consuming station stops to uncouple coaches at Cardiff and Swansea, the tail of the 'Red Dragon' did not meander into Carmarthen until ten minutes before midnight, and sometimes much later.

Under privatization the 'Red Dragon' departs Paddington on weekdays at 1800, terminating at Swansea at 2100. The only through train to Carmarthen is untitled, leaving Paddington at 1730 and arriving at Carmarthen at 2120. According to ancient legend, a red dragon was adopted as the emblem for Wales when Merlin was a youth in the town. He interpreted a fight between two dragons, in which a red dragon killed a white dragon, as signifying the eventual victory of Wales over England. The subsequent accession of Henry VII as King of England convinced Welsh bards that this tale was more than a myth.

From Carmarthen the train travels along the east bank of the Tywi to Ferryside station then beside Gwendraeth Bay to Kidwelly, where the remains of its castle stand high on a hill facing the sea. Crossing low-lying Towyn Burrows, the train stops at Pembrey & Burry Port station, with the Gower peninsula across mudflats of the Loughor estuary.

Although no longer a major port or railway junction, Llanelli remains an important industrial centre. Gowerton station is at the northern fringe of the Gower peninsula, the first land in Britain to be designated an area of outstanding natural beauty, with a rich variety of unspoilt country and seaside preserved in a small perimeter close to industrial centres of South Wales. We will get off the train at Gowerton in order to explore the Gower coast all the way to Swansea, where we will rejoin the train to continue our journey eastwards.

On the west side of Gower is Rhossili Bay, a popular beach for surfers when strong westerlies are blowing on its sandy shore, which extends for three miles to Worms Head, where Dylan Thomas would sit all day watching Atlantic waves marching in with their crests of spindrift, and declare that this was the wildest place he knew.

The remains of ships wrecked between Worms Head and Burry Holms may be seen protruding above the sands at low tide. Cliffs and caves extend east from Worms Head to Porteynon Bay, with its beach leading to more cliffs and rocks around the headland to Oxwich Bay.

One of the most picturesque of the Gower bays is Three Cliffs Bay, where the River Pennard, hemmed in by towering limestone cliffs, meanders down to the sea in wide loops around a ridge of sandhills, presenting a rich variation in colours, seen best at low tide when the sands, sculpted by the river outflow, are at their most spectacular. The only approach to this pristine bay is by footpath, which makes it even more attractive for the visitor, who may well find this beach deserted when others nearby are crowded.

Beyond Three Cliffs Bay are several smaller bays flanked by cliffs until we reach Mumbles Head, a popular holiday resort built around Mumbles Hill (252ft). The long promenade faces a wide expanse of sand leading to Oystermouth, whose Norman castle formerly guarded this part of the Gower peninsula. The famous Oystermouth Railway ran along this shore, and in 1957 became the first railway in the world to celebrate 150 years of passenger services. Unfortunately, the line closed in 1960.

The brown sands of Swansea Bay arc around the shoreline as far as the Tawe estuary, lined with docks, a fine marina, and modern industrial parks. Swansea's proximity to the Gower peninsula and to the Brecon Beacons National Park make the city a good touring base, with its rich cultural traditions and maritime heritage. Norse sailors named this place Sweyn's Isle a thousand years ago, and to the Welsh it is Abertawe, the mouth of the River Tawe.

In our detour to the Gower peninsula we have reached Swansea via the Mumbles. The train from Gowerton to Swansea enters the city from the west by descending the valley of the Tawe, with the bulk of Kilvey Hill looming across the valley as the tracks curve towards the terminus.

Swansea is the major commercial, administrative and shopping centre of west Wales, and in 1998 was selected as the new home of the Welsh Industrial & Maritime Museum. The road around Swansea Bay to the Mumbles still retains its terraces of boarding houses built during the great hundred years (1867-1967) of railway excursions to the seaside, when the Oystermouth Railway carried holidaymakers along the eastern fringe of the Gower peninsula, the closest a train could get to the beaches along its south shore.

In the summer of 1955, twenty-five years after the GWR had experimented with a short-lived Pullman service to Plymouth, the Western Region of BR introduced a new Pullman train to Swansea, the 'South Wales Pullman' comprising eight coaches in the famous chocolate and cream livery so admired on the popular SR 'Belles'. When trains between London and South Wales changed from steam to diesel in the 1960s, a blue and grey livery was used for the 'Blue Pullman', in which the front and rear coaches of the train contained diesel power units, later adopted as a design criterion for InterCity 125 HSTs.

Tradition lingers long in the railway world, and at the time of the 'Blue Pullman' there were those in the Western Region hierarchy who were determined to retain the much-admired GWR colours, similar to the original British Pullman livery. Since 1950 the 'Red Dragon' had proudly carried GWR colours into Wales, but it went to the sword in the 1960s. All 'Blue Pullman'trains were withdrawn in 1973, but to their credit they proved to be useful prototypes for the highly successful HSTs, whose longevity has yet to be written into the record books.

We leave the Swansea station by First Great Western train to Cardiff and Bristol Parkway. The coast between Swansea and Cardiff has long stretches of sands and dunes, but the train travels inland, and huge industrial facilities such as those at Port Talbot obscure the coastline. Bridgend is now the closest station to Porthcawl, which was first developed as a 19th century coaling port. It is now one of the leading resorts in South Wales, with a fine promenade, and one of Europe's largest seaside caravan sites.

Glamorgan's heritage coast extends for 14 miles from Porthcawl in the west to Aberthaw in the east, where land meets sea with a coastline of high cliffs and sandy beaches scoured by the Bristol Channel's wide range of tide levels. This was the first coastline of Wales to achieve 'Heritage Coast' status in 1972, and at Merthyr Mawr Warren can be seen some of the largest sand dunes in Europe.

Barry Island is the next station on the coast, reached via Cardiff. The 'island' is actually a small peninsula connected by causeway and railway to the town and port of Barry. Its main natural attraction is the fine beach at Whitmore Bay, a sheltered crescent of south-facing sands.

Nothing stands still on Barry Island, where the Vale of Glamorgan Railway Society operates preserved steam trains between the Valley Lines station and the recently-created rail heritage centre dedicated to 'The Age of Steam', evoking memories of courtesy, punctuality, and comfort of the GWR trains which served South Wales for over a century.

Barry is also known as the graveyard for hundreds of steam locomotives which were scrapped and suffered meltdown here in the 1960s. Fortunately, it was also a site of pilgrimage for railway preservationists, who persuaded a sympathetic owner to withhold the death sentence on some fine specimens until enough money had been raised to purchase them. We can now admire many classes of locomotives, paradigms of the great days of steam, which have been restored to their former glory to operate on the Railtrack network, as well as on preserved lines.

A quiet seaside town in the 18th century, Cardiff developed into the busiest coal-exporting port in the world at the beginning of the 20th century, with the GWR playing a major role in the process. Many of the old docks have been converted into leisure areas and marinas in this cosmopolitan city of wide-ranging attractions that include Cardiff Castle, the Civic Centre, the National Museum & Gallery, the Welsh National Opera, theatres, parks, as well as national sporting venues for rugby and ice-skating.

Contemporary and classical buildings mingle happily on Victorian and Edwardian streets leading to Cardiff castle with its Roman walls, Norman keep, and lavishly decorated Victorian residence built for the immensely rich third Marquess of Bute. The extensive Cardiff Civic Centre complex is one of Europe's finest groupings of neo-classical buildings, set beside wide tree-lined boulevards, while on both banks of the River Taff there are parks and gardens leading north to Llandaff Cathedral, two miles from the city centre.

At the city's pastoral outskirts, where Cardiff meets the Vale of Glamorgan, is the Museum of Welsh Life, with heritage buildings from all over Wales displayed in scenic parklands. The diversity of sights and attractions around Cardiff, mostly unseen from Central Station, deserve further exploration.

Four miles by train from Cardiff is Penarth, the city's "garden by the sea" with its attractive promenade and recently restored pier, one of the finest in Wales, overlooking the seafront and Cardiff Bay. Penarth succeeds in preserving the atmosphere of a small Victorian seaside resort, where a stroll along the pier and promenade is like taking a step back in time to an elegant, less hurried age. Close by are the green acres of Alexandra Park, and high above are clifftop walks with fine views across the Severn estuary to the islands of Flat Holm and Steep Holm.

Before leaving Cardiff, we recall one of the prestigious named trains introduced by BR in the 1950s to attract more passengers on the London-Cardiff service. The train was given the name 'Capitals United', a title which many considered more suited to a football team than to an elite express train. It had a relatively short life in those heady post-WW2 days when devolution was but a distant dream in the Welsh capital. The 'Capitals United' was withdrawn in the timetable amendments of the 1960s, a sad time for railway travellers, who at the start of the decade had high hopes for continuity of existing services throughout the network.

From Cardiff, the train to Bristol runs inland to reach Newport, then Severn Tunnel Junction, the last station in Wales before entering the tunnel leading to England. To complete the link in our railway journeys around the coasts of Britain, we change trains at Bristol to travel on a branch line to Severn Beach, above the railway tunnel which burrows below the English Stones Reef into Wales. While the shore is mostly tidal mud, the high sea wall provides a bracing walk, with views of the two Severn road bridges to the north, and across the water to Wales, three miles away.

Appendices

OPENING DATES FOR RAILWAYS TO THE SEA

PASSENGER SERVICES FROM LONDON UNLESS SHOWN THUS: Manchester–Liverpool

1807	Swansea (Mumbles) – Oystermouth	**1864**	Aberystwyth; Kingswear; Seaford; Hornsea; Shanklin
1817	Kilmarnock – Troon	**1866**	Barmouth; Tenby; Ventnor; Tywyn – Abergynolwyn
1830	Manchester – Liverpool; Canterbury – Whitstable	**1867**	Pwllheli; Aberdovey; Barmouth; Brixham
1834	Bodmin – Wadebridge	**1868**	Seaton; Golspie
1836	Pickering – Whitby; Blaenau Ffestiniog – Porthmadog	**1869**	Greenock
1837	Gwennap – Hayle; Glasgow – Ardrossan	**1870**	Bournemouth; Strome Ferry
1840	Southampton; Prestatyn; Fleetwood; Glasgow – Ayr	**1873**	Barnstaple; Skegness
1841	Bristol; Brighton	**1874**	Ilfracombe; Minehead; Wick; Thurso; Sidmouth
1842	Glasgow – Edinburgh; Gosport; Hull – Bridlington	**1876**	Fowey; Newquay; Ravenglass – Eskdale
1843	Folkestone; Redruth – Hayle	**1877**	St Ives; Felixstowe; Cromer
1844	Dover; Norwich; Yarmouth	**1878**	Birkenhead; West Kirby
1845	Carlisle – Maryport; York – Scarborough	**1879**	Southwold; Porthcawl
1846	Blackpool; Edinburgh – Berwick; Ramsgate; Teignmouth	**1880**	Oban; Newport – Sandown
1847	Newhaven; Lowestoft; Bridlington; Cockermouth – Workington	**1881**	Clacton
1848	Glasgow; Portsmouth; Plymouth; Torquay	**1884**	Bridport
1849	Edinburgh; Newquay; Morecambe	**1885**	Swanage; Walton-on-the-Naze; Whitby – Scarborough
1850	Cardiff; Swansea; Holyhead; Aberdeen	**1886**	Cardigan; New Brighton
1851	Hastings	**1890**	Fairbourne – Penrhyn Point
1852	Redruth–Penzance	**1894**	Fort William
1854	Harwich; Withernsea	**1897**	Kyle of Lochalsh; Budleigh Salterton
1855	Barnstaple – Bideford	**1898**	Bude; Lynton
1856	Southend; Milford Haven	**1899**	Padstow
1857	Weymouth; Grange-over-Sands	**1901**	Mallaig; Looe; Bideford – Westward Ho!
1858	Llandudno	**1902**	Devil's Bridge – Aberystwyth
1859	Penzance; Paignton; Yarmouth; Lowestoft	**1903**	Lyme Regis; Lybster; Ballachulish
1860	Moorswater – Looe Quay; Poole	**1906**	Fishguard; Turnberry
1861	Exmouth; Saltburn	**1908**	Gunnislake – Plymouth; Appledore
1862	Hunstanton; Watchet; Stranraer; Newport – Cowes	**1911**	Aberaeron
1863	Skegness; Falmouth		

THE STATIONS LISTED ARE A SELECTION BY THE AUTHOR

The photo of Minehead station was taken by the author in April 1995.

The 'Torbay Express' prepares to depart from Kingswear in 1959 on the first stage of what would be a very fast run from Exeter to London Paddington. Across the estuary is Dartmouth, reached by ferry and noted as having the only railway station in Britain never to have received a train.
(NRM - MWE58/8)

The 'Devon Belle' passes Cowley Bridge Junction, near Exeter. Operating for just eight summers from 1947 to 1954, this all-Pullman service linked London Waterloo with Ilfracombe and Plymouth. (NRM - SR/131)

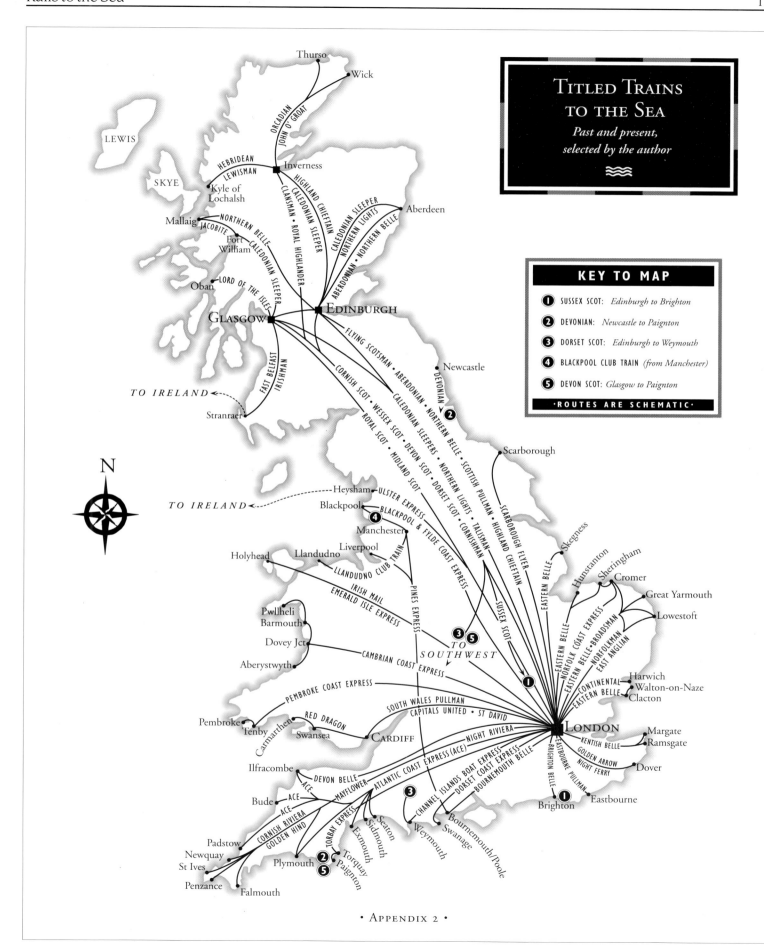

Thurso
Wick
LEWIS

ORCADIAN · JOHN O' GROAT

SKYE
HEBRIDEAN · LEWISMAN
Inverness
Kyle of
Lochalsh
HIGHLAND CHIEFTAIN
CALEDONIAN SLEEPER
CLANSMAN · ROYAL HIGHLANDER
Aberdeen
Mallaig
NORTHERN BELLE
JACOBITE
Fort
William
CALEDONIAN SLEEPER
CALEDONIAN SLEEPER
ABERDONIAN · NORTHERN LIGHTS
ABERDONIAN · NORTHERN BELLE
Oban
LORD OF THE ISLES

GLASGOW
EDINBURGH

FLYING SCOTSMAN · ABERDONIAN · NORTHERN BELLE

FAST BELFAST
IRISHMAN

TO IRELAND

Stranraer

CORNISH SCOT · WESSEX SCOT · DEVON SCOT · MIDLAND SCOT

CALEDONIAN SLEEPERS · NORTHERN LIGHTS · DORSET SCOT · CORNISHMAN

ROYAL SCOT · DEVON SCOT · MIDLAND SCOT

SCOTTISH PULLMAN · TALISMAN · HIGHLAND CHIEFTAIN

DEVONIAN

Newcastle

Scarborough

SCARBOROUGH FLYER

TO IRELAND
Heysham
ULSTER EXPRESS
Blackpool
BLACKPOOL & FYLDE COAST EXPRESS
Manchester

EASTERN BELLE

Skegness
Hunstanton
Sheringham
Cromer
Great Yarmouth
Lowestoft

Holyhead
Llandudno
Liverpool
LLANDUDNO CLUB TRAIN
IRISH MAIL
EMERALD ISLE EXPRESS
PINES EXPRESS

SUSSEX SCOT

EASTERN BELLE
NORFOLK COAST EXPRESS
EASTERN BELLE · BROADSMAN
NORFOLKMAN
EAST ANGLIAN

Pwllheli
Barmouth
Dovey Jct
Aberystwyth
CAMBRIAN COAST EXPRESS

TO
SOUTHWEST

Harwich
CONTINENTAL
EASTERN BELLE
Walton-on-Naze
Clacton

PEMBROKE COAST EXPRESS

SOUTH WALES PULLMAN
CAPITALS UNITED · ST DAVID

Pembroke
Tenby
RED DRAGON
Carmarthen
Swansea
CARDIFF

NIGHT RIVIERA

LONDON
Margate
KENTISH BELLE
Ramsgate
GOLDEN ARROW
NIGHT FERRY
Dover

EASTBOURNE PULLMAN
BRIGHTON BELLE

Ilfracombe
DEVON BELLE
ACE
MAYFLOWER
ATLANTIC COAST EXPRESS (ACE)
CHANNEL ISLANDS BOAT EXPRESS
DORSET COAST EXPRESS
BOURNEMOUTH BELLE

Bude
ACE
ACE

Bournemouth/Poole
Swanage
Weymouth
Seaton
Sidmouth
Exmouth

Brighton
Eastbourne

Padstow
CORNISH RIVIERA
GOLDEN HIND
Newquay
St Ives
TORBAY EXPRESS
Torquay
Paignton
Plymouth
Penzance
Falmouth

KEY TO MAP

1. SUSSEX SCOT: *Edinburgh to Brighton*
2. DEVONIAN: *Newcastle to Paignton*
3. DORSET SCOT: *Edinburgh to Weymouth*
4. BLACKPOOL CLUB TRAIN *(from Manchester)*
5. DEVON SCOT: *Glasgow to Paignton*

·ROUTES ARE SCHEMATIC·

The North Norfolk Railway, with its main station at Sheringham, recaptures much of the atmosphere of the old Midland & Great Northern Joint line. (John Hadrill)

'Terrier' tank at Smallbrook Junction on the Isle of Wight Steam Railway in 1994. Current proposals envisage steam operations from Newport, the island's capital, through to Ryde. (John Hadrill)

PRESERVED & NARROW GAUGE RAILWAYS TO THE SEA
≈

KEY TO MAP

1 WEST SOMERSET RAILWAY
2 PAIGNTON & DARTMOUTH RAILWAY
3 SWANAGE RAILWAY
4 ISLE OF WIGHT STEAM RAILWAY
5 ROMNEY, HYTHE & DYMCHURCH RLY
6 NORTH NORFOLK RAILWAY
7 WELLS & WALSINGHAM RAILWAY
8 CLEETHORPES COAST LIGHT RAILWAY
9 BO'NESS & KINNEIL RAILWAY
10 MULL & WEST HIGHLAND RAILWAY
11 RAVENGLASS & ESKDALE RAILWAY
12 WELSH HIGHLAND RAILWAY
13 FFESTINIOG RAILWAY
14 FAIRBOURNE RAILWAY
15 TALYLLYN RAILWAY
16 VALE OF RHEIDOL RAILWAY

NOTE

This listing is a selection by the author.

*Some of these railways operate seasonally.
Current timetables should be consulted.*

N

*The photo of a Ffestiniog Railway train leaving
Porthmadog station was taken by the author in 1997.*

VIEWS FROM THE TRAIN

The first generation of diesel units offered knowing passengers superb views from the front of the train. Here the driver will be braking carefully on the 1 in 39 descent to Robin Hood's Bay on the now closed Scarborough to Whitby line.

Today's air-conditioned rolling stock does not even have opening windows, although happily there are still exceptions. A passenger takes a breather as 'The Hebridean' pauses at Achnasheen on the scenic Inverness to Kyle of Lochalsh line. (John Hadrill)

THE FINEST SEA VIEWS FROM THE TRAIN IN BRITAIN

BETWEEN STATIONS	SEA VIEWS FROM TRAIN
• *Attadale – Kyle of Lochalsh*	Loch Carron, Inner Sound, Raasay, Scalpay, Skye
• *Lelant – St Ives*	St Ives Bay, Carbis Bay, Hayle Sands, Godrevy Lighthouse
• *Pwllheli – Dovey Junction*	Tremadoc & Barmouth Bays, Mawddach & Dovey Estuaries
• *Maryport – Arnside*	Irish Sea, Morecambe Bay, Isle of Man, Cumbrian Coast
• *Dawlish Warren – Teignmouth*	Devon Coast, English Channel, Teign Estuary
• *Lochailort – Mallaig*	Sands of Morar, Cuillins (Skye), Rhum and Eigg
• *Golspie – Helmsdale*	Dornoch Firth, Moray Firth, Dunrobin Castle
• *St Erth – Penzance*	St Michael's Mount, Mount's Bay, Lizard Point
• *Abergele – Bangor*	Irish Sea, Conwy Bay, Menai Strait, Anglesey
• *Ryde Pierhead – Ryde*	The Solent, Spithead, Isle of Wight, Hampshire Coast
• *Paignton – Kingswear*	Tor Bay, Goodrington Sands, Dart Estuary
• *Inverness – Muir of Ord*	Beauly Forth, Moray Firth, Black Isle
• *Carnoustie – Arbroath*	Buddon Ness, St Andrews Bay, Fife Ness
• *Topsham – Exmouth*	Exe Estuary, Devon Coast, English Channel
• *Minehead – Watchet*	Blue Anchor Bay, Bridgewater Bay
• *Dalmeny – Kirkcaldy*	Firth of Forth, Inverkeithing Bay, Inchkeith
• *Tain – Ardgay*	Dornoch Firth, Cambuscurrie Bay

THIS LISTING IS THE AUTHOR'S PERSONAL CHOICE, AND IS IN RANDOM ORDER.

TRAIN OPERATING COMPANIES SERVING THE COAST

- Anglia Railways

- Cardiff Railway

- Central Trains

- Connex

- First Great Eastern

- First Great Western

- Great North Eastern Railway

- Island Line

- Merseyrail Electrics

- Northern Spirit

- North Western Trains

- ScotRail

- South West Trains

- Virgin Trains

- Wales & West Railway

- West Coast Railway Company

IN THIS LISTING, SOME COMPANY TITLES HAVE BEEN ABBREVIATED.

RAIL DISTANCES FROM LONDON TO THE SEA (TO THE NEAREST MILE)

STATION	MILES	STATION	MILES
CHAPTER 4		RAMSGATE	79
PENZANCE	305	MARGATE	74
ST. IVES	304	HERNE BAY	63
FALMOUTH	292	WHITSTABLE	59
ST. AUSTELL	265		
PAR	261	**CHAPTER 6**	
NEWQUAY	282	SOUTHEND (CENTRAL)	36
LOOE	253	SHOEBURYNESS	40
PLYMOUTH	226	BURNHAM-ON-CROUCH	43
PAIGNTON	202	CLACTON	70
TORQUAY	200	FRINTON	67
TEIGNMOUTH	188	WALTON-ON-NAZE	71
DAWLISH	186	HARWICH	71
EXETER	174	FELIXSTOWE	82
EXMOUTH	188	WOODBRIDGE	79
BARNSTAPLE	214	LOWESTOFT	118
WESTON-SUPER-MARE	138	GREAT YARMOUTH	133
		CROMER	141
CHAPTER 5		SHERINGHAM	145
WEYMOUTH	143	KING'S LYNN	97
POOLE	114		
BOURNEMOUTH	108	**CHAPTER 7**	
LYMINGTON PIER	98	SKEGNESS	161
SOUTHAMPTON	80	CLEETHORPES	188
PORTSMOUTH HARBOUR	75	BRIDLINGTON	247
RYDE (INCL. FERRY)	79	FILEY	235
SHANKLIN	88	SCARBOROUGH	231
BOGNOR REGIS	68	WHITBY	272
LITTLEHAMPTON	63	SALTBURN	260
WORTHING	62	NEWCASTLE	268
HOVE	53	WHITLEY BAY	279
BRIGHTON	51	ALNMOUTH	304
NEWHAVEN	60	BERWICK	335
SEAFORD	59		
EASTBOURNE	66	**CHAPTER 8**	
HASTINGS	63	DUNBAR	363
FOLKESTONE	70	NORTH BERWICK	381
DOVER	78	EDINBURGH	393
DEAL	92	FORTH BRIDGE	403
		INVERKEITHING	406

LOST
CAUSES

Lynton station, perched 700ft above the resort of Lynmouth which it was intended to serve. Its remoteness was one of the factors leading to closure in 1935 of the much loved narrow gauge Lynton & Barnstaple Railway. (NRM - Soole 831)

Allhallows-on-Sea, just to the west of the Medway estuary in Kent, represented the last serious attempt to create a railway resort. Opened by the Southern in 1932, the branch failed to live up to expectations with seaside lovers preferring the golden sands further east. The terminus gained the unfortunate nickname 'Allhallows-on-Mud' and lasted less than thirty years until closure in 1961. (J.S Gilks)

RAIL DISTANCES FROM LONDON TO THE SEA (TO THE NEAREST MILE)

STATION	MILES	STATION	MILES
CHAPTER 8		BARROW	267
KIRKCALDY	419	GRANGE-OVER-SANDS	246
LEUCHARS	444	MORECAMBE	236
DUNDEE	453	BLACKPOOL	229
ARBROATH	470	SOUTHPORT	212
MONTROSE	484	LIVERPOOL	194
STONEHAVEN	508	NEW BRIGHTON	200
ABERDEEN	524	WEST KIRBY	204
NAIRN	582		
INVERNESS	568	**CHAPTER 11**	
DINGWALL	587	PRESTATYN	205
INVERGORDON	600	RHYL	209
GOLSPIE	652	ABERGELE	214
DUNROBIN	655	COLWYN BAY	220
HELMSDALE	670	LLANDUDNO JUNCTION	223
WICK	725	LLANDUDNO	226
THURSO	717	BANGOR	239
		LLANFAIR.PG	242
CHAPTER 9		HOLYHEAD	264
KYLE OF LOCHALSH	651	PWLLHELI	276
MALLAIG	566	CRICCIETH	267
MORAR	563	PORTHMADOG	261
ARISAIG	558	HARLECH	253
FORT WILLIAM	525	BARMOUTH	243
OBAN	503	FAIRBOURNE	240
GLASGOW	401	ABERDOVEY	278
GOUROCK	428	ABERYSTWYTH	234
WEMYSS BAY	432	FISHGUARD	262
LARGS	441	MILFORD HAVEN	260
ARDROSSAN	433	PEMBROKE DOCK	268
SALTCOATS	431	TENBY	255
		CARMARTHEN	220
CHAPTER 10		FERRYSIDE	214
TROON	435	PEMBREY/BURRY PORT	204
AYR	442	GOWERTON	195
GIRVAN	468	SWANSEA	192
STRANRAER	515	BARRY ISLAND	154
CARLISLE	300	CARDIFF	145
MARYPORT	325	BRISTOL	118
WHITEHAVEN	314	SEVERN BEACH	132
RAVENGLASS	296		

References

AA Book of the Seaside. Drive Publications Ltd 1972
Allen, Cecil J. *Titled Trains of Great Britain.* 6th Edition Ian Allan 1983.
Anderson, J. & Swinglehurst, E. *The Victorian and Edwardian Seaside.* Country Life 1978
Atterbury, Paul. *See Britain By Train.* AA Publishing 1989
Atterbury, Paul. *End of the Line.* Boxtree Publishing 1994
Atterbury, Paul. *Discovering Britain's Lost Railways.* AA Publishing 1995
Atthill, Robin. *The Somerset and Dorset Railway.* David and Charles 1967
Awdry, W. (Editor). *A Guide to the Steam Railways of Great Britain.* Pelham Books 1984
Baker, Michael H.C. *Railways to the Coast.* Patrick Stephens 1990
Bates, Darrell. *The Companion Guide to Devon & Cornwall.* Collins 1976
Brown, M. (Editor). *T.E.Lawrence: The Selected Letters.* W.W. Norton, New York 1989
Cavendish, Richard. *Explore Britain's Coastline* AA Publishing 1993
Cole, Beverley & Durack, R. *Railway Posters* Laurence King 1992
Cook, Chris. *A History of the Great Trains.* Harcourt Brace 1977
Davies, Hunter. *A Walk Along the Tracks..* Hamlyn Paperbacks 1983
Eagle, Dorothy. *The Oxford Literary Guide to the British Isles.* O.U.P. 1977
Fairclough, A. *The Story of Cornwall's Railways* Tor Mark Press, Truro (undated)
Frater, Alexander. *Stopping Train Britain.* Hodder and Stoughton 1985
Goldring, Patrick. *Britain By Train.* Hamlyn Publishing 1982
Hennessey, R.A.S. *Railways* Batsford 1973
Jordan, A & E. *Away for the Day.* Silver Link Publishing 1991
Joy, David. *Main Line Over Shap.* Dalesman Publishing 1975
Kingston, Patrick. *Royal Trains.* Octopus Publishing 1989
Lee, Hermione. *Virginia Woolf.* Chatto & Windus 1996
Marshall, John. *The Guinness Railway Book.* Guinness Superlatives 1989
Morgan, Brian. *The Great Trains.* Crown Publishers 1973
Mullay, A.J. *Non-Stop: London to Scotland Steam.* Alan Sutton 1989
Nock, O.S. *Speed Records on Britain's Railways.* Pan Books 1972
Nock, O.S. *150 Years of Main Line Railways.* David and Charles 1980
Nock, O.S. *British Locomotives of the 20th Century-Volume 3.* Patrick Stephens 1985
Palin, Michael. *Happy Holidays - The Golden Age of Railway Posters.* Pavilion Books 1987
Robinson, A., & Millward, R. *The Shell Book of The British Coast.* David & Charles 1983
Roche, T.W.E. *The Withered Arm.* Forge Books, Wokingham, Berks 1967
Simmons, Jack. *Railways: An Anthology.* Collins 1991
Snell, J.B. *Britain's Railways Under Steam.* Arthur Barker Ltd 1965
Thomas, David St John. *The Great Way West* David and Charles 1975
Thomas, John. *The Skye Railway.* David St John Thomas 1991
Thomas, John. *The West Highland Railway.* David St John Thomas 1984
Uncles, Christopher. *Lochaber and the Road to the Isles.* Richard Stenlake Publishing 1996
Way, R.Barnard. *Famous British Trains.* Ivor Nicholson and Watson 1936
Weir, Tom. *The Highland Line.* Famedram Publishers, Scotland (no date)
Westwood, John. *British Steam - The Classic Years.* Bison Group 1989
Whitehouse, Patrick. *The Great Western Railway-150 Glorious Years.* David & Charles 1985

Abbreviations

ACE	Atlantic Coast Express
BR	British Rail
CR	Cornish Riviera
DB	Devon Belle
FS	Flying Scotsman
GNER	Great North Eastern Railway
GWR	Great Western Railway
HST	High Speed Train (InterCity 125)
IOW	Isle of Wight
L&BR	Lynton & Barnstaple Railway
LBSCR	London, Brighton and South Coast Railway
LMS	London, Midland & Scottish Railway
LNER	London & North Eastern Railway
LNWR	London & North Western Railway
M&GNJR	Midland & Great Northern Joint Railway
NNR	North Norfolk Railway
NYMR	North Yorkshire Moors Railway
PLA	Passenger Luggage in Advance
R&ER	Ravenglass & Eskdale Railway
RCP	Rail Charter Partnership
RH&DR	Romney, Hythe & Dymchurch Railway
S&D	Somerset and Dorset Railway
SLC	Scenic Land Cruise
SR	Southern Railway
TOC	Train Operating Company
VSOE	Venice Simplon Orient Express
WHR	Welsh Highland Railway
WW1	World War One
WW2	World War Two

Acknowledgements

There are many tracks to the sea upon which enduring happy memories have been nurtured and recorded. In writing this book of railway journeys, I acknowledge the contributions of authors whose books are listed on page 186.

My family has encouraged me throughout my long absences on railway explorations around Britain during the past three decades, and I thank them for their patience and good advice while this challenging project was taking up so much of my time.

Public libraries have provided access to a rich store of railway information, and I am indebted to librarians in Britain, from Penzance to Inverness, from Whitby to Tenby; and in Canada from Halifax to Vancouver, for their courtesy and assistance. Their names are unknown to me, and they may have wondered who was spending so much time among their Class 385 bookshelves. Perhaps they will now know.

Special thanks to my daughter, Lisa Birrell, whose graphics have enriched this book; to Gillian Panton, who read and commented on all the chapters; to John and Gill Coady for supplying me with valuable reference material; and to David Joy, author, editor and publisher, whose guidance has shaped the book now in your hands. Any errors in this book are mine alone.

As a subscriber to 'The Railway Magazine' I gratefully acknowledge use of contemporary railway news, facts and figures contained in its excellent monthly issues, particularly regarding train services to the coast.

I thank all those whose kindness and hospitality have enabled me to complete more than a thousand journeys around Britain, exploring rail routes to the sea and collecting material for this book. I hope that my relatives and friends enjoy the ride as they bask in their own contribution to this railway odyssey, where serendipity has been my constant companion.

Throughout my railway travels during the past fifty years, I have neither sought, nor received, any privileges from British Rail or from the privatized railway companies. In casting aside the cloak of anonymity I have worn on my journeys, I hope that this volume will be found to be a worthy tribute to the great achievements of British railway companies and their personnel.

Vancouver, B.C
January 1999.

Index